M000222026

POVERTY AND INCENTIVES

The Economics of
Social Security

Bau# 21392

POVERTY AND INCENTIVES

The Economics of Social Security

RICHARD HEMMING

OXFORD UNIVERSITY PRESS
1984

Oxford University Press, Walton Street, Oxford OX2 6DP
London Glasgow New York Toronto
Delhi Bombay Calcutta Madras Karachi
Kuala Lumpur Singapore Hong Kong Tokyo
Nairobi Dar es Salaam Cape Town
Melbourne Auckland

and associated companies in
Beirut Berlin Ibadan Mexico City Nicosia

Oxford is a trade mark of Oxford University Press

Published in the United States
by Oxford University Press, New York

© Richard Hemming 1984

All rights reserved. No part of this publication may be reproduced,
stored in a retrieval system, or transmitted, in any form or by any means,
electronic, mechanical, photocopying, recording, or otherwise, without
the prior permission of Oxford University Press

British Library Cataloguing in Publication Data

Hemming, Richard
Poverty and incentives: the economics of social
security.
1. Social security—Great Britain
I. Title
368.4'00941 HD7167
ISBN 0-19-877164-9
ISBN 0-19-877165-7 pbk

Library of Congress Cataloging in Publication Data
Hemming, Richard.
Poverty and incentives.
Bibliography: p.
Includes index.
1. Social security—Great Britain. I. Title.
HD7165.H45 1984 368.4'00941 83-13468
ISBN 0-19-877164-9
ISBN 9-19-877165-7 (pbk.)

Set by ROD-ART, Abingdon, England
and printed in Great Britain
at the University Press, Oxford

PREFACE

IN preparing this book I have received help from many organizations and individuals. The Department of Health and Social Security, the Department of the Environment, and the Inland Revenue always treated my requests for information and explanation courteously. Stephen Clark, John Ermisch, Guy Fiegehen, Ken Judge, Stewart Lansley, and Lesley Rimmer provided help either with specific points of detail or by providing comments on individual chapters. I owe a great debt to my colleagues at the Institute for Fiscal Studies, and in particular Andrew Dilnot, John Kay, Nick Morris, and Neil Warren. I have drawn heavily upon their published work arising out of an Institute project on the distributional effects of fiscal policy. Nick Morris provided the data necessary to draw Figure 4.4. John Kay and I have been working on an Institute project on pension provision in Britain; Chapter 6 is based on our work. I must extend particular thanks to John Hills, who I worked with for too brief a period at the Institute for Fiscal Studies. He read the entire manuscript with an attention to detail which led to vast improvements in both content and presentation. Naturally I absolve all these organizations and individuals from any responsibility for errors and ambiguities which may remain. Barbara Lee typed successive drafts of the book with truly remarkable accuracy and good humour.

Most of this book was written during 1982. In the course of that year there were important though not fundamental changes to the structure of the social security system, and all benefit rates changed. The year 1982 was not untypical. Efforts have been made to ensure that all the information in the book is correct as of 1 January 1983. Although by the time this book is published there will have been further structural and rate changes, it is unlikely that these will invalidate the examples which have been constructed to show how the system works.

CONTENTS

LIST OF FIGURES

LIST OF TABLES

INTRODUCTION

BOOK titles often promise an encyclopaedic content not matched in practice. The title of this book has been chosen so as not to give a misleading impression of its content. 'Poverty and Incentives: The Economics of Social Security' deals with the structure, effectiveness, and reform of income support through social security. It contains little relevant economic and political history, no discussion of fundamental philosophical issues relating to state provision, and few if any references to the National Health Service and the personal social services (see instead Bruce, 1961, Pinker, 1979, and Wilson and Wilson, 1982). What remains is neither a benefit handbook nor a treatise on structural change, although it contains some measure of each. Many social security benefits are described in detail, and numerous reforms are discussed. However, the core of the book is an assessment of the performance of the current social security system.

Economic analysis plays a large though not overwhelming part throughout. Until very recently social security was a subject virtually ignored by economists. This has now changed, so much so that there already exists a book describing the economics of social security. What McClements (1978) means by the economics of social security is any part of economic theory which could prove useful to budding social security analysts. And this is a quite proper interpretation. Techniques of economic analysis, and perhaps more importantly the discipline they imply, are finding an ever-increasing range of applications. Their value is clearly demonstrated in the closely related books by Atkinson (1975) on inequality, by Kay and King (1981) on taxation, and by Le Grand (1982) on public expenditure. This book is written in the same spirit as these three; while all three rely on economic analysis none is written solely for economists. It is hoped that it will be read in conjunction with them, for the disturbing story they combine to tell deserves a much wider audience.

The plan of the book is as follows. In Chapter 1 an economic framework for social security analysis is developed; it will serve to focus the discussion in subsequent chapters. An overview of the structure of social security is provided in Chapter 2. Poverty is the subject of Chapter 3, and in particular the extent to which the benefits available reach those for whom they are intended. Benefits for low income working families interact with the taxes they must also pay in a complex fashion which is explained in Chapter 4. A neat way of doing this is to determine the benefits received and taxes paid by a particular family at different levels of earnings. This reveals very clearly the problems the interaction creates. Where helpful the position of hypothetical recipients of benefit is examined elsewhere in the book. In Chapter 5, dealing with unemployment, sickness, and disability benefits, this approach proves especially valuable. Spending on retirement pensions is by far the largest item of social security expenditure; a new state pension scheme has recently been introduced which in twenty years' time will begin paying pensions considerably more generous than those currently available. Working out the implications for expenditure of the new scheme occupies much of Chapter 6, although other pension issues are not ignored. The British social security system provides assistance with housing costs; but despite recent reform, serious problems remain. What these are, and how they might be overcome, is revealed in Chapter 7. Chapter 8 deals with proposals for social security reform, both radical and not so radical.

1

SOCIAL SECURITY ANALYSIS

WHY does Britain have a social security system? To answer this question properly we really have to know what arrangements would be made in its absence to protect from destitution those who fail to provide adequately for themselves and their families. Many counterfactual hypotheses can be formulated. For example, some may believe that the aged would rely on their children to support them, or past saving to support themselves in retirement; husbands would ensure that their widows are adequately provided for; the infirmed would be cared for by their families; the unemployed and temporarily sick would borrow against future earnings; and charitable giving would be adequate for those with no other means of support. Others may believe that everybody currently relying on social security benefits as their principal source of income would live a life of intolerable hardship.

However, most reasonable people will see the truth as lying somewhere between these two extremes. Clearly financial and domestic ties between members of what might be termed the 'extended' family — retired grandparents, working parents and children — have weakened, and the socialization of transfers between working and retired generations has played a part in this, but the extended family was never of any great significance (see Laslett, 1965). While some workers would have both the desire and the ability to save for retirement or to survive temporary absences from the workforce, others are myopic — taking little notice of what the future might bring — or do not earn sufficient to save very much. And when there is little prospect of the unemployed or sick returning quickly to the workforce, borrowing, except on informal and often ruinous terms, will be virtually impossible. Altruistic giving could hardly cope with the resulting demands for assistance. If there were no social security, many whom the system currently helps would be able to arrange adequate substitutes. But it is difficult to believe that there would not also be widespread and, in some cases, severe poverty.

Thus one reason for government intervention is to prevent the dire social conditions which preceded and unfortunately accompanied the earliest form of state provision, the Poor Law. Poor Law relief was no more than public charity; it was operated in a manner which was supposed to be demeaning, and many judged extreme misery a price worth paying to avoid it. When the seeds of the modern social security system were sown at the turn of the twentieth century, a guarantee of subsistence to those who could establish their inability to provide adequately for themselves remained its primary objective. But many subsequent developments have been a response to the emergence of wider objectives.

Developments in two directions are worth highlighting. First, and virtually from the outset of the modern system, many social security benefits − for the retired, widowed, unemployed, sick, and disabled − have been paid from a state-run social insurance scheme. When sufficient contributions to the scheme have been made, a right to contingent flat-rate benefits is established. Second, and much more recently, there has been a shift to, and some subsequent retreat from, earnings-related benefits. Intervention is often defended on the grounds that there are weaknesses in the market mechanism for which only the government can compensate. The arguments actually used when these developments occurred had little to do with these economic objectives. Of course, this alone does not deny their relevance and importance, although when we come to examine them we will see that they are of rather dubious merit. So it is worth while to ask whether the economic arguments which might be drawn upon to explain the existence of a social security system with a considerable insurance element, and providing some income continuity − through earnings-related benefits − as well as income maintenance − a guaranteed minimum − have anything to commend them.

Market failure and forced saving

If the future were certain, insurance would be unknown. But life expectancy is a random variable while widowhood, unemployment, sickness, and injury are all random events. Relatively sophisticated individuals can make arrangements enabling them to minimize the impact of these uncertainties. However, if people in general are risk averse there will be a tendency for them to prepare for the more pessimistic outcomes, and the overall level of protection will be too great. If risks are pooled in an insurance scheme, the overall level of protection will reflect the average outcome. A more detailed discussion of the advantages of risk-pooling is provided by Pauly (1968).

Although risk-pooling might be advantageous, it is far from axiomatic that insurance should be provided by the state. Only if the private market would fail in some way does the state have a role. Insurance market failure has two principal causes, which an everyday example, motor insurance, clearly reveals.

Assume that the insurer cannot distinguish between different risks, for example whether a prospective purchaser of comprehensive insurance is a reckless or careful driver. The insurer has no choice but to charge them both the same premium. This practice may have two consequences. Because there is no loading for reckless drivers the incentive to drive carefully is diminished. There will be more accidents, more claims, and insurance becomes increasingly costly. This is the moral hazard problem, and it occurs anywhere that an outcome is insurable without reference to its cause. It is overcome by introducing co-insurance, requiring that part of each claim is met by the insured. The absence of loading for reckless drivers might also lead those who think they are good drivers to the conclusion that comprehensive insurance is a bad deal, and to settle for the statutory minimum third-party insurance instead. Only the bad risks remain in the market, and costs inevitably rise. This is the adverse selection problem. In the motor insurance industry it is overcome by the use of proxies to determine exposure to risk — age, occupation, the type of car driven, etc. — and then reducing the premiums of those who do not claim — a no-claims bonus — and these appear to perform well.

It is fairly clear that both moral hazard and adverse selection problems can arise in the private provision of insurance cover for the risks now covered by social insurance. Co-insurance is possible where there is a moral hazard problem, for example by specifying an official retirement age with reduced pensions for those who retire earlier, and by refusing to pay benefits until a spell of unemployment or sickness has exceeded some minimum number of days. The social insurance scheme adopts this approach. Adverse selection is more challenging. It is widely argued that unemployment insurance sold on the private market would suffer from this problem — it would not be attractive to civil servants and this would force up the price for, say, building workers – and this explains why a private market does not and could not exist (see Disney, 1981). But retirement pensions, widows' pensions, sick-pay, and permanent health insurance (which covers long-term sickness and disability) are all available privately. This does not, however, imply that the adverse selection problem is exaggerated. By relying predominantly on a firm- or industry-wide basis for such schemes and, as the state would, demanding compulsory membership, the private market excludes the possibility. Unfortunately much of the work-force is disenfranchised by the private sector – not so much in the field of sick-pay but significantly as far as pensions are concerned and almost entirely in the case of permanent health insurance. Individual contracts can be struck but these might tend to be more expensive than actuarially fair policies when, for the reasons described, the good risks reject the opportunity to buy insurance. The extent to which this would happen is unclear. We would think it to be more likely to occur with insurance covering sickness and injury than with pension provision. Individuals probably regard themselves as much better judges of whether they are going to be regularly absent from work through sickness or whether they work in a dangerous occupation, than they are of how long they are likely to live.

Not only insurance markets can fail; so might capital markets. Take the case of someone saving for retirement. More than likely they will be faced with a bewildering choice of investment possibilities, and the following dilemma will be only too obvious. Secure returns – on cash deposits with the bank or building society, or government bonds – will not seem particularly generous; to increase returns, riskier assets – company shares, property unit trusts, or even gold – must be bought. Skilled investors can combine safe and risky investments to meet best particular objectives. Most people not only lack this ability but also rarely know where to turn for advice. In this sense the capital market may be seen to fail the small inexperienced investors seeking to get the best out of their retirement savings.

There is a second very closely related and much more important respect in which the capital market fails those saving for their retirement. In the presence of inflation a pension of a fixed nominal amount declines in purchasing power over the retirement period. Private capital markets – and in particular companies – do not offer indexed investments. There may be many reasons for this: indexed debt being a bad business risk and the artificial barriers facing those who wish to make it available are often mentioned. The exact reason or reasons for the absence of indexed investments is neither here nor there. What is important is that the prospect of seeing even large sums of money put aside during a working life, rendered worthless in retirement through inflation makes saving for retirement an unappealing proposition. Yet it is a proposition which could not be rejected. For it would be the only way of providing for an aged future.

Our discussion of insurance and capital market failure does not yield clear-cut conclusions. Insurance market failure cannot be taken as read, although government concern for the unemployed, sick, and disabled looks justifiable for this reason alone. And capital market failure indicates that the government may be justified in providing some measure of protection for recipients of social security and small savers against the ravages of inflation.

A social insurance scheme is no more than a forced saving programme. However, forced saving need not be justified by reference to market failure on its own. We have already suggested that it is not unreasonable to assume that where the government accepts a responsibility to provide a floor to living standards many who would otherwise be reasonably self-reliant come to depend upon social security instead. This indicates a strong case for a forced saving programme, possibly social insurance, with benefits set at a level capable of sustaining the minimal standard of living. Market failure may strengthen the case for forced saving. The interesting question to ask then is whether those who might have bought more insurance on the free market, if there were one, should be forced to save more. There are arguments which suggest that a forced saving programme should have this feature.

We have identified myopia as a cause of inadequate saving and a forced saving programme compensates for this affliction; the reason that the myopic are forced to save is a belief that they will ultimately be grateful when the time comes for them to need to draw upon their savings. Now, if the degree of short-sightedness does not diminish as income increases, it is possible that those with higher incomes would desire larger benefits than those with lower incomes, and hence ought to be willing to save more. Similarly the capital market may not be forthcoming with the types of assets individuals are looking for, but if such assets were available, more might be purchased by those with higher incomes. These arguments might be seen to constitute a case for earnings-related benefits; however, they are not very persuasive. Population heterogeneity suggests that while in the absence of intervention the insurance and capital markets might fail many, a social security system which provides earnings-related benefits for all, may force a large number of people to save too much. The more ambitious a forced saving programme, the more likely it is that it will impose costs which far exceed its benefits.

A more convincing argument for earnings-related benefits is based upon the recognition that an unexpected change in circumstances which may last some time cannot be assimilated instantaneously. It takes time to adjust to the lower standard of living which can be supported by benefits and to relieve oneself of burdensome financial obligations taken on in better times, for example loan repayments or school fees. Short-term, earnings-related benefits therefore minimize the immediate upheaval resulting from having to leave the work-force or no longer being able to depend upon a member of the work-force for support. They also smooth the transition to a lower standard of living for those who will eventually have to depend upon social security in the longer term. If this argument is at all compelling, its most crucial implication must be emphasized. Earnings-related benefits should only be provided for those whose circumstances change quite unpredictably. Being made unemployed, being widowed before retirement, becoming sick, or getting injured are typically unpredictable occurrences. Having to retire is the reasonable expectation of most of us; and because women typically outlive their husbands most women whose husbands live to retirement age must anticipate widowhood. There is nothing in this argument to support the state provision of earnings-related retirement pensions.

Equity considerations

We take it to be the primary objective of the social security system to relieve and ultimately eliminate poverty. This can be attempted in a number of ways, and some will be more successful than others. Because Poor Law relief was widely regarded as undignified by many of those it could have helped, it was an abysmal failure. In this sense great strides have since been made, although social security benefits still fail to reach everybody they are intended for because a large number must be claimed. The practice of claiming still so offends the dignity of some potential benefit recipients that they do not bother with it. Only if the need to claim were removed would social security be a completely effective weapon for attacking poverty. But if claiming is judged desirable the right of claimants not to be forced into suffering unnecessary violations of their self-esteem should be respected.

Social security also has a wider equity objective. Before any taxes have been paid or any social security benefits have been received, the distribution of income would be unequal. How unequal is a difficult question to answer. We argued above that it cannot be concluded that the extent of poverty in the absence of social security can be ascertained by computing income before social security benefits have been received and examining how much poverty there would be. People might be capable of making other financial arrangements. Similarly, the distribution of gross income in the absence of income taxes and cash benefits cannot properly be gauged by assuming that taxes were not levied and transfers did not take place. People might behave differently − for example, do more work − if there were no tax and benefit system. However, both in determining the impact of social security on poverty and the distributional impact of the tax and benefit system, there is no practical alternative to assuming that behaviour is unaffected by these arrangements. Yet, even given this strong assumption, the extent to which poverty or income inequality is reduced will depend upon how it is measured. Poverty measurement will be discussed in Chapter 3; for the moment we will focus on the measurement of inequality only.

Income inequality can be measured in a number of ways. The most commonly used measure is the Gini index, which is a statistical indicator of the concentration of incomes. It is computed in the following way. Individuals, families, or households can be ranked by their incomes, beginning with the poorest and ending with the richest. We then calculate the percentage of total income Y received by the worst-off X per cent of income recipients, with X running from 0 per cent to 100 per cent. Y increases with X. The pairs of numbers so produced can be plotted on a graph to form a Lorenz curve, as in Figure 1.1. If the distribution of income is perfectly equal, the Lorenz curve coincides with the diagonal line. If income is unequally distributed the Lorenz curve will be as drawn. The Gini index is the ratio of the area between the Lorenz curve and the diagonal to the area below the diagonal. It equals zero when there is no inequality, and unity with complete inequality (all income being received by one individual, family, or household).

Figure 1.2 shows Lorenz curves for the distribution of household income in 1980 according to three definitions of household income.

Original income is income before any cash benefits have been received· or any taxes have been paid. Gross income includes benefits. Disposable income is gross income less income tax and national insurance contributions. In moving from original to disposable income the Gini index falls by about a third; three-quarters of this fall occurs in moving from original to gross income and is therefore due to social security benefits.

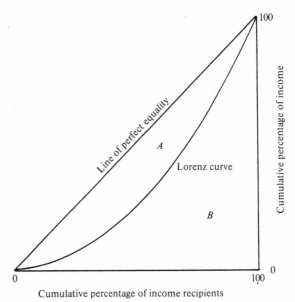

FIG. 1.1. The Lorenz Curve and the Gini Index
Gini index = $A/(A+B)$ = 0 with perfect equality.
= 1 with complete inequality.

The Gini index is widely criticized. Consider two societies with identical unequal income distributions but where the first does not care about inequality and the second does. It has been argued that these different attitudes to inequality should be reflected in an inequality measure. The Gini index, being a purely statistical device, cannot do this. Atkinson (1970) has suggested how inequality can be measured such that the compassionate society can have its strong dislike of inequality expressed in a measure of inequality. This involves measuring the 'cost of inequality', which is the proportion of aggregate income that society would be willing to forgo in order to achieve perfect equality. As well as information about the distribution of income the cost of inequality depends upon a parameter reflecting society's attitude to inequality. In practical work this parameter is obviously imposed, and since the range of possibilities is speculative so is the estimated cost of inequality. Kay and King (1980, Table 14.2) report some simple calculations which reveal the cost of inequality in 1977 to have been in the extraordinarily wide range 6–99 per cent. But these same calculations show that the impact of taxes and benefits is always to reduce the cost of inequality by two-thirds to three-quarters. Social security benefits consistently explain two-thirds to three-quarters of this reduction.

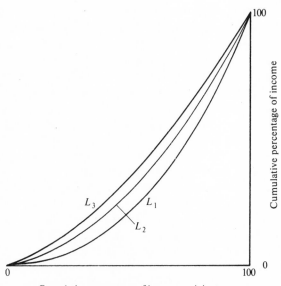

Cumulative percentage of income recipients

FIG. 1.2. Income Inequality in the United Kingdom: 1980
Lorenz curve L_1, original income;   Gini index = 0.46.
Lorenz curve L_2, gross income;   Gini index = 0.36.
Lorenz curve L_3, disposable income;   Gini index = 0.33.

Source: CSO Economic Trends, January 1982.

Social security is clearly integral to achieving a more equal distribution of income. It redistributes in two principal ways. In attempting to fulfil its principal objective – relieving poverty – money is transferred to the poor from the non-poor. It also redistributes amongst the non-poor. Society's redistributive objectives may well require that those who are not necessarily poor – for example, all families with children – have their incomes enhanced. The British tax system is not designed to make these payments, although it could be restructured to do so. Social security is the mechanism by which these payments are currently made. We shall see that some 60 per cent of total social security expenditure is received by the non-poor. It is by examining the redistributive impact of the tax and benefit systems together that we judge whether society's redistributive objectives are met, and not by reference to the tax system or the social security system alone.

Specifying this wider redistributive role for social security, where social security is treated simply as an extension of the tax system, confirms our interest in 'vertical' equity – the treatment of the rich relative to the treatment of the poor. Vertical equity is closely related to the concept of progressivity, indeed the two are often conflated. This is understandable, and a significant simplification. However, they are quite distinct, and it is worth making the distinction clear. Take the case of an income tax. The proportion of income paid in tax is referred to as the average tax rate; the proportion of each increment of income paid in tax is referred to as the marginal tax rate. If the marginal tax rate always exceeds the average tax rate the average tax rate increases with income, and the tax is progressive. All progressive taxes are vertically equitable; they redistribute from the rich to the poor, and the Lorenz curve shifts inwards. We will see that the average tax rate in Britain does not rise continuously with income. Over a certain range of income the average tax rate falls and the tax system is locally regressive. Yet the tax system is still vertically equitable, in the sense that the Lorenz curve of the distribution of post-tax income lies everywhere inside the Lorenz curve of the distribution of pre-tax income. And a wholly progressive tax could be less redistributive. When one tax system is described as being more progressive than another it does not follow that it is also being claimed that it is more redistributive; however, this is the general intention of such claims.

In discussing the characteristics of a good tax structure it is usually claimed that 'horizontal' equity is also desirable; it should treat fairly those who are judged to be equally rich or poor. This should be required of the social security system as well, and thereby the tax and benefit system as a whole. We will discover examples of horizontal inequity in the social security system. It is sometimes argued that an insuperable problem arises in attempting to repair these. For if equals are treated unequally, any attempt to treat them more equally will itself imply horizontal inequity. An example demonstrates this alleged catch-22 situation.

Take two equally wealthy people. One invests in stocks and shares, pays tax on his investment income, and the rent on his house is met from the remainder. The other owns his own home, and prior to 1963 would have had to pay tax on the income he could have received if that house had been let on the private market. The abolition of tax on the imputed income from owner-occupied housing was horizontally inequitable, favouring owner-occupation. Now both people will have made investment and housing decisions which reflect the tax concession; but if one still rents while the other is an owner-occupier, to remove the concession would itself be horizontally inequitable. This example, and others like it, are often referred to in defence of the status quo. But they tend to confuse a comparison of two alternative states of the world, one preferable to the other, with the movement between them. We will see in Chapter 7 that the taxation of imputed income is desirable. If this were done the tax system would be more equitable.

Taxation, social security, and incentives

Much of the discussion of incentives is concerned with the impact of income taxation on labour supply. In our discussion of the relationship between progressivity and redistribution we distinguished between average and marginal tax rates. An income tax affects labour supply in two ways. First, there is an income effect which depends upon the average tax rate; the larger the proportion of income paid in tax, the worse off a taxpayer will be, and the more work that must be done if customary living standards are to be protected. Second, there is a substitution effect which depends upon the marginal tax rate; the greater the proportion of any increase in income paid in tax, the lower the amount of disposable income being rejected by working a little less and enjoying some more leisure. The impact of income taxation on labour supply depends upon the net outcome of the income and substitution effects, and is therefore affected by both average and marginal tax rates. Any income tax will result in an income effect; it is the inevitable consequence of having to impose a tax at all. Only an income tax which requires tax payments to vary with income has a substitution effect. A differential lump-sum tax — say a fixed proportion of income earned when working forty hours — which must be paid no matter how much work is done, imposes no tax on increments of income and therefore has no substitution effect. The substitution effect is therefore the consequence of imposing a particular type of tax.

Reference is often made to the disincentive effect of taxation. In much popular discussion this is usually taken to mean that high marginal tax rates are associated with a lower level of labour supply than low marginal tax rates. We know that this is not necessarily the case; if high marginal tax rates are accompanied by high average tax rates the income effect could outweigh the substitution effect and labour supply might increase with high marginal tax rates. But just because labour supply is not reduced by high marginal tax rates this cannot be taken to indicate that there are no disincentive effects. Every taxpayer could be required to contribute exactly the same amount to tax revenue as under the income tax, through differential lump-sum taxes. These will only have an income effect, and more work will be done. By imposing a tax with high marginal tax rates rather than equal-yield, differential lump-sum taxes, labour supply is less than it potentially could be, given the tax burden and its distribution. This is the sense in which it can correctly be claimed that high marginal tax rates have disincentive effects. And the higher the marginal tax rate the greater the disincentive effect, because additional leisure looks even more attractive relative to work.

Although the popular belief about the impact of taxation on labour supply is only one of the possibilities suggested by economic theory, the eventual outcome is important. Labour supply responses to redistribution through taxation may lead to such a large reduction in total income that the redistribution which can be achieved is severely limited. How does labour supply respond to changes in marginal tax rates? We can gain some idea from examining how hours of work vary between taxpayers with different net (after tax) wage rates and different levels of unearned income. We therefore begin with a simple labour supply function $H = H(w,U)$, where H is hours of work, w is the net wage rate and U is unearned income. The way in which H varies with w is given by H_w and the way in which H varies with U is given by H_U. H_w is the overall effect on H of a small change in w and is referred to as the price effect. H_U is the income effect. We know that the price effect separates into an income effect and a substitution effect, which is the price effect when U adjusts to leave the worker no worse off. We denote this H_S. However, it does not follow that $H_S = H_w - H_U$ since the effect of a change in the net wage on income depends upon how many hours are worked. We therefore have, $H_S = H_w - H \cdot H_U$. Price, income, and substitution effects can be expressed as corresponding elasticities: $E_w = H_w \cdot w/H$; $E_U = H_U \cdot U/H$; and $E_S = H_S \cdot w/H$. The advantage of reporting the elasticities is that they are independent of units of measurement; for example, the magnitude of the price effect depends upon whether the net wage rate is measured in pounds or pence while the price elasticity does not.

Empirical estimates of these elasticities for Britain have been derived from the results of a survey of the wages and hours of a small sample of married weekly-paid males, undertaken in 1971. Typical results are those of Brown, Levin, and Ulph (1976), which show that at the sample mean $E_w = -0.13$, $E_U = -0.01$, and $E_S = 0.22$. However, the estimation of labour supply functions is extremely complicated, and the problems the exercise presents can be overcome in a number of ways. Brown (1981) describes the alternative approaches in considerable detail and reports the range of elasticity estimates that different approaches entail. Many are close to those just reported, but some are much removed, although not sufficiently so to alter the conclusion that the general order of magnitude of the various elasticities can be agreed to be rather small. For example, the elasticities reported above imply that a 10 per cent reduction in the net wage rate at the sample mean, from 50p to 45p an hour, will increase hours of work by 1.3 per cent, which at the sample mean is only 37 minutes a week. The popular belief therefore lacks a firm foundation in practice as well as in principle. However, it cannot be confidently concluded on the basis of these results that the limits to redistribution are nowhere near being reached.

Much has been learned from work which has gone into deriving elasticity estimates, but this probably relates far more to technical estimation issues than to the behavioural responses of taxpayers to changes in wage and tax rates. Further work will reveal how good the preliminary elasticity estimates are, and in particular whether labour supply elasticities are small for all types of worker and at all earnings levels. Certainly the US evidence suggests that at very low incomes where average tax rates are negative and both the income and substitution effects operate to reduce labour supply, the adverse impact is very small (see Watts and Rees, 1977), while high earners face so many non-financial incentives – power, prestige, respect – that a high level of taxation does not deter work effort (see Holland, 1969). But this latter finding serves to indicate that the response of hours of work to financial rewards is only one aspect of the complex way in which behaviour might be influenced by taxation. Instead of doing fewer hours less well paid workers might simply make less of an effort. However, the aspect of behavioural responses to taxation which has recently attracted much attention is the apparent growth of an underground, or black, economy.

Activities in the black economy are unrecorded, and the income so derived does not attract tax. By their very nature very little is known about the extent of these activities. In 1979 the Inland Revenue suggested that the black economy was 7½ per cent of gross national product. The basis of this figure is unknown; it has been described as 'one of the most famous guesses ever to emerge from Somerset House' (*The Guardian*, 4 March 1981). It is now admitted by the Inland Revenue that one cannot be as precise about the size of the black economy as this figure suggests; the revised estimate is 6–8 per cent! Dilnot and Morris (1981) have matched the income and expenditure records of individual househoulds who responded to the Family Expenditure Survey. However, it is difficult to believe that those engaged in fraudulent activities are going to provide accurate information in a government survey. Their suggestion that the black economy is only 2–3 per cent of gross national product has therefore to be treated with some caution. But there is little that can be achieved from arguments about the precise size of the black economy. It is certainly small, and if it remains so it is not something that is necessarily harmful: 'The existence of small amounts of economic activity on which the marginal tax rate is zero, much of which would not be undertaken at all if it were confined to the formal economy, may reduce the disincentive effects of taxation and add to social relationships. When this achieves proportions which encourage wide scale fraud or lead to a cumulative collapse of the moral force of the tax system, our reactions should be rather different' (Dilnot and Morris, 1981, p. 72).

We have concentrated upon the impact of income taxation on labour supply, and the associated disincentive effects which result from the way in which we choose to tax income. Social security bears upon this discussion in two ways. First, most of those in work pay income tax. They also have to pay national insurance contributions which finance some social security benefits, mainly retirement pensions; the remainder are financed from general taxation. Thus the tax burden imposed upon the working population reflects the scope and generosity of the social security system. Second, some working families with low earnings qualify for social security benefits, and these tend to be income related. As earnings fall, benefit entitlement increases. Conversely as earnings increase, benefit entitlement falls, and the withdrawal of benefits is therefore equivalent to a tax on income. Social security also raises other issues concerning incentives.

It should not occasion surprise if the social security system is capable of replacing a large proportion of the earnings in relatively lowly paid jobs, and being in work therefore offers little apparent financial advantage. Indeed it has been suggested that unemployment in Britain would be lower if the benefits paid to the unemployed were lower. This is a controversial issue, which we will explore in Chapter 5.

Disincentive effects are not confined to labour supply. We have suggested that private voluntary saving may be lower in the presence of social security, because social security removes the need for individuals to make any provision for periods of unemployment, sickness, or retirement. Social security is not funded, and national saving and investment could be lower as a consequence. However, there may be offsetting influences; the most obvious is early retirement. The net effect on national saving is in general ambiguous. The argument that social security substitutes for private saving, and depresses national saving and investment, is most compelling in respect of retirement pensions. The extent to which this view is justified, the impact of a shift towards funding, and the influence of retirement pensions on the labour force participation of older workers, will be investigated in Chapter 6.

Assessing social security

The success or failure of the British social security system, or of any particular part of it, can only be judged once the objectives of the system have been clearly specified. It is unlikely that any particular set of objectives will command universal approval. But from the preceding discussion three objectives have clearly emerged, and we would doubt that they are controversial. First, social security should provide an effective means of dealing with poverty, and it should do so in a manner which preserves the dignity of the poor. The simpler the system the more likely it is to be effective. Second, society's wider equity objectives should be served by the system. And third, it should be efficient, in other words, disincentive effects should be minimized. We do not attach any importance to the view that social security should have a large insurance element, nor the view that benefits should be earnings-related other than in the short term for the unemployed, sick, and injured.

It is with these three objectives in mind that we undertake our analysis of the social security system. However, there will be a recurring problem. The objectives appear to be inconsistent, and in particular it is necessary to reach a compromise between what is required from equity and efficiency standpoints. This is a classical dilemma. But how important is it? Thurow (1981) for one is not convinced. He notes the reluctance of many countries to expand their social security systems and effect further redistribution, and the desire of some to cut back in this direction. This is justified by the need to improve economic performance. However, a comparison of economic growth and redistribution in a dozen developed countries leads him to conclude that: 'Some good performers have a high degree of inequality and no redistribution; others have a low degree of inequality and substantial redistribution. Poor economic performers are equally mixed in terms of the degree of inequality and the extent of their redistributional effort. Whatever the connection between equity and efficiency it is not a simple one where the willingness to tolerate inequality guarantees efficiency or is necessary to achieve efficiency' (Thurow, 1981, p. 138). Only two interpretations can be placed upon the attitudes of governments worried about the consequences of further redistribution. They either have little faith in the facts, or the limits to redistribution are not economic at all, but political.

International comparisons can be uninformative and even misleading. During the 1960s and 1970s the growth rate in both France and Norway was twice that in Britain; France achieved far less redistribution than Britain, and Norway far more. Would Britain's growth rate have been twice as high only if we had redistributed as little as France, or, if the growth rate had been twice as high would we have been able to redistribute as much as Norway? And the message from labour supply studies is equally unclear. What empirical information is available suggests that the economic limits to redistribution are far from being reached. But labour supply studies are still in their infancy; and even the most confidently defended labour supply elasticity estimates would only tell part of the full disincentives story. Perhaps the facts as they are should be taken lightly, and in view of the limitations of our knowledge the more pessimistic outcomes should not be ignored. Indeed, they should perhaps be the favoured basis on which we should choose to proceed.

This is the attitude which will be taken throughout this book, not because of any belief that the facts are mistaken but rather because it is known to be a firmly-held view of the current government, most of its supporters, and many others. The limits to redistribution may genuinely be thought economic in origin, even though such a conclusion has only the most slender basis in fact. Or it may simply be felt that anything more than only a moderate interference by government in the activities of individuals is unwarranted, and efficiency arguments are used to disguise a political assessment of the limits to redistribution. For our purposes there is no need to distinguish between these arguments. It is the views which are held, and not why they are held, that matter. Disincentive effects may be trivial, but if the social security system fails badly to meet its equity objectives, improvements which involve heavier taxation for a significant proportion of the working population would be politically unpopular with a government elected on a tax-cutting platform, even though little has been achieved in this direction. Social security reform should not be conditional on a change to a government willing to achieve equity improvements unhindered by an obsession with efficiency considerations.

2

THE STRUCTURE OF SOCIAL SECURITY

THE Poor Law, even after the reform of 1834, sought to do no more than make available a minimal but still abysmal standard of living to the sick, the idle, and the incompetent, which often had to be endured in the notorious 'workhouses'. Poor Law relief was financed from local rates, and given that the improved condition of the poor was supposed to remain worse than that of the most unhealthy, lazy, and untalented person fortunate enough to be in gainful employment, total expenditure was low. Since then, and principally since the mid-twentieth century, social security expenditure has soared broadly in line with general social welfare expenditure: this can be seen clearly from Table 2.1. At some time during his or her life social security payments will

TABLE 2.1

The Social Security Sector: 1950–80
(£ million, 1980 prices)

	1950	1960	1970	1980
Gross national product	99,479	127,407	186,541	225,522
Government expenditure	34,969	37,742	75,452	103,720
Social welfare expenditure	9,385	12,623	36,755	55,444
Social security expenditure	5,227	8,034	14,158	22,221

Sources: CSO National Income and Expenditure.
CSO Economic Trends: Annual Supplement.

be made on behalf of everyone in the population. In this chapter we are going to describe the development of the social security system since the Poor Law, and the structure which has ultimately arisen.

The development of the social security system

The first departure from the principles of the Poor Law came around the turn of the twentieth century. The 1897 Workmen's Compensation Act made earnings-related compensation, subject to limits, payable to those incapacitated as a result of an injury sustained at particular types of work. Compensation was paid directly by employers. Rights to compensation could be established through the courts. By 1906 such compensation was available in most spheres of employment. Two years later, in 1908, the Old Age Pensions Act allowed for the provision of a means-tested pension, albeit a small one, to people aged over 70. This was followed in 1911 by the National Insurance Act, which introduced compulsory insurance against unemployment for workers in specific industries, and against the medical costs and earnings lost by low-paid workers during periods of sickness. These benefits were available as of right in return for contributions; there was no means test. They were financed by contributions made by those covered, their employers, and an Exchequer supplement. The 1934 Unemployment Act introduced a means-tested benefit for those unemployed not covered by national insurance.

Apart from a reduction in the pension age to 65 for men and to 60 for women the period up to the end of the Second World War saw no significant further developments in social security legislation. But immediate pre-war society had still been an unequal and divided one to which few wished to return. The war created upheaval, and life in post-war Britain was inevitably going to be very different. The political consensus was that the new Britain should be a 'welfare state' where those who could not guarantee an adequate standard of living for themselves would be helped with dignity; where those risks which were faced by all – sickness, injury, unemployment, old age – were pooled in a social insurance scheme; and access to suitable housing, education, health care, and, most of all, employment was secured by all.

In 1942 a detailed investigation into the existing social security arrangements, and suggestions for their reform, were published. Perhaps surprisingly, in the midst of war, the now famous Beveridge Report (1942) fired the public imagination and became an instant best seller in both Britain and America. Beveridge's major goal was the 'abolition of want', and this was to be achieved by a social security system which would protect the individual 'from the cradle to the grave'. The main recommendation of the Beveridge Report was that the disorganized system for the provision of social insurance and assistance which existed before the war should be replaced by a unified system. Underlying the form this unified system should adopt were three critical assumptions. Firstly, poverty resulting from the commitment to children should be averted by a system of family support. The 1945 Family Allowances Act provided such a system. Secondly, governments would adhere to a full employment policy; mass unemployment, and therefore its high cost in terms of reduced income from contributions and increased insurance and assistance payments, would be avoided. Full employment was indeed to be a political watchword for more than twenty years. Thirdly, it was assumed that health and rehabilitation services would be widely available, as indeed was guaranteed in the 1948 National Health Service Act. Beveridge was therefore free to focus the nation's attention on the arrangements for the elderly, unemployed, sick, disabled, and widowed.

The corresponding risks would be covered by a single national insurance scheme to be administered by a central authority, the Ministry of Social Security. Adult benefits would be at a fixed rate with a supplement for dependants. They would be paid only to those not in work and those, except in the case of the aged, unable to work. There would be a fixed contribution, split between employees and employers, which Beveridge recognized would place a heavier burden on the low-paid, but was the necessary feature of any national insurance scheme which pooled equal risks and paid flat-rate benefits. Contributions, together with an Exchequer supplement, would be the sole source of finance for the national insurance scheme. Exactly enough money would be raised in any year to pay for benefits being met from the scheme. In order to qualify for benefits a claimant had to have a satisfactory contribution record. There was no means test. The national insurance scheme was to operate in conjunction with a back-up national assistance scheme. For those who could not satisfy the contribution requirements for national insurance – mainly because of the suggested twenty-year transitional period – or for whom the benefits were inappropriate, a means-tested benefit would be available. Once the national insurance scheme had matured, national assistance would rarely be used. Most of Beveridge's recommendations were incorporated into the 1946 National Insurance (Industrial Injuries) Act. The Beveridge scheme was administered by the Ministry of Pensions and National Insurance. With the passing of the 1948 National Assistance Act, the Poor Law was officially committed to the grave;

the National Assistance Board was created to administer non-insurance benefits.

Beveridge was wedded not only to an insurance principle but also to a subsistence principle. In turn the subsistence principle required not only that benefits should be adequate but also that they should be no more than adequate. The former requirement follows directly from a desire to abolish want. The latter has a rather more complex justification. Certainly Beveridge was faced with a situation where if flat-rate contributions were not going to be over-burdensome for those on low incomes, they had to be fairly low, while at the same time the scheme had to be financially sound. With his belief that the Exchequer supplement should only be 20 per cent of joint contributions in the early years of the scheme these conditions dictated fairly restrictive benefits. Beveridge was also very wary of the possible effects of an organized social security system on the national economy, as a result of it demanding too large a share of general revenues and also affecting national output more directly. The scheme, while not being limited in coverage, should be modest in a financial sense. But, as Kincaid (1973) has pointed out, these opinions had the same implications as Beveridge's general social philosophy: he was a libertarian, and felt that government intervention should impinge upon the freedom of the individual as little as possible in seeking to fulfil its defensible objectives. Subsistence benefits were not only demanded for reasons of good housekeeping but were also in themselves desirable, and therefore a merit of the scheme. Individuals would remain free to provide more than the minimum for themselves and their families.

Having established a case for subsistence benefits, albeit maybe an uneasy one, it was then necessary to establish how subsistence levels were to be determined. Beveridge relied on calculations undertaken by Rowntree (1941), which were based upon his observations of the living standard and working conditions of the lower classes in York. In an earlier study (Rowntree, 1901), Rowntree's view of a subsistence income was determined by a relationship between basic physiological needs and budgetary efficiency. Primary poverty was evidenced when an efficiently spent income could not cover basic needs; secondary poverty was evidenced when a small amount of inefficiency in spending income led to the same result. Basic physiological needs were elaborately differentiated and converted into monetary amounts. On this basis Rowntree established the existence of standards of living in York that even the most careful reorganization of spending could not prevent from appearing fairly horrific in the eyes of all reasonable people. But by the time of his second study, current convention had superseded survival, and a varied diet and some non-essentials were included in the subsistence standard.

Nevertheless, Beveridge recommended that benefit levels be set slightly below the new subsistence levels established by Rowntree. He would not pay for travel to and from work, despite the fact that the same costs would probably be incurred by an unemployed man looking for work. Benefit recipients presumably also had no need of haircuts, entertainment, or postal services, since these were not provided for. However, to allow for some inefficiency in budgeting the full cost of personal sundries was not subtracted from the Rowntree estimates.

These reformed social security arrangements ran into trouble virtually from the moment they were implemented, although this did little to diminish the solidarity in political support for the post-war reforms. First, although Beveridge envisaged a twenty-year transitional period, political expediency led to full pension rights being given immediately to all existing pensioners. Second, when National Assistance came into operation in 1948 the full benefits payable exceeded the National Insurance benefits being paid, which had been set at an even lower level than intended by Beveridge, and most National Insurance beneficiaries also qualified for the National Assistance. National Assistance was fulfilling a far from subsidiary role. In the longer term there was a demographic trend which saw the ratio of the working population to the retired declining, and which thus forced up contribution rates. Beveridge was aware of this trend but his intention was that there should be some scope to increase the Exchequer supplement; the Treasury did not share this sentiment and the burden tended to fall on employees and employers (see Field, Meacher, and Pond, 1977). Political pressure ensured that benefits were periodically increased. At the same time earnings of the low-paid failed to keep up with those of the work-force in general. Not surprisingly it became increasingly difficult for successive governments to justify flat-rate contributions, because they were bearing unfairly and to an intolerable degree on the low-paid. For example, in 1958 the flat-rate employee contribution was 10 shillings or 50p. Average weekly earnings for male manual workers stood at £12.77, and the contribution therefore represented 3.9 per cent of these earnings. But for a low-paid worker earning £5 a week this rose to 10 per cent, while for an affluent worker earning £25 a week the contribution demanded only 2 per cent of earnings. A way out of this dilemma was sought.

It was found in the 1959 National Insurance Act, the Boyd–Carpenter plan. The Conservative government introduced a graduated pension scheme in 1961, operating it as a supplement to the existing National Insurance scheme. A small earnings-related pension was earned in return for earnings-related contributions set at a level far in excess of the level needed to finance the contemporaneous benefits. This was not surprising since the whole scheme was felt by many simply to be a method of financing existing National Insurance benefits by deception. The scheme was therefore wildly unpopular.

In 1966 the Ministry of Social Security replaced the Ministry of Pensions and National Insurance, and it became responsible for National Assistance, which at the same time was renamed Supplementary Benefit. Supplementary Benefit was to be administered directly by the Supplementary Benefits Commission. By 1968 the Ministry of Social Security had been merged with the Ministry of Health to create the Department of Health and Social Security.

In our discussion of the role of social security we emphasized the need to relieve poverty. Subsistence benefits should achieve this objective; the extent to which in fact they do so will be studied at a later stage. We also suggested that there may be a case for a public programme of earnings-related benefits. By the mid-1960s there was a growing political awareness that just as subsistence benefits had been the answer to the problems of the 1940s and 1950s, so earnings-related benefits would meet the different demands of the 1960s and after. In the aftermath of the depression of the 1930s the public's views about a minimal standard of living were conditioned by the severity of that depression, and what in the 1940s were judged to be subsistence benefits would have offered considerable improvements in living standards to those who suffered in the 1930s. Later the protection of customary standards began to be suggested as a primary objective of social security. The cynical might look upon the expression of these wider objectives as simply an attempt to provide a defensible excuse for the graduated pension scheme. But an earnings-related supplement was extended to other national insurance benefits in 1966 and 1975. And numerous White Papers describing proposed social security reforms affirmed the belief in earnings-related benefits.

In 1969 the Labour government outlined an ambitious blueprint for the merging of flat-rate and earnings-related benefits – the

Crossman plan (DHSS, 1969) – but before it could be implemented the Labour government had fought and lost an election. In 1971 the Conservative government announced its own intentions, the Joseph plan (DHSS, 1971). These plans focused attention on retirement pensions, and in particular the role that ought to be played by the state at a time when occupational pension schemes were growing in their coverage. Crossman argued for a dominant role for the state, and specified extremely complex arrangements by which employers offering good pension coverage to employees could contract out of – that is, withdraw their employees from – part of the fully earnings-related state scheme. This arrangement was already a feature of the graduated pension scheme. Joseph, on the other hand, emphasized the subservient role of the state. There would be universal coverage by a flat-rate scheme with a back-up state reserve scheme, offering an earnings-related arrangement to those employees whose employers provided no, or insufficient, private coverage. Like the Crossman plan the Joseph plan suffered at the hands of the voting public in 1974 despite having reached the statute-book in the previous year.

While these plans were being discussed some changes were made to social security arrangements. Most notably in 1971 a new means-tested benefit was introduced, Family Income Supplement, which was payable to families with dependants, and whose head was in full-time work, while means-tested housing benefits for those not in receipt of Supplementary Benefit, in which case housing costs were fully taken into account, became widely available after the passing of the 1972 Housing Finance Act. These, combined with the graduated pension scheme and other earnings-related National Insurance benefits, meant that there was now a major difference between the social security system in operation and that envisaged by Beveridge. Indeed, his guiding principles seemingly exercised little influence over social security arrangements. In 1974 the Labour government outlined further proposals for earnings-related pensions with contracting-out – the Castle plan (DHSS, 1974) – and these came into effect from April 1978 consequent upon the passing of the 1975 Social Security Pensions Act. They remain in effect despite a change of government. Contributions have been fully earnings-related since 1975. But there has been some subsequent retreat in the provision of earnings-related benefits to non-pensioners. The arrangements for child support have also been changed. Family allowance was abolished in 1977, and child benefit phased in over the next two years, as arrangements for child support through the tax system were withdrawn.

The 1980 Social Security Act brought changes in the administration of the Supplementary Benefit scheme; the scheme is now commonly referred to as the 'new' Supplementary Benefit scheme. Under the 1982 Social Security and Housing Benefits Act, the system of housing benefits was administratively rationalized from April 1983, and in the first eight weeks of sickness and injury, 'statutory sick pay' is paid in place of existing sickness or injury benefits.

Social security expenditure 1980–1

Social security expenditure in the year ending March 1981 totalled £22.4 billion, around 10 per cent of gross national product and 21 per cent of total government expenditure. Social security expenditure splits conveniently into two categories, that on contributory National Insurance benefits and that on non-contributory benefits. A breakdown of expenditure is given in Table 2.2. With 9 million retirement pensioners out of 12 million recipients of National Insurance benefits,

TABLE 2.2

Expenditure on Principal Social Security Benefits: 1980–1
(£ million)

National Insurance Benefits	
Retirement Pensions	10,541
Unemployment Benefit	1,281
Invalidity Benefit	1,150
Widow's Benefit	688
Sickness Benefit	596
Others	657
Total	14,863
Non-Contributory Benefits	
Child Benefit	3,005
Supplementary Benefit	2,859
Others	1,637
Total	7,501
Total Benefit Expenditure	22,364

Source: DHSS, *Social Security Statistics*, 1982. (Supplied in advance of publication by DHSS Central Office, Newcastle upon Tyne.)

it should not be too surprising that retirement pensions demand a large share of National Insurance expenditure. And of the 11 million payments of non-contributory benefits 7½ million were of child benefit in respect of 13 million children, and 3½ million of Supplementary Benefit. These figures refer to an average week in 1981. With 2.8 million unemployed the expenditure on unemployment benefits may seem surprisingly low. But only about 1 million unemployed actually received unemployment benefit; 1.3 million received Supplementary Benefit instead, because unemployment benefit is only paid for a restricted period, or as well, because they are entitled to both. The unemployed on Supplementary Benefit received £2,200 million in benefit, making the total cost of benefits to the unemployed more like £3,500 million rather than the £1,300 million spent on unemployment benefit. Thus, all in all, payments to the retired, to the unemployed, and in respect of children accounted for about three-quarters of total social security expenditure in 1981. About half of the remainder went to the sick and disabled. Family Income Supplement cost only £43 million. (All the above figures are taken from DHSS Social Security Statistics, 1982.)

This expenditure is financed in two ways. Contributory National Insurance benefits are paid out of the National Insurance fund. The fund derives its income predominantly from National Insurance contributions charged to employees and employers, although an Exchequer contribution provides some 17 per cent of the total. Income should roughly match expenditure – the National Insurance scheme is financed on what is often known as a pay-as-you-go basis – but the National Insurance fund tends to carry forward a surplus each year. In 1981 this was a little less than £½ billion, and in March of that year the fund stood at £5 billion. A few very small non-contributory National Insurance benefits are paid out of the National Insurance fund, but non-contributory benefits are as a rule financed out of general revenue, often referred to as the Consolidated Fund.

Social security benefits

We have drawn the distinction between contributory National Insurance benefits and non-contributory benefits. Associated with the former are a set of contribution conditions which will be outlined shortly. We have also seen that the principal contributory benefits are retirement pensions, unemployment benefit, widow's benefit, sickness benefit, and invalidity benefit. The others are maternity benefit, death grant, and a child's special allowance, paid when maintenance payments cease on the death of an ex-husband. Guardian's allowance, industrial disablement benefit, and industrial death benefit are the non-contributory National Insurance benefits. Nearly all National Insurance benefits are paid at a weekly flat rate: the exceptions are two lump-sum payments – death grant and maternity grant (which is part of maternity benefit) – and the earnings-related pension paid under the state earnings-related pension scheme, which is in addition to the flat-rate basic pension. Earnings-related supplements to unemployment benefit, sickness benefit, and maternity allowance (the other part of maternity benefit), and the earnings-related addition to widow's allowance (part of widow's benefit) were abolished with effect from January 1982. A distinction can be drawn between short-term and long-term benefits. Unemployment benefit is paid for 52 weeks, sickness benefit for 28 weeks, widow's allowance for 26 weeks, and maternity allowance for approximately 18 weeks. When these benefits cease, claimants can be switched to a long-term National Insurance benefit which is paid indefinitely – invalidity benefit after sickness benefit, widowed mother's allowance or widow's pension after widow's allowance (these are the three components of widow's benefit) – or Supplementary Benefit.

Some non-contributory benefits are paid as of right. Child benefit, and where appropriate an additional one-parent benefit, is paid in respect of every child. Various benefits – attendance allowance, mobility allowance, and invalid care allowance – are paid to the physically and mentally disabled, and those who care for them. There are some non-contributory pensions, also invalidity and age additions to pensions, and all pensioners receive a lump-sum Christmas bonus.

Other non-contributory benefits are means-tested; that is, they are only paid if claimants can prove that their financial situation justifies payments. Supplementary Benefit is paid to those not in full-time work (working less than thirty hours a week) and makes up the difference between a family's requirements and its resources, the former being reflected in an appropriate 'scale rate' plus an addition for full housing costs, and the latter requiring the independent assessment of income from different sources according to detailed rules. Only the man in a married or unmarried couple can normally claim supplementary benefit. Additional payments, made regularly to cover the costs of heating, a special diet, or essential domestic help, or as a lump-sum grant to purchase necessary domestic appliances, furniture, or clothing, will be made to those who qualify for them. Prior to 1980 they were discretionary. Separate long-term scale rates apply to retirement pensioners – for whom Supplementary Benefit is referred to as supplementary pension – and those who have received Supplementary Benefit for 52 weeks without being required to make themselves available for work. Family Income Supplement is paid to a family when the head is in full-time work, and makes up half the difference between a qualifying level and gross weekly income, both of which are subject to suitably elaborate calculations. Recipients of Supplementary Benefit and Family Income Supplement are entitled to (or have a 'passport' to) a wide range of non-cash, means-tested benefits, for example free prescriptions, free milk, free school meals, free or cheap NHS dental treatment and glasses, and refunds of fares to hospital. Others may also qualify for these and other non-cash benefits.

Supplementary Benefit payments reflect housing costs; those not on Supplementary Benefit have to rely on a system of means-tested rent and rate rebates and rent allowances. Although these have not formally been part of the social security system in an accounting sense, they are an important element of income support. In 1981 they were paid out to about 3½ million households and cost £600 million (a breakdown of expenditure is provided in Chapter 7). They are widely viewed as social security benefits, and legislation and accounting convention do now largely reflect this. Council tenants are eligible for rent rebates, rate-payers for rate rebates, and private tenants for rent allowances. Rebates and allowances again rely upon complicated formulas to compute the needs allowance and gross weekly income which determine the benefit payable. After April 1982 many Supplementary Benefit recipients – those who are not council tenants and those whose Supplementary Benefit is less than their housing costs – qualify for rebates and allowances rather than Supplementary Benefit housing payments.

Some benefits are taxable: these are retirement pensions, widow's benefit, unemployment benefit and Supplementary Benefit paid to the unemployed and strikers, and statutory sick pay (which is also subject to National Insurance contributions). However, the retired and widows receive some tax concessions over and above those afforded all other taxpayers. But retirement pensions may be subject to an earnings rule, whereby once earnings reach a certain limit the pension is reduced, initially by 50p per pound of earnings, and then quickly by a pound in the pound.

Only a cursory look at the range of social security benefits currently available has been attempted above. We will be examining some of the principal benefits – retirement pensions, unemployment benefit, sickness benefit, disablement benefits, child benefit, Supplementary Benefit, Family Income Supplement, and housing benefits – in considerable detail, and others a little less fully. We therefore postpone a more complete description of benefits until then. But even then we will not go into the details of each and every benefit. Those with limitless time and patience can discover all there is to know about the 31 principal benefits (28 social security benefits and 3 housing benefits) by reading the appropriate statutes and department leaflets. However, we would recommend that instead they consult the excellent handbook to the benefit system provided by Mathewman and Lambert (1982).

Benefit levels

In 1948 social security benefits were set at levels which were close to, and if anything slightly below, subsistence level. Table 2.3 reveals that,

TABLE 2.3

The Real Value of Social Security Benefits: 1948-80
(£, April 1981 prices)

	July 1948	April 1961	September 1971	November 1975	November 1980
Unemployment benefit[a]	19.64	26.88	34.96	36.47	35.61
Retirement pension[a]	19.64	26.88	34.96	42.96	46.32
Supplementary Benefit[b]	17.93	25.31	33.39	35.10	36.65
Child support[c] – one child	4.87	4.36	4.27	3.67	4.84
Child support[c] – three children	17.60	16.62	15.36	13.81	13.44

[a] Standard rates for a couple.
[b] Scale rate for a couple (housing costs are provided for separately).
[c] Including the value of support provided through the tax system. Figures are for April of each year.

Source: DHSS, *Social Security Statistics,* 1981.

of the major items of social security expenditure, only child support has not increased in real terms (relative to prices). The real value of other benefits has more or less doubled. However, Table 2.3 only shows the long-term trend. For extended periods in the 1950s and 1960s

benefit levels were fixed while prices rose, and real values fell correspondingly. Recent years have also seen reductions in the real level of
some benefits.

Current practice — as a result of the 1975 Social Security Act —
requires that most social security benefits are reviewed each March
in the light of inflation which has occurred over the previous four
months and the level of inflation which is expected over the next
eight months. Benefits are then uprated from the following November.
Only a few benefits — most notably Supplementary Benefit — do not
have to be reviewed, although they have not as yet been excluded.
Table 2.3 shows that the real value of retirement pensions has leapt
forward in recent years. During the 1970s most benefits have been price
protected — approximately indexed to retail prices — but between
1975 and 1980 flat-rate pensions and other long-term benefits were
indexed to whichever was the faster rising of earnings and prices, which
turned out to be earnings. Since 1980 long-term benefits have been
indexed only to prices. However, short-term National Insurance
benefits have not kept up with prices. They suffered a cut of 5 per
cent (officially referred to as an abatement) in 1980. The 5 per cent
cut was supposed to be in lieu of benefit taxation, although only an
impending general election has brought any indication that, now
taxation of short-term benefits has begun, the cut will be restored.
Upratings are based on inflation estimates, and there is no legal requirement that shortfalls are made good, nor that overpayments are
recovered. There was an overshoot of 1 per cent in the case of retirement pensions in November 1980, and this was deducted from the
November 1981 uprating. There were shortfalls in the uprating of most
benefits in 1979, 1980, and 1981 which achieved considerable savings.
Only the 2 per cent shortfall in 1981 will be restored from November
1982; at the time of writing (October 1982), it looks as though there
could be a significant overshoot in 1982–3. It has been indicated that
this will be recovered in the November 1983 uprating, although again
a late 1983 general election may prevent (or delay) this.

While short-term National Insurance benefits have suffered in recent
years, some other benefits have been fully protected relative to prices.
The real value of Supplementary Benefit has been maintained, and
some of the child rates have increased in real value, although housing
is now removed from the retail price index for uprating purposes
because the housing costs of Supplementary Benefit recipients are met
in full; this depresses the index when housing costs increase faster than

prices in general. Whether this practice will be continued should real housing costs begin a continued fall – as there is some indication they have done – is not certain. The qualifying level for Family Income Supplement has also increased in real terms. But other elements of family support have suffered even more than the main National Insurance benefits. Child benefit was not restored to its April 1979 value in the following November, and is now worth nearly 10 per cent less in real terms than in April 1979. And from November 1981 the method of calculating the child additions to National Insurance benefits was changed, with the effect that these were drastically cut. There is a widespread feeling that this benefit-cutting strategy will be continued under the current Conservative government, except when politically inexpedient.

National Insurance contributions

Contributions are divided into four classes, but Class 1 contributions which are made by employees and their employers are the major source of revenue. Class 1 contributions are based on all earnings below an upper earnings limit but are relieved if earnings do not exceed a lower earnings limit. Those who satisfy the contribution conditions are entitled to the full range of National Insurance benefits. Broadly speaking a benefit will be paid at its standard rate if Class 1 contributions equal in value to fifty times the weekly lower earnings limit were paid in the tax year preceding the calendar year in which a benefit is claimed. Benefit will be paid at a reduced rate if contributions amount to twenty-five times the weekly lower earnings limit. These are exactly the terms under which unemployment benefit would be paid to a person with an unbroken employment record prior to his or her claim. However, they do not apply to all benefits. For example, maternity grant can be paid if contributions amount to twenty-five times the weekly lower earnings limit. And a standard retirement pension requires contributions amounting to fifty-two times the lower weekly earnings limit in nine out of every ten years of a working life. Where an employment record is broken, say by unemployment or sickness, a person can be credited with contributions, in which case credits can be substituted for payments, but, again broadly speaking, the required contributions must have been paid in any one tax year. Where a period of time is spent raising or caring for the elderly, sick, or disabled at home there is provision for home responsibility protection. The number of qualifying years are amended accordingly.

Married women and recipients of widow's benefit have in the past been allowed to pay a reduced contribution rate. They then forfeit their rights to all benefits other than those they can receive on their husbands' contribution records and industrial injury benefits. Women who entered the work-force after April 1977 were not offered this choice. Lower Class 1 contributions are also paid by both employees who are contracted out of the state earnings-related pension scheme by virtue of their membership of a good occupational pension scheme, and their employers, but only on earnings above the lower limit.

In addition to Class 1 contributions, since 1977 most employers have also had to pay a National Insurance surcharge. Levied on the same earnings as contributions this was initially set at 1.5 per cent, then rose to 3.5 per cent, and since August 1982 has been 2 per cent. Over the period 1977–80 the surcharge raised on average £2.3 billion which was paid directly into general revenue: over the same period the Exchequer contribution to the National Insurance fund averaged £2.15 billion. There was never any explicit rationale given for the surcharge, and there may well be some truth in the apocryphal claim that it was introduced to offset the Exchequer contribution. Certainly the elaborate piece of accounting implied by the existence of these two forms of financing has little apparent rationale.

Class 1 contribution rates for 1982–3 are reported in Table 2.4, along with the earnings limits. The rates and earnings limits are adjusted to meet each year's revenue requirements. The fixed point is the lower earnings limit, which the 1975 Social Security Pensions Act requires to be roughly equal to the basic state pension at the start of the financial year. Contribution rates are fixed from April to April, and benefit rates, including pensions, from November to November. Thus the financial year coincides with the contribution year. There is some flexibility over the upper earnings limit which has to lie between 6½ and 7½ times the lower earnings limit. It has tended to be closer to the higher figure so that any level of expenditure can be financed with lower contribution rates.

Class 2 contributions are flat rate and paid by the self-employed: a satisfactory contribution record entitles them to most National Insurance benefits, the exceptions being unemployment benefit, industrial injury benefit, or any earnings-related benefits. The self-employed also have to pay profits-related Class 4 contributions to consolidate their benefit entitlement. Flat-rate Class 3 contributions are voluntary, and are made to repair a broken Class 1 or Class 2 contri-

bution record, although this normally has to be done within two years
of the end of the relevant tax year.

TABLE 2.4

National Insurance Contributions: 1982–3

Earnings limits	£ per week
Lower earnings limit	29.50
Upper earnings limit	220.00
Rates	percentage
Contracted in	
Employee	8.75
Employer[a]	12.2
Contracted out	
Employee	6.25
Employer[a]	7.7
Reduced rate for married women	3.2

Note: Not all National Insurance contributions find their way into the National
Insurance fund; there is a total contribution of 1.9 per cent into the redundancy
fund and to the National Health Service.

[a]Including 2 per cent surcharge.

Social security administration

For much of its life the National Insurance scheme was overseen by
a body of National Insurance commissioners. Because entitlements to
National Insurance benefits are laid down in law, all decisions regarding
benefit payments have to be made in the light of this law. Appeals
could be made to the commissioners, all judges, on points of law, and
their rulings set up legal precedents. The National Assistance Board,
and subsequently the Supplementary Benefits Commission (mainly
academics and representatives of various welfare agencies), has been
responsible for the National Assistance/Supplementary Benefit scheme,
and Family Income Supplement. These bodies had extensive discretionary powers, shared by the benefit officers and local tribunals
which implemented their policies, although benefit officers and local
tribunals did not have to abide by these policies. Claimants had no
legally enforceable rights, and could only appeal to a higher authority,
the High Court, when natural justice had been violated.

This obviously unsatisfactory state of affairs was changed with the passing of the 1980 Social Security Act. The Supplementary Benefits Commission was abolished, and replaced by the Social Security Advisory Committee: this Committee must be consulted by the Secretary of State for Social Services on all legislative matters. A set of legally binding Supplementary Benefit regulations has been created. And the National Insurance commissioners have been renamed social security commissioners, a change which reflects the widening of their role. Appeals can be made to them on points of both National Insurance and Supplementary Benefit law.

While the administration of the National Insurance scheme and Supplementary Benefit is now more fully integrated than ever before, the distinction between these two parts of the social security system is as important as it was when the Beveridge Plan was implemented. Beveridge believed that the insurance principle would be popular because voluntary insurance had previously been widespread and it would avoid the need for a means test by establishing claims as of right; this principle has been the most pervasive legacy of Beveridge. The extent to which the National Insurance scheme can be viewed as operating according to the same principles as private insurance will be discussed in Chapter 8. While Beveridge envisaged a situation in which the National Assistance scheme would become practically redundant, the failure of National Insurance benefits to measure up to subsistence standards prevented that ever being the case.

The purpose of means-testing is to guarantee that non-contributory benefits are paid only to those in need; hence the comparison of needs and resources. In principle a means test could be fairly simple: but we have already noted that each means-tested benefit relies on a different means test, and the formulas used to compute needs and resources are different, and equally convoluted, for each. There is no clear correspondence between Supplementary Benefit scale rates, the Family Income Supplement qualifying levels, and the needs allowances for housing benefit. The Supplementary Benefit definition of resources includes payments of child benefit, while the Family Income Supplement definition of gross income does not; those with over £2,500 in savings are disqualified from receiving Supplementary Benefit, while the Family Income Supplement definition of gross income includes the imputed income from those savings. The means tests for free dental and optical treatment, free prescriptions, free milk, etc. operate broadly along Supplementary Benefit lines, but tend to set against income items disallowed when claiming the latter, for example hire-purchase payments. Some local authorities can enhance housing benefits, and the means test for free school meals varies from locality to locality. To determine whether a family is entitled to a benefit, and if they were how much they would get, would tax the author's abilities, even though the various schemes have been analysed in some detail. It is not difficult to imagine the horrors the schemes hold for the innocent claimants whose ability to feed themselves and their children depends upon their decision about what to claim and upon how much benefit they receive.

Means-testing adds considerably to the administrative costs of social security. Table 2.5 reveals that National Insurance benefits and the principal non-contributory, non-means-tested benefit, that is child

TABLE 2.5

Administrative Cost of Social Security Benefits

Benefit	Date	Administrative cost ÷ total benefit (percentage)
National Insurance[a]	1981–2	3.1
Child benefit[a]	1981–2	2.5
Supplementary Benefits[a]	1981–2	11.0
Family Income Supplement[a]	1981–2	4.0
Housing benefits[b] – rent rebates	1975–6	5.2
rent allowances		11.1
rent rebates		15.4

Sources: [a] House of Commons Hansard (23 February 1982). The 3.1 per cent figure excludes industrial injury benefit, for which the ratio of administrative cost to total benefit is 12.0 per cent.
[b] Meade Committee (1978).

benefit, require about 2½–3 per cent of total benefit expenditure to administer them: this is about half the cost at the outset of the National Insurance scheme (see Meade Committee, 1978) – reflecting improved benefits and some improvements in efficiency – but more than double the cost (relative to revenue) of administering income tax. But means-tested benefits are considerably more expensive, in the range 4.0 per cent, for Family Income Supplement, to 15.4 per cent, for rate rebates.

Means tests are not only difficult to understand and expensive to administer but also deter people from claiming. Both official and un-official estimates of take-up confirm that a significant proportion of those entitled to benefits do not receive them. Table 2.6 shows us that for no benefit is non-take-up below 25 per cent, and perhaps most staggering is the failure of nearly 50 per cent of qualifying families to claim the Family Income Supplement to which they are entitled. However, it is estimated that only some £15 million lies unclaimed, and with

TABLE 2.6

Take-Up of Means-Tested Benefits

Benefit	Date	Take-up (percentage)
Supplementary Benefit[a]	1977	74
Family Income Supplement[a]	1978–9	51
Housing benefits[b] – rent rebates	1979	72
rent allowances		50
rent rebates		70
Free school meals[c]	1978–9	61

Sources: [a] SSAC (1982).
         [b] House of Commons Hansard (13 February 1980).
         [c] Wilson (1981).

£50 million actually claimed this suggests that many of the sums forgone are relatively small, averaging slightly less than £3 a week. If families are ignoring these small sums because they regard them as trivial there is little cause for concern: some families will freely choose more modest life-styles than others. But if they do not know about their entitlement, if £3 is an indicator of the average financial cost of claiming, or if claimants feel degraded by the means test we should indeed be concerned. Were consumer ignorance the only problem, an effective advertising campaign would probably cost only a small fraction of the unclaimed benefit. Certainly claiming will often require bus fares (or other travel costs) to be paid, and if benefit is too small to cover the cost of claiming it, this nonsense is easily remedied. However, it has been clearly established that means tests are stigmatizing (except that for higher education grants, which are claimed mainly by the middle classes), and this is likely to influence take-up far more than consumer ignorance or piffling entitlements. If most non-take-up can be attributed to the damage done to the pride of those who ask for help and to a fear of being regarded as a burden on society, the prospects of significantly improving take-up are bleak.

   While there would appear to be no reasonable argument which could be used to defend complication on the grounds that it leads to incomplete take-up, measures to improve take-up would aggravate what in 1982 became a serious problem. Increasing unemployment has highlighted staff shortages in benefit offices to such an extent that during the year there were strikes all over the country, with the West Midlands particularly badly affected. To alleviate the work-load the Department of Health and Social Security introduced a measure of self-assessment for Supplementary Benefit. It consists of a form containing some 140 questions – although the question 'Are you a registered blind person?' will be irrelevant to most – many of which are so detailed that it is confidently expected by benefit office staff that so many forms will be incorrectly completed that it will increase and not reduce their work-load.

Social security abuse

Social security claimants have a bad reputation. The discovery of an unemployed man or woman who is work-shy – suffering from a non-existent backache or deliberately creating an unfavourable impression at job interviews – or who has a part-time job on the side, or of a single mother living with a man who is in work yet still claiming benefit, is often described as the 'tip of a fraud iceberg' by certain elements of the press and less responsible politicians and members of the judiciary. Social security fraud is taken very seriously, and some ministers at the Department of Health and Social Security, most notably Ian Sproat, Reg Prentice, Patrick Jenkin, and now Hugh Rossi, have been particularly enthusiastic in their fight against the fraudulent. Derek Rayner, in the course of his review of efficiency in government spending, endorsed such campaigns and recommended that additional funds be channelled in this direction to reduce the estimated 8 per cent of benefit payments made to those in work (DE and DHSS, 1981). In aggregate, fraudulent payments must therefore amount to around £2 billion, which is about two-thirds of the estimated loss resulting from tax evasion. And like that number it is complete guesswork. Only detected fraud can be measured, and this is small. In 1980–1 detected fraud and unwitting abuse amounted to only £171 million, a trivial sum compared to total social security expenditure, and it cost £33 million to trace that.

The social security system is policed in two distinct ways. In the Department of Health and Social Security great reliance is placed on informants, for example those who believe that their window-cleaner has told his regular employer that he is ill and is drawing sickness benefit, or that the unmarried mother living over the road is being kept by her boy-friend and claiming Supplementary Benefit. All information is followed up. Their fraud investigators have been treated with some public contempt mainly because the cohabitation rule – whereby unmarried couples living together can be treated as if they were married – is applied in what appears to be an arbitrary fashion; inconsistent decisions, and the hardship these sometimes create, have been well publicized. The conduct of Department of Employment fraud investigators attracts less opprobrium. They tend to be peripatetic, and are required to develop considerable cunning to seek out fraudulent claims of unemployment benefit. Instances of claimants turning up at benefit offices with a ladder on the roof of their car, or other blatant indicators of being in work, are rare. A number of investigators are therefore ex-policemen. A small proportion (5 per cent) of unemployment and single parent claims can be selected for detailed investigation by a Specialist Claims Control unit. Any unemployed claimant whose work history suggests possession of a skill marketable on the black economy or who has a suspiciously high standard of living, and any single parents who do not take court action to recover unpaid maintenance or who have children of school age, all of which might indicate that claimants are also working, tend to be the subject of investigations.

The methods of fraud investigation worry those who have studied them. For example, Robinson and Wainwright (1981) describe the way in which non-prosecution interviews by Specialist Claims Control investigators – intended simply to elicit information from claimants when there is no evidence but only a suspicion of fraud – often result in claimants withdrawing claims and repaying benefit under implicit threat of prosecution. In September 1982, 'Operation Major' in Oxford involved the indiscriminate interrogation of nearly 300 claimants by Thames Valley police and local Department of Health and Social Security officers, and the arrest of a third of those who were suspected of giving false addresses to secure extra benefit. Sections of the press likened the ingenuity and execution of the operation (and possibly its entertainment value for their readers) to the monumental confidence trick which was the subject of the successful film *The Sting*; others recognized that it raised very serious issues concerning the policing of the social security system. Only some months later did detailed information about 'Operation Major' become available. Franey (1983) is firmly of the opinion that neither the police, the Department of Health and Social Security, nor the Courts can take much pride in 'Operation Major'; it is concluded that, 'in justifying Specialist Claims Control, the Government has said that the innocent have nothing to be afraid of. Those arrested on September 2 know emphatically that the innocent do have reasons to fear' (Franey, 1983, p. 76). If there were even the most remote chance that the innocent lived in fear of fraud investigation there would be a need for a critical exploration of the techniques employed. The lesson learned from 'Operation Major' would seem to be that this is a matter of some urgency.

Since we do not know the extent of social security fraud, the success of fraud investigation cannot be gauged. While in terms of recovered money per investigator the Inland Revenue's specialist investigation units are far more successful (in 1980 spending only £5 million to recover £200 million in unpaid tax), little attention is paid to such comparisons. We would judge that, like detected fraud, undetected fraud is trivial, and that the government's emphasis on fraud investigation as a means of saving money is misplaced. Yet equally we believe that fraud should be investigated — but with a vigour at least matched by diligence, promptness, and sympathy in delivering benefits to those who should receive them — because the few fraudulent have, with some assistance, brought the social security system into disrepute. All claimants are thus affected, and the fear of being regarded, quite wrongly, as a cheat may deter many from claiming the benefits which they require and to which they are, after all, legally entitled.

3

POVERTY IN BRITAIN

HOW much poverty is there in Britain? Who are the poor? How poor are they? The answers to these questions will provide some indication of the quality of the social security system. But before they can be answered important methodological issues must be considered. The importance of these issues – which concern the appropriate poverty standard and the measurement of poverty – is reflected in the fact that the first half of this chapter is devoted to them. The picture of poverty we present reflects the way in which these issues are resolved. Ideally we would like to be really up to date, but this is difficult. We are forced to rely upon survey data which take a long time to collect, process, and analyse; it is often five years before results from suitable surveys are available. We have to be satisfied with data collected in the early 1970s. There has been one major development since then which would require us to modify the conclusions of say 1975 quite substantially, unemployment; we cannot be certain what impact a large increase in unemployment has had, but we can form a good idea.

The meaning of poverty

'Behind the door on which we knocked we found a married couple and four of their children, including one young daughter with a wan little baby of her own. A teenage boy, recently returned from an institution of some sort, had some reasonable clothes and bedding. His father had some worn through reasonable clothes, but no bedding. No-one else had any proper bedding or any clothes in which they could decently be seen in the street. They were sleeping under old coats and rags. The mother of the family, with a broken leg encased in plaster to the hip, was sleeping on a battered settee. There was no cot and no clothes for the baby, and no food in the larder. A fire was burning in the grate, but gas and electricity had been cut off, and both meters had been broken into. The back door swung lop-sidedly on one hinge. The place stank. Indoors and outdoors it was frosty cold. This was an extreme case, but every visiting social security officer meets one like it from time to time' (Donnison, 1982, p. 96).

In Britain today there are families — like the one described above — who everyone with knowledge of their living standards would agree experience intolerable hardship. Their life-style is so severe that no observer could fail to feel ashamed that they live in a society permitting such extreme poverty. There is also a large 'grey' area, within which people would be unable to agree which families were poor and which were not. A family unanimously agreed not to be poor is likely to have a life-style substantially more comfortable than that which most of us enjoy. Yet if we intend to regard the relief of poverty as a principal motivation for a social security system, and the extent to which this is achieved as an indicator of its success, the poor have to be identified. This clearly requires the specification of a poverty standard which will allow the poor to be separated from the non-poor.

It has been suggested by some that this is impossible; perhaps Orshansky (1965) has provided the most authoritative expression of this opinion. The problem would appear to be that since there are likely to be a wide variety of views about the precise nature of poverty, and value judgements cannot form the basis of descriptive exercises, the poor cannot be identified in any policy-relevant sense. But it may equally be argued that a descriptive exercise requires neither that a universally agreed poverty line is established nor that there exist convincing rules for reaching a consensus from divergent individual views. It is sufficient to be able to justify ignoring the opinions of each and every member of society, and instead focus on identifying the established standards of adequacy in a particular society (see Sen, 1979).

If poverty is indeed no more than a value judgement, the dispassionate investigator of poverty in Britain may be easily persuaded in no event to entertain the prospect of attempting to identify the poor. But such submission would reflect not the moral force of the argument against the exercise, but an unwillingness to face up to the difficult problem of selection it imposes. For, while recognizing that in saying, for example, that there is too much poverty in Britain, or that India is a poorer country than Britain, different individuals can conclude these statements from numerous ethical standpoints, it is none the less valuable to be able to describe the contemporary standards of adequacy such statements generally imply. Ascertaining them may require some crude approximations given disagreement as to what ought to be meant by poverty — and it is difficult to defend failure to disclose these, or to masquerade them as some pseudo-scientific procedure for moving from individual to social expression — but this does not invalidate the exercise. Indeed, it is only such approximations which will allow us to move from popular usage to a workable poverty standard, and only then can poverty in Britain be described.

While the possibility of a descriptive exercise has always been widely acceptable in Britain, it is perhaps not too surprising that there has been some disagreement as to what constitute adequate standards of decency. Two distinct approaches can be identified. One defines poverty in an absolute sense, with no reference to general living standards, and the other defines it in a relative sense, and does take account of general living standards.

In his study of poverty in York at the end of the nineteenth century Rowntree (1901) associated absolute poverty with a failure to maintain physical efficiency. Although modified in the interim the poverty standard established by Rowntree eventually formed the basis of the social security benefits paid under the Beveridge system. Yet it possessed fundamental weaknesses; in particular it was arbitrary. Physical efficiency could be maintained with a diet which did not vary with the type of work done; some beer, tobacco and a holiday were features of a subsistence standard of living; actual housing, if above a minimal standard, was always regarded as subsistence housing. Any precision that Rowntree's standard would appear to possess is totally misleading. It is clear that poverty has an irreducible core, and that there is a life style which in any society would be regarded as poverty. And this is really the only interpretation which can reasonably be placed upon the term absolute poverty. Rowntree was obviously more generous than this, and became increasingly so, no doubt influenced by what he saw around him in York. To be influenced in this way is widely acceptable, and it allows us to say that there are poor families in both India and Britain, despite the fact that the poor in Britain would not be regarded as poor in India. Although Rowntree initially defined his poverty standard in absolute terms, he ultimately measured relative poverty.

The notion of relative poverty can be interpreted in a number of ways. For example, it can be seen to imply that the poor are a fixture, say the bottom 10 per cent of the income distribution. But this is not what is generally meant by the term. While poverty will in any practical sense always imply income inequality, the reverse is not necessarily true. Relative poverty will normally be defined with respect to a standard of living related to the average for society, and which increases as the average increases. This is the sense in which the poverty standard is relative. However, it is quite possible that nobody is below the poverty standard. Clearly there is considerable overlap between the concepts of poverty and inequality, but to suggest the usurping of one by the other is to reduce our ability to describe fundamental characteristics of a society with any accuracy in terms which would be commonly understood.

A relative poverty standard, distinct from income inequality considerations, is generally related to what established rules of decency render appropriate. But while this has been recognized in principle, in practice little importance has been attached to it. One crucial reason for this is that the existence of an official poverty standard – as reflected in the minimum income the state guarantees a family – can be seen to obviate the need for the selection exercise referred to above; indeed a number of important poverty studies have been based upon this approach. Another attraction of the use of the official standard is that it allows the success of social security policy to be judged against a bench-mark that governments themselves determine. While there are many problems which arise as a result of adopting this approach, and some will be considered shortly, perhaps the most fundamental criticism it attracts is that deviations of income from the official poverty standard, or even more generous standards, are a flawed indicator of the deprivations which create poverty.

Townsend (1979) emphasizes inadequate social functioning as a guide to poverty. He attempts to characterize a style of living widely shared or approved of in society, and then relates the extent to which this style of living is not achieved to resources. Poverty occurs when a small reduction in resources is accompanied by a disproportionate increase in deprivation: poverty is defined only in terms of relative deprivation. Using data from a specifically commissioned household survey, Townsend constructs a provisional deprivation index, based upon a dozen household characteristics reflecting their social functioning. This index is then compared with household income, and it was discovered that there existed a threshold of income below which disproportionate deprivation occurs; this was around 50 per cent above the official poverty standard.

Townsend's approach has clear technical deficiencies: in particular, his claim that there is a poverty threshold has no statistical basis. But, more importantly, it has crucial conceptual defects. The provisional index of deprivation is misleading, since it reflects not only the absence of opportunity for efficient social functioning, but also different preferences for the form social functioning takes. Many households do not wish to eat meat, take a holiday, or socialize, even though they can; others do not have the opportunity. Townsend sees both groups as experiencing similar deprivations. He is free to do this, but not to then claim, as he does, that his findings have relevance for policy. They are the product of a view of poverty which bears little relationship to either popular conception, or the opinions expressed in the numerous case studies Townsend so meticulously documents.

In discussing the extent of poverty in Britain, Townsend compares the picture which emerges using his poverty standard with two others; the first is the official standard, and the second a relative income standard, where the poverty line is expressed as some fixed proportion of average income. The arbitrariness of the second of these is emphasized. But the first is treated most sympathetically. For Townsend recognizes that where one is interested in appraising the social security system, or elements of it, the poverty standard which could be regarded as that accepted by society itself, and which should be attained by all as a result of government policies reflecting the wishes of that society, should rightly be the corner-stone of that appraisal. Thus the official poverty standard plays a large part in Townsend's study. However, this standard has inherent weaknesses which cannot lightly be assumed away.

We shall see that the official standard moves with the general level of incomes, albeit erratically: in this sense it captures the relative nature of poverty. But it does so in a rather mechanical manner, one which ignores important questions concerning both the meaning of relative poverty and the mechanism which should be relied upon to relieve poverty. We shall also see that the majority of those at risk of poverty rely on the state to provide most of their income. However, it is quite reasonable to argue that society believes this income should in part reflect what is necessary to avoid poverty, plus some share in the growth of the economy and incomes as a whole. In other words, it is possible that poverty can be relieved through economic growth which leaves relative incomes unchanged. To adhere rigidly to the official poverty standard assumes away this possibility, and only a change in relative incomes can reduce poverty. And it is clearly a paradoxical implication of equating poverty standards to minimum income guarantees, that any attempt by the government to help the poor through *ex gratia* increases in their state income automatically increases the incidence of poverty. And as a corollary the incidence of poverty is reduced if the state decides to be less generous. But perhaps most importantly the official poverty standard may not correspond to the standard which society deems to be appropriate. The government may well recognize the standard it ought ideally to apply but is successful in conveying the opinion that only something more modest is feasible. Thus the official standard reflects what society will attempt to eliminate, and not what society disapproves of when claiming there to be too much poverty.

Despite these weaknesses it still seems right that the social security system should be judged in the light of the official poverty standard. For the true test of a mechanism designed to guarantee a specified minimum standard of living is the extent to which it delivers what it promises. Whether what is promised is adequate is an important question, and one to which we will return; but it is quite a separate question, requiring us to make our own judgements as to how society as a whole interprets adequacy.

Poverty measures

When the official poverty standard is accepted as the basis of poverty measurement it is usual for a family to be regarded as poor when its net income falls below that standard. Studies which have adopted this approach tend to focus attention on poverty incidence: they have attempted to 'count the poor', and the proportion of the population they represent – widely referred to as the head-count ratio – has provided a measure of poverty in Britain. The extent to which the head-count ratio is reduced in moving from a comparison based on income ignoring the effect of social security, to one based on income allowing for the effect of social security, is treated as the principal indicator of the success of the social security system (see, for example, Atkinson, 1969). However, it has always been accepted that the picture of poverty this approach produces is deficient in a serious respect. It indicates exactly the same extent of poverty when all the poor have

incomes only a little way below the poverty line as when the same
number of poor have incomes substantially below it. Thus if all the
poor were paid a sum of money equal to half the difference between
their income and the poverty line, the fact that this cannot affect the
numbers living in poverty implies no reduction in poverty. This is so
despite the obvious relief the poor receive, and it is difficult to believe
that a poverty measure should not reflect the fact that the poor are
now better off. Beckerman (1979) and others subsequently have shown
that information on income shortfalls – the extent to which income
falls below the poverty line – very usefully supplements that contained in estimates of poverty incidence. These income shortfalls
are often known as poverty gaps.

If the average poverty gap is expressed as a proportion of the
poverty line, we have a measure of the average depth of poverty: if
the aggregate poverty gap is expressed as a proportion of gross national
product, we have a measure of the relative cost to the country of
relieving poverty. Both of these are useful indicators of social progress,
and each will indicate that paying the poor half the difference between
their income and the poverty line reduces measured poverty – each
index is halved – even though the number of poor is not reduced. We
will refer to these indicators as the poverty gap ratio and the poverty
relief ratio respectively. It is worth emphasizing that these measures
should be used in conjunction with the head-count ratio: just as the
latter is inadequate when used alone so are the poverty gap measures.
With the average poverty gap fixed, the poverty gap ratio is independent of the number of poor, and with the aggregate poverty gap fixed,
the poverty relief ratio is independent of the number of poor. But the
number of poor is still an invaluable piece of information; hence the
need to combine a poverty gap measure with the head-count ratio.

Although the poverty gap measures correctly reflect the impact on
poverty of money transferred to the poor, they cannot distinguish between money transferred to those suffering different degrees of
poverty. Neither the poverty gap ratio nor the poverty relief ratio can
differentiate between the cases where the total income of the poor is
equally distributed, and those where some of the poor have incomes
only a little way below the poverty line while the rest have negligible
incomes. It may be that in general we would prefer to direct limited
resources towards those in greatest poverty, and poverty measurement
should therefore take account of not only average poverty gaps but also
how poverty gaps are distributed amongst the poor. Thus, in principle,

we would want to say that a redistribution of income amongst the poor, from the least poor to the poorest, will reduce poverty.

Sen (1976) was the original champion of this view, in the belief that the important dimensions of poverty are its incidence, the average deprivation experienced by the poor, and relative deprivation. Poverty incidence is reflected in the head-count ratio and average deprivation in the poverty gap ratio. Relative deprivation occurs when some gaps are larger than others, and the feeling of deprivation increases disproportionately as gaps increase: relative deprivation is therefore increasing with the degree of inequality in the distribution of poverty gaps. Note that the term relative deprivation is being used in a sense somewhat different to that employed by Townsend (1979); in the definitive treatment of the subject, Runciman (1966) adopts an interpretation somewhere between the two. Sen also suggested an ingenious method by which these three dimensions of poverty could be integrated to produce a composite poverty index; this involves computing the Gini index of the distribution of income amongst the poor, and combining this with the head-count ratio and poverty gap ratio in such a way that the resulting index possesses certain desirable properties.

The Sen index has been widely commented upon, and much modified. Most notably Takayama (1979) has suggested that it embodies only a limited notion of relative deprivation. Specifically, concentrating on the distribution of income amongst the poor implies that in assessing their feelings of deprivation it is assumed that the poor compare their situation only with those of other poor who are more or less deprived. Takayama argues that in assessing the experience of deprivation the non-poor, all of whom have an income at least equal to the poverty line, should enter the comparison directly. To assess relative deprivation the Gini index of an augmented distribution — where the non-poor are allocated an income equal to the poverty line — is computed. This inequality index depends in part on the number of non-poor and the average poverty gap; thus there is no need to combine it with the head-count ratio and the poverty gap ratio to yield a composite index. The inequality index serves as a poverty index. As it turns out, the Takayama index reduces to a combination of the head-count ratio, the poverty gap ratio, and the Gini index of the distribution of income amongst the poor, but is a different combination to that suggested by Sen. The composite indices are recent developments and as yet have not been widely used to measure the extent of poverty in Britain. Clark and Hemming (1981) have com-

puted Sen and Takayama indices using the official poverty standard
and their results are reported later in this chapter.

The official poverty standard

Poverty will be assessed relative to the Supplementary Benefit scale
rate: this is a widely practised and, as we have already argued, justifiable procedure. Few new results will be offered. The picture of
poverty which emerges will obviously be one of the principal influences
on the discussion of social security which follows. For this reason it is
essential that certain qualifications which bear upon the results
reported here are appreciated.

It is important to note that Supplementary Benefit scale rates are
defined exclusive of housing costs. Both within any region and across
regions there is price variation for items in a family's budget (see
Williams, 1977), and housing is the item of expenditure for which this
variation is most extreme. It is also the one over which families have
least discretion. Current housing expenditure is determined largely
as a result of decisions made a long time in the past, and the structure
of the housing market does not make it easy for low income families
who are spending too much on housing to do very much about it.
The measurement of poverty normally involves a comparison of
net income and the Supplementary Benefit scale rate, and net
income should naturally be defined not only exclusive of the usual
deductions – income tax and National Insurance contributions – but
also of housing expenditure.

It was pointed out earlier that Supplementary Benefit scale rates
have their origins in the estimates derived by Beveridge of the expenditure required to sustain subsistence living standards. However, relative
to that of the working population, the standard of living Supplementary Benefit can support is now somewhat higher than it was on the
introduction of the Beveridge Plan. Figure 3.1 traces the evolution of
the National Assistance/Supplementary Benefit scale rate (for a married
couple) relative to the average net earnings (less average housing costs)
of male manual workers. The trend is generally upward, although the
relationship between the scale rate and net earnings is erratic. It should
perhaps come as no surprise that many of the larger relative increases
have come at around the time of general elections, and in one case a
notorious political scandal. These larger increases are normally compensated for in subsequent years.

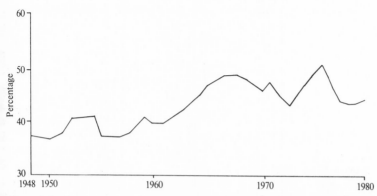

FIG. 3.1. Ratio of National Assistance/Supplementary Benefit Scale Rates to Net Earnings (Less Average Housing Costs): 1948–80 (Married couple below retirement age).

Sources: RCDIW (1978) for data up to 1976, and own calculations based on data from DHSS, *Social Security Statistics* and the *Department of Employment Gazette* for subsequent years.

Despite the fact that the relative value of the scale rate has tended to rise over time, with the average relative value increasing from 38 per cent in the 1950s to 45 per cent in the 1960s and 1970s, it should not be inferred that Supplementary Benefit does, or ever did, provide an adequate poverty standard. Figure 3.1 draws attention to the fact that when we look at changes in poverty over time, the poverty standard being applied is itself changing. Poverty is being measured with a poverty standard which in the long-term has become more demanding. But this reflects only the increasing generosity of the scale rates. From this one can infer that official policy requires poverty to be defined consistently as a phenomenon with a large element of relativity. That the standard of living of Supplementary Benefit recipients is one which can be generally regarded as minimally acceptable does not follow at all.

The Supplementary Benefit scale rates for different families embody equivalence scales, which attempt to take account of the fact that if expenditure per head is fixed, family composition will influence a family's standard of living per head. Thus the scale rate is lower for a married couple than for two single individuals, and lower for a couple with a child than for a couple and a single adult, etc. The equivalence scales implicit in recent scale rates are shown in Table 3.1. They are

TABLE 3.1.

Equivalence Scales

	Supplementary Benefit scale rates[a] 1981	Beveridge Plan	Family expenditure estimates[b]
Single person	62	59	–
Married couple	100	100	100
Couple with one child	121–49	122	130–58
Couple with two children	142–98	144	160–216
Couple with four children	184–296	188	220–332

[a] Payments for children depend upon their age: ranges are minimum and maximum payments.
[b] Scales depend upon age of child, total expenditure, and whether there are economies of scale in food expenditure: the lower figure assumes children are under 5, there are economies of scale, and a total weekly expenditure in 1970 prices for an adult couple of £10; while the higher figure assumes children are over 5, there are no economies of scale, and expenditure is £30.

Sources: DHSS, *Social Security Statistics.*
              Beveridge (1942).
              Muellbauer (1979).

accompanied by those recommended by Beveridge and by those derived from data on family expenditure over the period 1968-73. A clear picture emerges. Apart from the increased generosity to older children evident in 1981, a response to the notion of a 'teenage cost peak' (Wynn, 1970), the Beveridge scales still underlie Supplementary Benefit scale rates. These scales have been criticized because they do not accurately reflect the actual expenditures of families of different composition (Nicholson, 1949). This is not surprising. The equivalence scales suggested by Beveridge exactly reflect the manner in which his poverty standard was derived, and thus share its principal weakness. The absolute poverty standard, and Beveridge's scales, are arbitrary. A number of attempts have been made to construct equivalence scales (usually for children only) based on actual expenditures: examples are McClements (1977), Fiegehen, Lansley, and Smith (1977), and Muellbauer (1979). There is some dispute as to how such scales should be estimated properly, but the differences are of a highly technical nature and there would be little point in attempting to resolve these here. The equivalence scales estimated by Muellbauer are the best currently available and are the scales reported as the family expenditure estimates in Table 3.1. While the expenditure-based scales indicate that children cost slightly more than allowed for by the Supplementary Benefit scales, it is difficult to conclude that the latter are wildly inappropriate.

Data sources

Official statistics provide the main sources of evidence about poverty in Britain. Some of the earliest estimates were based upon Inland Revenue (IR) statistics on the distribution of annual income: these are derived from a random sample of tax records. However, IR data are deficient in the crucial respect that they do not include information on those with low incomes, who are not subject to an income tax assessment, nor on the non-taxable social security income of those who are. For a number of years, but not since 1972–3, the Central Statistical Office supplemented these data from alternative sources, notably the Family Expenditure Survey (FES), and a number of researchers made use of these modified IR data to provide estimates of poverty. However, the majority of poverty studies simply rely on the Family Expenditure Survey.

The FES is an annual survey of the income and expenditure of some 7,000 households in a single two-week period with interviews spread over a calendar year. Its principal purpose is to provide information to calculate the expenditure weights required in the construction of the retail price index. However, this is one of its least well publicized uses: it is with the analysis of poverty and income redistribution that the FES is most often associated. FES data are not perfect for either its main purpose or the alternative uses to which it is put: the sample is small, and while the response rate is 70 per cent, which is quite good, response rates differ quite markedly between different groups of respondents. This has the result that the sick, disabled, and retirement pensioners are under-represented, while children are over-represented, and some sources of income, mainly from investment and self-employment, and some expenditures, notably on drink and tobacco, are under-reported. For further discussion of the quality of FES data the reader is referred to Kemsley, Redpath, and Holmes (1980). Despite these problems the FES is one of the best sources of data on poverty we have, and because the survey has been undertaken since the mid-

1950s, it is the only one which permits fairly long-term trends in poverty to be discerned.

The General Household Survey (GHS) has also provided data for poverty analysis: these data have been collected since 1971. The GHS sample is slightly larger than the FES sample, but it is far less ambitious in its coverage and the major weakness is that its income data are poor. Not only is income under-reported, but also no other information than that on gross annual income is collected: the GHS does not therefore permit the checks of internal consistency that are possible with the FES, which collects information on net income and deductions quite separately. In most other respects the GHS appears to be at least as reliable as the FES.

Poverty incidence

Our measure of poverty incidence is the proportion of the population who are poor. Table 3.2 summarizes the results of the majority of post-war studies of poverty in Britain. It simply updates a similar table provided by Atkinson (1975). When FES data are used the reported estimates are based upon 'normal' net disposable weekly income, which is personal disposable income defined in the familiar way minus actual (net) housing expenditure and, sometimes, work expenses. Normal income is distinguishable from the alternative concept used in the FES, 'last week's income', by the way in which employment income and social security benefits are treated. When earnings during the survey period are affected by irregular bonuses or short hours the employee's assessment of normal income is used. When an individual has been away from work for thirteen weeks or less, normal income when last employed is used in place of the short-term benefits actually received. All other things being equal, this definition of weekly income should provide poverty estimates which are broadly comparable with those relying on IR and GHS data, which base their estimates on annual income.

However, in Table 3.2 all other things are not equal, which explains why the studies using IR and GHS data produce far larger poverty estimates. The IR figures are probably an overestimate: there are more tax units than families or households, and so students or children with taxable income may be classified as poor; also, those with incomes at the Supplementary Benefit level tend to be regarded as poor, and when tax units change composition in the course of a year they are often mis-

TABLE 3.2

Poverty Estimates for Great Britain* and the United Kingdom: 1953–75

Year	Study	Data source	Unit	Poverty incidence (%)	Number of poor (millions)
1954	Gough and Stark	IR	tax unit	12.3	6.3
1959	"	"	"	8.8	4.6
1963	"	"	"	9.4	5.1
1953–4	Abel-Smith and Townsend	FES	household	1.2	0.6
1960	"	"	"	3.8	2.0
1967	Atkinson[1]	"	"	3.5	2.0
1969	Atkinson[2]	"	"	3.4	2.0
1968–9	Townsend	Own survey	"	6.4	3.8
1971	Fiegehen et al.	FES	"	4.9	2.6
1975	Beckerman and Clark*	"	"	2.3	1.3
1975	Layard et al.*	GHS	"	8.7	4.6
1975	Berthoud and Brown	GHS	"	11.3	6.1

Sources: Gough and Stark (1968), Table iv.
Abel-Smith and Townsend (1965), Table 25.
Atkinson[1] (1969), Table 2.2.
Atkinson[2] (1974).
Townsend (1979), Table 7.1.
Fiegehen, Lansley, and Smith (1977), Table 4.1.
Beckerman and Clark (1982), Table 3.2.
Layard et al. (1978), Table 3.1.
Berthoud and Brown (1981), Table 2.7.

classified. The estimates by Layard *et al.* are extraordinarily high, but this is readily explained. The Supplementary Benefit scale rates include a long-term addition, and in most studies this is allowed for in assessing pensioner poverty. But Layard *et al.* use the long-term rate for all household groups, a procedure defended because the income concept is long-term. However, prior to 1980 the long-term rate was only paid to those under retirement age who were not unemployed and who had been in continuous receipt of Supplementary Benefit for two years (now one year). It is quite reasonable for Layard *et al.* to argue that the long-term scale rates accord with their view as to an appropriate poverty standard, but otherwise the long-term rates are only an official standard with certain qualifying conditions. They certainly do not reflect the income which would be received by the majority of non-pensioners if they had to rely on Supplementary Benefit for the period over which income is assessed, in this case a year. For a married couple the long-term rate is 25 per cent greater than the ordinary rate.

The studies by Abel-Smith and Townsend, and by Townsend on his own, have shown that if the poverty standard is 40 per cent greater than the Supplementary Benefit scale rates then the number in poverty slightly more than triples. The estimates of Layard *et al.* are consistent with this. Using the same data as Layard *et al.*, Berthoud and Brown (1981) estimate that 11.3 per cent of individuals were poor in 1975. They too use the long-term Supplementary Benefit rate to determine whether a household is living in poverty. This procedure is defended by reference to: the fact that under the Beveridge Plan National Assistance did not guarantee poverty relief; the medical evidence that the ordinary scale rates could not provide adequate nutrition for children; the claims by the Supplementary Benefits Commission that many Supplementary Benefit recipients were poor; and the non-participating life-style, described by Townsend (1979), of those living close to the poverty line. To take account of the inadequacy of the scale rates for children, Berthoud and Brown compute an addition for children which bears an exact relationship to the difference between the long-term and ordinary rates for adults. This largely explains their much higher poverty estimate.

Comparing the results for 1953–4 and 1960, Abel-Smith and Townsend concluded that: 'On the whole the data we have presented contradicts the commonly held view that a trend towards greater equality has accompanied the trend towards greater affluence' (Abel-Smith and Townsend, 1965, page 66). Atkinson was more circumspect: '. . . there is no clear indication in recent years of a trend towards the elimination of poverty. . . . poverty in Britain has remained a problem of considerable magnitude throughout the past twenty years' (Atkinson, 1975, page 198). The more recent poverty estimates do not require the picture to be modified very much. That of Fiegehen, Lansley, and Smith is somewhat higher than those immediately preceding it, and higher than that of Beckerman and Clark, which in turn is lower than the estimates based on the FES for the 1960s. The difference between the two Abel-Smith and Townsend estimates reflects mainly a change in methodology and cannot in any way be explained by improved Supplementary Benefit scale rates relative to net earnings; the scale rates remained much the same, and the fact that they were higher but still stable in the late 1960s explains Atkinson's similar estimates for 1967 and 1969. The years 1971 and 1975 were much like 1967 and 1969, in the sense that the relative value of the Supplementary Benefit scale rates were similar. It seems that the most likely explanation of the differences between the Atkinson, Fiegehen-Lansley-Smith, and Beckerman-Clark estimates is to be found in the sensitivity of poverty estimates to minor changes in the small numbers of poor in FES samples, rather than in any trends. On the basis of evidence from the FES we would judge that Atkinson's conclusion remains appropriate.

Townsend's estimate is also high, nearly twice that of Atkinson for the same period. It is based on an independent survey which has two distinct advantages over the FES. Firstly, although information was collected for only 3,260 households, the survey collected detailed information about the resources and life-style of those at the greatest risk of poverty. In particular a careful attempt was made to trace the income of respondents over the previous twelve months, an attempt which should provide a more reliable estimate of 'normal' income for those with changing circumstances than the guess often relied on in the FES. Secondly, considerable care was taken to guarantee that those groups most susceptible to poverty were not underrepresented in the sample. While we have been rather dismissive about Townsend's preferred approach to poverty measurement there does not appear to be any good reason to reject his estimate of poverty incidence using the official poverty standard. It certainly appears to be on the high side, but perhaps only because we have been conditioned by the much lower estimates regularly indicated by the FES. The temptation to reject instead the FES estimates is easily avoided, but only because the Townsend survey is a one-off affair. If a similar survey were repeated, and revealed much higher poverty estimates than the FES, this position would have to be reviewed.

Some further methodological issues

Supplementary Benefit provides a source of weekly family income. These three words 'weekly', 'family', and 'income', are associated with the most interesting methodological issues raised in attempting to measure poverty; in addition to the issue of the exact measures that should be applied and that of the poverty standard to be adopted. The problems associated with the first two words are fairly well documented (see Fiegehen, Lansley, and Smith, 1977) and it is necessary only to provide a reminder of their significance.

Looking at poverty on a weekly basis has both advantages and disadvantages. Naturally some of those families identified as being poor in any particular week would be poor in most other weeks of the year. However, others may simply be down on their luck in that particular week, and over a year they should certainly not be regarded as poor. Now both permanent and temporary poverty are interesting phenomena, but the weekly perspective does not allow us to distinguish between them (whereas the annual perspective ignores temporary poverty). Sometimes data do allow these two phenomena to be separated − by comparing income in a particular week with 'normal' income − but it is often necessary to supplement the information provided with an analysis of the characteristics of the poor.

Most poverty studies attempt to estimate the proportion of the population living in poverty. If all households consisted of families, we could simply identify poor families or households and see how many individuals they contain. However, this in itself may give a misleading picture of poverty. In a poor family some members may secure an adequate standard of living at the expense of others; in a non-poor family some family members may have a very low standard of living. The extent of income sharing between family members is difficult to ascertain. Rimmer (1980) has reported examples of families where income sharing is far from complete, but cannot claim that this is at all widespread. Therefore the view that it is family poverty alone which is of interest seems for the moment sensible and practical. This view may need modifying, should poverty within the family be proved a problem of some magnitude. Where some households contain more than one family unit, say a family living with grandparents, a similar problem emerges. If income is shared within the family but not within the household, measuring poverty on a household basis, as is usual when using FES data, will produce misleading estimates. We would expect them to be too low. Little is known about income sharing within the household; however, it would be surprising if it were not less complete than within the family.

We have little information about how Supplementary Benefit income is supposed to be budgeted, although it has to be presumed that there exists a bundle (or bundles) of goods which it can finance, and which yield an adequate standard of living. The purpose of Supplementary Benefit is to provide the opportunity for an adequate standard to be achieved, but it does not guarantee that it is achieved. For example, some families may be financially inept or irresponsible, and therefore fail to reach this standard; families may face different prices, and thus some are prevented from attaining the standard; other families

may choose an extremely low standard of living, although not necessarily one they find unpleasant. We should be concerned about all these
families, and if we gauged poverty using a consumption poverty
standard — identifying those families who fail to achieve the minimal
consumption standard — we might judge them all to be poor. But this
would be misleading. Many demonstrably non-poor families may
choose low standards of living, and their income could be substantially
increased without much affecting their standard of living. The common
conception of poverty does not admit this possibility. There may be
a case for some limited retreat from the income concept of poverty.
However, the social security system is designed with the achievement of
a guaranteed minimum income as its objective, and using an income
basis for poverty measurement is therefore appropriate when assessing
that system. But, given the employment of the income basis, comple-
mentary information which details how this income is used is of
interest, and an effort to remove obstacles to its efficient use or
minimize its misuse should naturally be considered.

Fiegehen, Lansley, and Smith (1977) have examined the sensitivity
of their poverty estimates (for 1971) to some of the underlying assumptions. Their results are summarized in Table 3.3, and those involving the
substitution of last week's income for normal income, or the tax unit,
which broadly corresponds with the family, for the household, clearly
demonstrate how responsive poverty incidence is to changes in each

TABLE 3.3

Poverty Estimates Under Alternative Assumptions: 1971
(percentages)

	Poverty incidence
Initial estimate	4.9
Substituting:	
Last week's income for normal income	6.5
Tax unit for household	8.8

	Proportion of households living in poverty
Initial estimate	7.1
Substituting:	
Expenditure for normal income	9.4

Source: Fiegehen, Lansley, and Smith (1977), Tables 4.3, 4.5, and 4.6.

assumption. The effect of moving from income poverty to expenditure poverty is assessed only for estimates of the number of poor households, but marked responsiveness to the change is again revealed. And what is particularly interesting in this is the fact that of the 9.4 per cent of households which are poor on an expenditure basis, only 2.9 per cent would be poor on an income basis. The switch therefore affects not only the incidence of poverty but also the composition of the poor. The choice between income and expenditure bases is therefore important.

The justification for employing the expenditure basis is that it tells one more about standards of living. We have argued that since the official poverty standard is an income standard, the success of the social security system should primarily be judged by looking at its ability to eliminate income poverty. We have agreed, however, that information about the standards of living of the poor, and those in danger of poverty, is of considerable value. But what does expenditure tell one about standards of living? The most fundamental measure of standards of living, or economic welfare, is consumption, the benefits derived in any period from goods and services purchased in that period and from goods and sources purchased in previous periods which still yield consumption benefits. Weekly or annual consumption is not the same as weekly or annual expenditure. The distinction is clearest in the case of consumer durables: a television set obviously yields consumption benefits for some considerable time after it is purchased. Less obviously, and becoming increasingly so, do a suit, a paperback novel, and a restaurant meal. Expenditure is clearly closely related to consumption, but because nearly all goods have some durability, expenditure on any good is a poor guide to concurrent consumption of that good. It follows that even information on expenditure may not provide a reliable guide to standard of living. However, research is in progress which promises to allow a measure of consumption, and thereby standard of living, to be derived from household expenditure data.

The characteristics of the poor

The mid-1960s saw a rediscovery of poverty in Britain. Not that poverty had not existed prior to this; rather the possibility that the Beveridge plan had failed was one many were reluctant to contemplate. Yet Abel-Smith and Townsend (1965) were the first to demonstrate that it clearly had, and in ways which might not have been expected.

They found pensioners to be the most numerous among the poor, and being a pensioner carried with it the greatest risk of poverty. Many pensioners failed to claim the supplementary pensions, payable because National Insurance pensions were set at a level below the official poverty standard, to which they were entitled. The Ministry of Pensions and National Insurance (1966) confirmed the extent and causes of poverty among pensioners.

But the number of non-pensioner two-parent families in poverty was surprising (see also DHSS, 1971). For Beveridge had believed that wage income would nearly always be sufficient to maintain two adults and one child, and that family allowances would cover the cost of additional children. However, many families with their head in full-time work were poor, and they were not predominantly large families. A special government inquiry, Ministry of Social Security (1967), showed that of those poor families with two or more children, 57 per cent only had two or three children. There were three reasons for this. The first was low pay: contrary to Beveridge's expectation many workers failed to earn sufficient to leave their net earnings at the official minimum for a small family. The second was the low level of family allowances, which were initially set at a level below that recommended by Beveridge, and have then remained fixed for prolonged periods while prices have risen. Third, those liable to income tax were allocated a child tax allowance, a tranche of income free of tax which increased with the number of children, a second element to child support. But this allowance was of more value to those with high earnings than to those with lower earnings, and of no value whatsoever to the poorest families who were not liable to tax. Since the mid-1960s Family Income Supplement and housing benefits have been introduced, and child tax allowances and family allowances have been superseded by child benefit, mainly in response to the emergence of poverty among families where the head was in full-time work.

As well as families where the head was in full-time work, other families, in receipt of state benefits, were poor. One reason for this was the operation of the wage stop. The wage stop was designed to guarantee that the unemployed and temporarily sick did not receive state income in excess of their normal net earnings when in work. As a result of consistent pressure, largely from the Child Poverty Action Group, it was withdrawn in 1975. Also many of those entitled to benefits were not receiving them, again for reasons we have already outlined. Another group at severe risk of poverty, more so than others below retirement age but at less risk than retirement pensioners, were single-parent families. Finer (1974) showed that there were half a million such families in 1971. In a quarter of these the single parent was a widow or widower eligible to receive a National Insurance pension; and a half were divorced or separated, many of whom would have been awarded maintenance but some of whom did not receive it nor any Supplementary Benefit. The remainder were predominantly unmarried mothers relying on Supplementary Benefit.

A detailed study of the characteristics of the poor, as defined by the official poverty standard, has been undertaken by Fiegehen, Lansley, and Smith (1977). Some of their findings are summarized in Table 3.4. The results bear out much of what we have already said. The poor were predominantly retirement pensioners, the unemployed,

TABLE 3.4

The Characteristics of the Poor: 1971

Household characteristic		Proportion of poor individuals in households with each characteristic (percentage)
Number of adults:	1	36.9
	2	54.7
	more than 2	8.4
Number of children	0	58.2
	1	9.7
	2	10.8
	3	6.2
	more than 3	15.1
Status of head of household		
Age: 16–34		21.3
35–54		20.6
55–64		12.3
65 and over		45.8
Sex: Male		62.0
Female		38.0
Employment status:	Employee	14.4
	Unemployed	10.3
	Self-employed	12.0
	Retired	47.5
	Unoccupied	15.9
Main source of income		
Employment or self-employment		23.3
Social security		67.3
Other		9.4

Source: Fiegehen, Lansley, and Smith (1977), Tables 5.1, 5.3, and 5.4.

low-paid workers, single parents, and anyone else relying on social security; a fact which reflects the impact of non-take-up and the operation of the wage stop. In low-paid families with children, there were more children in poor small families than in poor large families.

The statistics in Table 3.4 on the distribution of the poor relative to the age of the head of the household, indicate that there may be a life cycle of poverty. Jackson (1972) has suggested that a distinction should be made between the high risk of poverty which occurs because of unforeseen circumstances, such as unemployment, sickness, or the absence of one parent, and that which is associated with predictable features of the life cycle, principally retirement and caring for children, and also being a dependent child. It certainly appears to be the case that there are relatively few poor households where the head is aged 35-64, which is the fundamental prediction of the life-cycle story. However, the interesting question is whether two or possibly three substantial periods of poverty is the reasonable expectation of a significant number of people who were in poor families as children. The reported characteristics of the poor do not contain the answer to this question. And so it is a difficult one to answer precisely; but the evidence suggests that the answer is more likely to be 'yes' than 'no'. Parental socio-economic background, education, and earnings are inextricably linked; Phelps-Brown (1977) summarizes the evidence. Occupational pension scheme coverage is better amongst non-manual than manual and unskilled workers (Government Actuary, 1978), and asset holdings tend to reinforce income inequality (Townsend, 1979). Someone who is poor as a child is more likely to be poor at some subsequent stage of the life cycle.

The only explicit study of the transmission of poverty has been undertaken by Atkinson, Maynard, and Trinder (1980). Rowntree undertook three poverty surveys in York, the last in 1950. Atkinson, Maynard, and Trinder traced the fortunes of a surprisingly large proportion of the respondents to the 1950 survey and their sons and daughters. They found that of children from families which were poor in 1950, 11.5 per cent were in poor families in 1975-6, and another 33.9 per cent were on the margins of poverty, that is with an income below 140 per cent of the appropriate long-term Supplementary Benefit scale rate. Of those children in families on the margins of poverty in 1950, 33.6 per cent were still there in 1975-6, and 6.4 per cent were unambiguously poor. While there had been some upward income mobility, the life cycle of poverty would appear to be a reality for a significant proportion of the York sample.

Using 1975 GHS data, both Layard *et al.* (1978) and Berthoud–Brown (1981) examine the characteristics of the poor. Because of their different definition of poverty – one not really appropriate to our study – they get slightly different quantitative results to Fiegehen, Lansley, and Smith (1977). Yet their qualitative results are similar, although there is an important difference. We have noted that low-paid large families did not contribute greatly to the number of poor in 1971; low pay provided a better explanation of the number of small families in poverty. Layard *et al.* and Berthoud–Brown find the reverse to be true. Few poor families were supported by an adult in full-time work: those on low pay tended to be women who were second earners, while when the head of a poor family was in full-time work he was generally fairly well paid, but the family was large. If the father was low-paid his wife often worked. There is little to indicate that low pay was a receding problem in the first half of the 1970s. But Table 2.3 showed that the real value of family support declined appreciably. Hence the increase in the number of poor larger families, a situation which is unlikely to have been reversed. The different findings for smaller families are probably a result, not of any fundamental changes in the composition of the poor, but of a more careful comparison of family earnings and family poverty.

There is one important respect in which the picture formed of poverty for the early 1970s will have by now changed, possibly quite dramatically. In 1971 and 1975 there were about one million unemployed; by early 1983 this figure has now risen to three and a half million. In 1971, 20 per cent of households where the head was unemployed were poor (Fiegehen, Lansley, and Smith, 1977, Table 5.3). If the 'risk of poverty' has not changed since then, there will now be an additional half a million poor households – containing a million to a million and a half individuals – who owe their plight to unemployment. It is a speculative contention, but with the figure of two and a half million poor which we have taken as the central estimate from earlier studies, and with little to indicate that poverty has fallen amongst other groups, it seems quite reasonable to suggest that the 1982 Family Expenditure Survey, when it becomes available, will reveal there to be about four million poor in Britain.

We have an idea how many poor there are, and who the poor are – pensioners, the unemployed, single parent families, large families, and many other social security recipients – and we now intend to see how poor the different groups are likely to be. We have discussed the issues which arise in attempting to answer this question. Unfortunately the household types for which the poverty indices that we discussed have been estimated do not exactly coincide with the breakdown of the poor just mentioned. Nevertheless the estimates in Table 3.5 are

TABLE 3.5

Poverty Indices by Household Type: 1975

Household type	Head-count ratio	Poverty gap ratio	Sen index	Takayama index
Single pensioners	0.159 (1)	0.104 (8)	0.030 (2)	0.016 (2)
Pensioner couples	0.062 (3)	0.116 (7)	0.012 (3=)	0.007 (4=)
Single non-pensioners	0.030 (4)	0.311 (5)	0.012 (3=)	0.009 (3)
Non-pensioner couples	0.013 (7=)	0.316 (4)	0.005 (7)	0.004 (7)
Couples (1–2 children)	0.016 (6)	0.347 (3)	0.007 (6)	0.005 (6)
Couples (3 or more children)	0.020 (5)	0.364 (2)	0.008 (5)	0.007 (4=)
Single parents	0.079 (2)	0.372 (1)	0.036 (1)	0.028 (1)
Others	0.013 (7=)	0.136 (6)	0.003 (8)	0.002 (8)

Source: Clark and Hemming (1981), Table 2.

informative. They are based on 1975 FES data, and use a poverty line reflecting official standards. Estimates of the head-count ratio, which shows the proportion of households of any type which is poor, reveal very clearly those who are at greatest risk of poverty, pensioners and single parents. The figures in brackets beside each estimate indicate the ranking of household types from the poorest (1) to the least poor (8). The estimates of the poverty gap ratio, which expresses the average deviation of net income from the poverty line as a proportion of the poverty line, are interesting. While many pensioners are poor, their poverty gaps are small, because unclaimed supplementary pensions are themselves small; while when non-pensioners are poor, in particular families with children, they tend to have large poverty gaps. Worst affected are single parents. Composite poverty indices take account of both the head-count ratio and the poverty gap ratio, and in addition inequality in the distribution of income amongst the poor. The Sen index gives more weight to the head-count ratio than does the Takayama index, but this is only just revealed by the data (compare pensioner couples against couples with more than three children).

Despite their small poverty gaps the composite indices still reflect the extent of poverty amongst pensioners as a group. But the indices agree that single parents are poorest, not only because they are at great risk but also because they risk more extreme poverty.

Inflation and the official poverty standard

We have noted the practice of uprating Supplementary Benefit each November to reflect inflation over the last twelve months. Inflation continues through the benefit year, but there are no explicit statements as to when Supplementary Benefit is at the real level which reflects the official poverty standard. For example, if this is at the date of uprating, then for the remainder of the year Supplementary Benefit must be below the official 'real' standard. Beckerman and Clark (1982) assume that this is indeed the case, and undertake their detailed study of poverty on this basis. They index Supplementary Benefit by increasing it each month to compensate for inflation since the last uprating. Their poverty line is shown in Figure 3.2, which is constructed on the assumptions that inflation occurs at a constant monthly rate

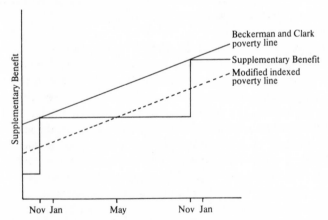

FIG. 3.2. Indexing Supplementary Benefit for Within-Year Inflation.

and that each November Supplementary Benefit is completely indexed. The impact of this procedure is to increase their poverty estimate in Table 3.2 by 107 per cent. While there may be a case for within-year adjustment — especially at high rates of inflation when there is a reasonable case for more frequent upratings — the Beckerman and Clark procedure is arbitrary. They have to guess the official intent in setting Supplementary Benefit rates, and the doubling of the estimated number of poor which results, shows that it is a guess with quite devastating implications.

Alternative guesses are equally plausible. Say, for example, that over a year the real level of Supplementary Benefit is supposed to be correct only on average. It is too high at the beginning of the benefit year and too low at the end. The low-paid and benefit recipients are supposed to make the financial provisions which are necessary to avoid poverty. This alternative indexation procedure might imply the modified indexed poverty line drawn in Figure 3.2. If the appropriate financial provisions are made — basically saving at the start of the benefit year and dissaving at the end — it is possible that using this poverty standard there will be fewer poor than when the unindexed Supplementary Benefit standard is used and all income is spent immediately it is received. This is certainly what Hemming and Harvey (1983) find in an analysis of poverty among retirement pensioners.

Inflation raises interesting issues when discussing poverty measurement, and they are worth mentioning. But they are not central to our analysis of poverty, with its modest intentions. It is because of their fairly consistent application of the indexed poverty line that we have not made more references to the detailed estimates of poverty provided by Beckerman and Clark.

The cost of poverty relief

We have concluded that a significant minority of the population is poor by official standards, and has remained so for the last twenty or thirty years. We have identified the members of this minority. Our findings give cause for concern. But they also tend to mask the success of the social security system in taking a vast number of people out of poverty. For example, Beckerman and Clark (1982), using an unindexed poverty line, show that in 1975, 15.8 per cent of the population would have been poor if they had not received social security benefits nor made other arrangements which would enable them to avoid poverty. The aggregate poverty gap would have been £3,276 million, an average of £7.33 per week (with average net earnings of around £40 per week). Social security expenditure in 1975 was £8,038 million, which had the effect of reducing the incidence of poverty to 2.3 per cent of the population, and the aggregate poverty gap to £114 million, an average of £1.75 per week.

While there are many who would take considerable pride in this achievement, life for those still living in poverty is one of some hardship. Yet it appears to be hardship which would not be expensive to relieve. £114 million is less than one-eighth of one per cent of gross national product — this is the poverty relief ratio referred to earlier — or 10p a week per working person. This sum of money is clearly trivial. However, £114 million is the direct cost. We have noted that it costs £8,038 million to reduce the aggregate poverty gap by £3,162 million: there is an indirect cost of £4,876 million which arises because of the way in which we choose to relieve poverty. This is money paid to the poor over and above that needed to eliminate their poverty, money paid to the non-poor, and administrative costs. If social security has disincentive effects, or stigmatizes claimants, these are also indirect costs. If the direct costs were the dominant element in the burden of relieving the poverty which remains, the problem would be easily remedied; unfortunately it is the indirect costs of achieving only a little more redistribution which are substantial.

4

WORKING FAMILIES

BEVERIDGE did not anticipate that working families, that is families where the head is in full-time work, would suffer poverty. Earnings and child support were expected never to yield an income below that which could be received from the state. We have seen that history has proved Beveridge to have been over-optimistic. Being a working family does not guarantee an adequate standard of living, and as a consequence there have been important developments in the social security system in order to provide means-tested benefits for low income families with a working head. In this chapter most attention will be focused on these means-tested benefits. For it is perhaps a surprising feature of the position of working families that those poor enough to receive benefits are none the less often not sufficiently poor to be relieved of the obligation to pay income tax and National Insurance contributions. The implication of this overlap between the tax system and the social security system is that some families can find themselves worse off, not better off, if they attempt to improve their standard of living. To appreciate why this perverse situation emerges, it is necessary to explain how the net family income associated with any particular level of gross earnings is computed.

The British tax system

Income tax has a fairly simple structure. Tax is levied on earnings in excess of personal allowances, which for tax year April 1982 to April 1983 stand at £1,565 a year for a single person and £2,445 a year for a married man. Personal allowances have been more or less continuously eroded by inflation, with the result that an increasing number of low-income families are taxed. In 1977 the Rooker–Wise amendment to the Finance Bill of that year led many to believe that the government were committed to indexing personal allowances to the retail price index, but in 1981 this was proved a false hope when personal allowances were not increased at all, although they were increased in 1982 to their current levels. The first £12,800 of taxable income is taxed at a constant marginal tax rate (or basic rate) of 30 per cent. Thereafter marginal tax rates rise, reaching 60 per cent when taxable income exceeds £31,500. All but 5 per cent of taxpayers pay tax at the basic rate. A married couple with one earner will only pay higher rates of tax if their earnings exceed £15,245. For those paying the basic rate, average tax rates rise as income increases: if earnings are £5,000 only 15.3 per cent of income will be paid in tax, the average rate then increases to 19.5 per cent at £7,000, 22.7 per cent at £10,000, and 25.2 per cent at the top of the basic rate band.

There are some complications. When a wife works, her income is usually aggregated with her husband's for tax purposes. However, 'wife's earned income relief' is available, and she can receive her own personal allowance — that for a single person — which is set against her earnings, but not any investment income she receives. Her husband retains his married man's allowances, and continues to pay tax on her investment income. Alternatively a working wife can opt to be taxed separately on her earned income though her husband forgoes his married man's allowance. Such an option is only worth while if a husband and wife taxed jointly would pay significant amounts of tax at higher rates. Investment income in excess of £6,250 attracts a surcharge of 15 per cent. Taxpayers who have taken out a mortgage to purchase their own home get full tax relief on interest payments for mortgages up to £25,000; this has long taken the form of an increased tax allowance which depends upon the size of these payments; however, after April 1983 lower interest payments, reflecting the value of this tax concession, are to be required from borrowers with mortgages which do not exceed £25,000. Those with larger mortgages will continue to receive an additional personal allowance. Widows, single parents, and the aged receive additional personal allowances.

National Insurance contributions are an important tax. This may seem a surprising assertion, and at best it is really only 'almost true'. They would be a pure tax if benefits received were completely independent of the amount previously paid in contributions. This has never been entirely the case. We have seen that earnings-related contributions paid between 1961 and 1978 established an entitlement to meagre earnings-related pensions, although the few who received earnings-related supplements to other National Insurance benefits found these more substantial. But these supplements have been discontinued. With the introduction of the State Earnings Related Pension Scheme, earnings-related pensions will eventually become more generous, even for contracted-out employees. However, these pensions will be based on earnings in the best twenty years in a working career. Thus in a typical male working lifetime of 49 years, 'contributions' will be paid in twenty years and 'taxes' in the remaining 29. Which years are which will not be known until the full 49 have elapsed.

Of course, taxpayers do not make this distinction. National Insurance contributions will be regarded by some as a tax, some as a pension contribution, and by others as an indistinguishable mixture of both. While it would be slightly misleading to regard them wholly as one or the other we believe that they are most commonly regarded as a tax by those who pay them, and are going to treat them as such. We cannot provide evidence in justification of our decision, but equally we can find little to indicate that we have been misled. A contracted-in employee therefore pays an additional marginal tax rate of 8.75 per cent on earnings up to £11,440 per year (£220 per week × 52) in 1982-3, unless earnings fall below £1,534 per year (£29.50 per week × 52), in which event no National Insurance contributions are payable. Note that the marginal tax rate at the lower earnings limit is exceptionally high, with £2.58 being deducted immediately weekly earnings reach this level.

National Insurance contributions are also paid by employers. Now while it is certainly true that the employer actually sends a cheque to the Inland Revenue (who collect the money for the Department of Health and Social Security), reflecting his own contributions, the cheque he sends also includes those of his employees. Nobody would claim that he is actually paying his employee's contributions, and it is not obvious that he is even paying his own. An employer can 'shift' his contributions, to his employees, by holding down their wages, or to consumers in general, by increasing the prices of the goods he sells or the services he provides. The extent to which employer contributions are shifted is difficult to detect, as is how they are shifted. But shifted they certainly are, and probably almost wholly on to employees. We imagine the situation where employers are concerned about gross labour costs and employees worry about take-home pay: if this is a fairly realistic scenario, in the long run the distinction between employer and employee contributions is of no significance. The employer's National Insurance contribution for a contracted-in employee is 12.2 per cent, including the surcharge, charged on the same earnings as the employee's contribution. But the employer's contribution is not to be regarded as an additional 12.2 per cent charged against the marginal income of the employee. The employer's contribution has to be treated as the income of the employee: the appropriate rate of tax on the employee is 12.2/112.2 = 10.9 per cent. In order to compute the overall marginal tax rate implied by the systems of income tax and National Insurance contributions, the rates of 30 per cent and 8.75 per cent have to be converted to tax rates on total income (including the employer's contribution). These become 26.7 per cent (30/112.2) and 7.8 per cent (8.75/112.2) respectively. The overall marginal tax rate is 45.4 per cent. These figures are easily amended for contracted-out employees. But it must be remembered that they pay into occupational pension schemes, where joint contribution rates are often in the range 15–20 per cent of earnings. Because occupational pensions are largely independent of career earnings – they are usually based on final salary – there is possibly a case, although a flimsy one, for regarding these contributions as taxes.

In Table 4.1 we show the distribution of marginal and average tax rates implied by systems of income tax and National Insurance contri-

TABLE 4.1

Overall Marginal and Average Tax Rates (Income Tax and National Insurance Contributions): 1982-3
(Married couple with one earner)

Annual earnings (£)	Marginal tax rate (percentage)	Average tax rate (percentage)
Less than 1,534	Nil	Nil
1,534 – 2,445	18.7	18.7
2,446 – 11,440	45.4	37.7
11,441 – 15,245	30.0	36.1
15,246 – 17,545	40.0	36.6
17,546 – 21,545	45.0	38.0
21,546 – 27,745	50.0	40.6
27,746 – 33,945	55.0	43.1
Above 33,945	60.0	48.4 (at £50,000)

Note: Annual earnings are defined excluding employer's National Insurance contributions, and average tax rates are computed at the upper earnings levels shown.

butions. The picture which emerges is rather surprising. Among tax-payers the lowest marginal tax rate is faced by those earning between £11,440 and £15,245 a year, and only when earnings reach £21,545 does the marginal tax rate exceed that faced by the bulk of taxpayers who earn below £11,440. Marginal tax rates do eventually reach 60 per cent, but higher tax rates affect only a very few taxpayers. The average tax rate generally rises, although the fact that the basic rate band extends beyond the upper earnings limit implies that average tax rates fall between £11,440 and £15,245 a year. While the system of income tax and National Insurance contributions can be described as progressive, in that pre-tax earnings are more equally distributed than post-tax earnings, part of the system is regressive.

Before concluding this discussion two extensions of the analysis are worth noting. British taxpayers pay indirect taxes (value added tax, taxes on drink, tobacco, and petrol, etc.), in addition to the direct taxes (income taxes and National Insurance contributions). Set against this many receive an additional tax allowance because they pay mortgage interest. Dilnot and Morris (1982) have estimated that for a couple with one earner the marginal tax rate on income which emerges from the typical expenditure pattern is 13.7 per cent. Mortgage interest relief is the equivalent of a 2 per cent reduction in the marginal rate of income tax, to 24.7 per cent. The overall marginal rate for a basic rate taxpayer is therefore a staggering 57.1 per cent. It may therefore come as a shock to learn that even ignoring employer's National Insurance contributions, indirect taxes, and mortgage interest relief, the marginal tax rates faced by those on low earnings who are entitled to social security in order to supplement their earnings are almost twice as high as this. To understand why, the benefits for which low earners may be eligible have to be described in detail.

Benefits for working families

Child benefit is a flat-rate benefit, in 1982-3 £5.85 a week, payable for each child under 16, or under 19 if still at school. When a child lives with both parents child benefit is paid to the mother, normally through post offices. A single parent is at the same time paid an additional one-parent benefit of £3.65 for the only or eldest child.

Family Income Supplement can be claimed by a family with one or more children where the head is in full-time work and family income is low. It is equal to 50 per cent of the subtraction (qualifying level – gross weekly income) a week. The qualifying level in 1982–3 is given by: £73.50 + (£9 × number of children). Gross weekly income is gross weekly earnings (before tax and National Insurance), averaged over the five weeks preceding a claim if weekly paid, or over two months if monthly paid, except where these periods are obviously untypical. Averaged weekly amounts of all other forms of income are included, but there are exceptions, most notably child benefit, rent rebates and allowances, and rate rebates. Payments must exceed 10p but cannot exceed £19 + (£2.00 × number of children). Once an award has been made, Family Income Supplement will be paid for 52 weeks; the amount will not be amended if circumstances change, although it will be if the qualifying levels or maxima are changed. After 52 weeks a further claim can be made.

Free school meals of a standard normally provided at school are automatically received by children whose parents are on Family Income Supplement. Other families can apply to their local authority to receive free school meals. A free school meal is roughly equivalent to a grant of £3 per week per child, although in many local authorities the school meals service has been drastically cut back and the value imputed to free school meals should reflect this.

Free milk will be given to those Family Income Supplement recipients with a child under five years and one month. This benefit is worth approximately £1.50 per child per week. It may also be provided to other families, subject to a means test.

Rent rebates take the form of a deduction from the rent of council tenants and *rent allowances* are a cash payment to private tenants. Rebates and allowances must comply with a minimum standard reflected in a basic national formula. According to the basic national formula the rebate or allowance is equal to:

   60 per cent of weekly rent
 + 25 per cent of (needs allowance – gross weekly income, if positive)
 or – 17 per cent of (gross weekly income – needs allowance, if positive).

There are three components to this calculation. Weekly rent is rent paid with a deduction for rates, rent receipts, and payments for furniture and a garage. In the case of a rent allowance, rent is based on a fair rent, which is either registered as such by a local rent officer or rent tribunal, or assessed by the local authority when a claim is made. The needs allowance depends upon family size, the 1982–3 scale being:

Single person	£41.40
Couple/single-parent	£61.00
Child addition	£11.40

with further additions if the claimant is blind or disabled. Gross weekly income includes income from all sources, the most notable exception being the first £18 of the claimant's earnings and the first £5.00 of a partner's earnings. A rent rebate or rent allowance is paid for six months (or a year for pensioners) but can be amended or discontinued if circumstances change. The minimum payment is 20p a week and payment cannot exceed rent paid, with an overriding maximum of £30 (£35 in Greater London).

Rate rebates can be paid to owner-occupiers and tenants who pay rates directly or make an earmarked contribution to rates. The formula for a rate rebate bears a close relationship to that for a rent rebate or rent allowance. The rebate is equal to:

    60 per cent of rates
  + 8 per cent of (needs allowance – gross weekly income, if positive)
or – 6 per cent of (gross weekly income – needs allowance, if positive).

The scale of needs allowances is as above, and gross income is defined as for rent rebates and allowances. A rate rebate is paid for nine months (or a year for pensioners) and can be amended or discontinued if circumstances change. The minimum payment is 10p a week and payment cannot exceed rates paid, with an overriding maximum of £5.50 (£9 in Greater London).

Consider a one-earner couple with two children, one aged four and one aged six. Only the older child attends school. The family rent their home from a local authority, paying £15 a week in rent and £5 a week in rates. The father earns £80 a week before any deductions. What is this family's net income in January 1983 if they receive all the benefits to which they are entitled? The necessary information to compute

net income can be found in this and the previous section. The
calculation is as follows.

Deductions
(1) *Income tax* is computed on an annual basis. Annual
    income is 52 × 80 = £4,160. The married man's
    allowance is £2,445, and the annual income tax
    liability is 30 per cent of (4,160 – 2,445) = £514.50.
    Averaged over 52 weeks this is a weekly payment of
    514.50 ÷ 52 =   £ 9.89
(2) *National Insurance contributions* are made at the
    employee rate on weekly earnings. The weekly con-
    tribution is 8.75 per cent of 80 =   £ 7.00
                                    Total deductions = £16.89

Benefits
(3) *Child benefit* at £5.85 a week per child =   £11.70
(4) *Family Income Supplement* is based upon a qualifying
    level which is 73.50 + (9 × 2) = £91.50, and gross
    weekly earnings of £80. The amount paid is 50 per
    cent of (91.50 – 80) =   £ 5.75
(5) *Free school meals* for the eldest child =   £ 3.00
(6) *Free milk* for the youngest child =   £ 1.50
(7) *Rent rebate* depends upon rent paid, £15, the needs
    allowance, 61 + (11.40 × 2) = £83.80, and gross
    weekly income, 80 + 11.70 (child benefit) + 5.75
    (Family Income Supplement) – 18 = £79.45. The
    amount paid is 60 per cent of 15 + 25 per cent of
    (83.80 – 79.45) =   £10.09
(8) *Rate rebate* is 60 per cent of 5 + 8 per cent of (83.80 –
    79.45) =   £ 3.35
                                      Total benefits = £35.39
            Net benefits = total benefits – total deductions
                        = 35.39 – 16.89 =   £18.50
            Net income = gross income + net benefits
                        = 80 + 18.50 =   £98.50

While this family pays both income tax and National Insurance contributions they are entitled to benefits which exceed their deductions by
£18.50 a week.

The interaction between taxes and benefits

To see how low earners can face much higher marginal tax rates than those in Table 4.1 consider the following example. Assume that the father of the family just described earns his £80 a week by working 40 hours at £2 per hour. Now suppose that his employer had offered him the opportunity of remaining behind for an hour each Friday night for an extra £4 a week. How much better off would he and his family have been if he had accepted the offer of overtime? The calculations are straightforward.

Deductions
(1)	Income tax =	£11.09
(2)	National Insurance contributions =	£ 7.35

Total deductions = £18.44

Benefits
(3)	Child benefit =	£11.70
(4)	Family Income Supplement =	£ 3.75
(5)	Free school meals =	£ 3.00
(6)	Free milk =	£ 1.50
(7)	Rent rebate =	£ 9.59
(8)	Rate rebate =	£ 3.19

Total benefits = £32.73
Net benefits = £14.29
Net income = £98.29

Without doing the overtime the family's net income is £98.50; if the offer had been accepted it would be £98.29. A £4 increase in earnings leaves our family 21p worse off. Taking the tax and benefit systems together the total amount of 'tax' paid on the additional £4 is £4.21, a marginal tax rate of 105.25 per cent. Tax payments consist of income tax and National Insurance contributions paid, and benefits withdrawn.

Marginal tax rates on low earnings can be much higher than 105.25 per cent. Free school meals and free milk are worth £4.50 a week. A family is entitled to them if it receives Family Income Supplement; if this entitlement is lost when Family Income Supplement is no longer received, this loss alone when an additional hour of work is done for £4 implies a marginal tax rate of 112.5 per cent. However, these benefits can continue to be received even though Family Income Supplement has been discontinued, subject to their own means tests.

Thus separate marginal tax rates might apply at different earnings levels; these are 75 per cent for free school meals and 37.5 per cent for free milk. Wherever these occur the marginal tax rates which low-income families face are considerably increased. We will assume that these benefits are withdrawn with Family Income Supplement.

The exact marginal tax rates faced by families at different levels of earnings depend upon the rates at which different benefits are withdrawn. In Figure 4.1 we show how means-tested benefits vary with

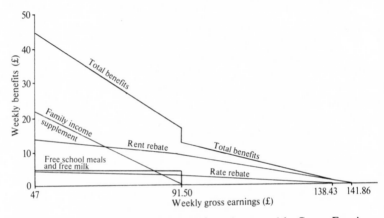

FIG. 4.1. How Means-Tested Benefits change with Gross Earnings: 1982–3 (One earner couple with two children aged four and six).

gross earnings for our example family; the range of gross earnings considered is from £47 a week, at which point income tax is first paid (i.e. 2,445 ÷ 52 = £47.02) up to £141.86 when the last remaining benefit, rent rebate, is ultimately withdrawn in full. If a family is receiving Family Income Supplement, rent rebate is withdrawn at a rate of 50 per cent; if it earns less than £88.70 — where gross weekly income equals the needs allowance according to the means test for housing benefits — rent rebate is withdrawn at a rate of 25 per cent and rate rebate at a rate of 8 per cent. When a family receives Family Income Supplement this is included in gross weekly income when rent and rate rebates are calculated. The implication of this is that when gross earnings are between £47 and £88.70 a week, the rate of withdrawal is not 50 + 25 + 8 = 83 per cent. At gross earnings level E, in the range £47 to £88.70, housing benefits are given by:

$$60\% \text{ (rent + rates)} + 33\% \{83.80 - (E-18) + 11.70 - 50\% (91.50 - E)\}$$

from which it follows that if earnings were ΔE higher, housing benefits would be reduced by $(33\% \times 50\%) \Delta E = 16.5\% \Delta E$. The rate of withdrawal of benefits is therefore 66.5 per cent. Income tax and employee National Insurance contributions amount to 38.75 per cent, and the marginal tax rate is therefore $38.75 + 66.5 = 105.25$ per cent, exactly as in our example above.

At higher earnings levels the marginal tax rate is at first lower. Between £88.70 and £91.50 a week the withdrawal rate for housing benefits is only 23 per cent, implying a marginal tax rate of 100.25 per cent. However, at £91.50 Family Income Supplement ends, and if free school meals and free milk are withdrawn the marginal tax rate becomes a staggering 212.75 per cent. Thereafter only housing benefits remain to be withdrawn, and the marginal tax rate is 61.75 per cent. Rate rebate runs out at £138.43 a week, and the marginal tax rate falls to 55.75 per cent, where it stays until rent rebate runs out at £141.86 a week. The marginal tax rate is then 38.75 per cent. These marginal tax rates are summarized in Table 4.2: also reported in the table are the

TABLE 4.2

Marginal Tax Rates on Lower Earnings: 1982–3
(One earner couple with two children aged four and six)

Annual gross earnings (£)	Excluding employer's National Insurance contributions (percentage)	Including employer's National Insurance contributions (percentage)
2,445–4,612	105.25	104.7
4,613–4,758	100.25	100.2
4,759–7,198	61.75	65.9
7,199–7,377	55.75	60.6
above 7,377	38.75	45.4

corresponding overall marginal tax rates, which include employer's National Insurance contributions, associated with various levels of annual gross earnings. These are comparable with the rates shown in Table 4.1.

What is the implication of the schedule of marginal tax rates shown in Table 4.2 for the gains in net income which result from higher levels of gross earnings? Figure 4.2 provides the answer. If gross earnings are

£47 a week, net income is £100.22 (the calculation follows the earlier examples). Because initial marginal tax rates exceed 100 per cent, net income is lower at successively higher levels of gross earnings, with a large difference at £91.50 a week, when free school meals and free milk are withdrawn. Thereafter net income is higher, because marginal tax rates are less than 100 per cent, but not until gross earnings reach £109.00 does net income match that corresponding to gross earnings of £47 a week.

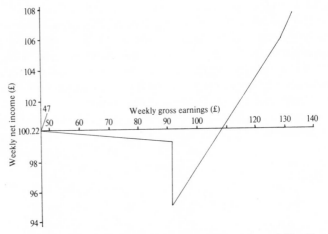

FIG. 4.2. The Relationship between Gross Earnings and Net Income (One earner couple with two children aged four and six).

The poverty trap

In his Open University pamphlet on the subject, Pond (1978) uses the term poverty trap to describe a situation where 'a family loses more in terms of extra taxes paid and reduced benefits received than it gains from a pay increase which brought them about' (p. 8-9). Relevant earnings increases are generally assumed to be small. Our one earner family with two children is firmly in the poverty trap; it would be 21p a week worse off if the father accepted an increase in gross earnings of £4. All families whose gross earnings are in the range where overall marginal tax rates exceed 100 per cent find themselves in the poverty trap. For marginal tax rates to exceed 100 per cent an earner must be paying income tax and National Insurance contributions, and receiving Family Income Supplement and housing benefits (except at the point where Family Income Supplement runs out and passport benefits are therefore withdrawn, in which case housing benefits need not be received). It follows that the poverty trap is a fairly recent phenomenon, a direct consequence of the introduction of Family Income Supplement and housing benefits in the early 1970s, the heyday of the growth of means-testing.

From Table 4.2 we can see that the poverty trap encompasses the range of earnings £47 to £91.50 a week; but this only applies to the particular family considered. If that family had one more child the qualifying level for Family Income Supplement would be raised to £100.50 and the poverty trap would be extended by £9, as it would be for each additional child. The lower end is determined by the tax threshold, the earnings level at which income tax is first paid. This will generally be £47 a week, in 1982-3 but if both husband and wife are working, the wife's earned income relief implies that this figure will rise to £77. However, when husband and wife both work, the family is most unlikely to earn sufficiently little to qualify for Family Income Supplement. The additional personal allowance for single parents is equal to the difference between the married man's allowance and the single person's allowance, viz. 2,445 - 1,565 = £880 a year, and there is consequently no distinction between the poverty trap for two-parent families when the head is in work and single parent families when that parent works full time.

The poverty trap has been around for ten years: has it become larger or smaller in that time? Figure 4.3 provides the answer for a one earner, two child family. It charts the real difference – adjusted for earnings growth – between the qualifying level for Family Income Supplement and the appropriate tax threshold, expressed as a weekly amount. The 'real' poverty trap is larger at the end of the ten years than at the beginning. The real value of the qualifying level for Family Income Supplement has held up quite well, and over-indexation in recent years has made up for less than complete indexation in the past. Meanwhile the real value of the tax threshold has, except in a few recent years, followed a downward trend: the personal allowance for a married couple was 40 per cent higher in real terms in 1971 than in 1981. In the middle of the period the child additions to the qualifying level were revised downwards as child benefit came in; hence the downward shift in the graph in 1976 is a once-and-for-all structural break.

FIG. 4.3. The 'Real' Poverty Trap' 1971–81
(One earner couple with two children).

Estimates of the number of families in the poverty trap are not particularly reliable – see Pond (1978) for a review of the statistical basis of numerous estimates – but even the most conservative will come as a surprise to many, given the attention paid to the poverty trap. We have said that families in the poverty trap have to be receiving Family Income Supplement; the latest estimate, for December 1981, is that there are 132,000 recipients of Family Income Supplement (Treasury and Civil Service Committee, 1982, Evidence from the Low Pay Unit). In terms of coverage it is a very small benefit. But not all of these families will be in the poverty trap. Some will not pay any income tax, because their earnings are below the tax threshold. In 1981, 20 per cent did not pay tax; therefore 105,600 families had earnings which were between the tax threshold and the qualifying level for Family Income Supplement. This is a good guide to the number of families in the poverty trap in 1981; it will however be a slight overestimate to the extent that some families will receive maximum rent and rate rebates, and will not have these withdrawn as income increases, while a few others will receive a rate rebate but not a rent rebate or allowance.

The number of families in this position is not stable. Table 4.3 shows how the number of families estimated to be in the poverty trap has changed since 1974. The general increase does not reflect improved take-up of Family Income Supplement: estimates of take-up have changed over the period but this change reflects different measurement techniques, and anyway the revisions are usually downward. In fact, the figures in Table 4.3 bear a reasonably close relationship to the size

TABLE 4.3

Number of Families in the Poverty Trap: 1974–81

April	1974	15,000
April	1975	12,300
April	1976	27,740
April	1977	46,400
April	1978	59,470
December	1979	63,730
April	1981	84,000
December	1981	105,600

Source: Treasury and Civil Service Committee (1982), Evidence from the Low Pay Unit.

of the real poverty trap, as shown in Figure 4.3. Given that the structure of earnings has remained relatively stable throughout the 1970s, and that, if anything, the relative earnings of the low-paid have fallen slightly, it is only to be expected that as the range of earnings over which marginal tax rates of 100 per cent plus apply increases, so must the number of families who face them.

Before one claims that there were 105,600 families in the poverty trap in December 1981 the meaning of this claim should be well understood. In discussing the poverty trap a careful distinction between long-term and short-term increases in earnings has to be made. The pattern of high marginal rates described in Table 4.2 correctly reflects the situation facing a family which increases its long-term earnings, in our example by working an hour extra every Friday for an additional £4. It is not the pattern necessarily facing a family which increases its short-term earnings, say by only doing overtime before Christmas or the summer holidays. This distinction arises because Family Income Supplement, once awarded on the basis of five weeks' or two months' earnings, is paid for a period of 52 weeks. Only if those additional short-term earnings are received in the five weeks preceding a new award, and possibly not even then, can they imply marginal tax rates as high as in Table 4.2. At any other time, marginal tax rates applicable to short-term increases in earnings are substantially below 100 per cent in the earnings range over which Family Income Supplement is payable. And those who face the very highest marginal tax rates because their long-term earnings increase, may find that it is nearly a year before they are actually exposed to them.

The distinction between the long-term and short-term positions has led Department of Health and Social Security officials to refer to the above estimates of the number of families in the poverty trap as 'theoretical', a term which is meant to be far from complimentary. They would contend that far fewer than 105,600 families are in the poverty trap, because not all families, and possibly relatively few, face marginal tax rates in excess of 100 per cent. There are a number of comments to be made on this view, and on the views of those who argue that a poverty trap only affecting 105,600 families is not a serious problem. The first is that a quarter of a million families have earnings below the qualifying level for Family Income Supplement, and 80 per cent of these are entitled to the benefit. Only half receive it. The poverty trap is potentially far more serious than the estimate of 105,600 suggests; campaigns to improve take-up will make it worse.

Furthermore, the poverty trap affects far more families than those facing marginal tax rates in excess of 100 per cent. While Figure 4.2 showed that almost any one earner, two child family earning between £47 and £91.50 a week would be in the poverty trap, it also showed that many of those families earning between £91.50 and £109 a week could be better off if they earned quite a lot less, although not necessarily if they earned a little less. Figure 4.4 shows the distribution of gross weekly income by family size, and it indicates that there could be something like 300,000 families in the extended poverty trap, and therefore about 400,000 families who could be better off if they earned less. However, the extended poverty trap is a double-edged sword. It can be used to show the wide range of earnings over which it pays to do less work (in the poverty trap and extended poverty trap), to refuse a slightly better-paid job and do a little more work on a regular basis (in the poverty trap), or to seek only those jobs which allow additional work to be done sporadically (also in the poverty trap). On the other hand it can equally be used to demonstrate how many families who could be better off if they worked less, reject these courses of action. But then the question which naturally arises is, 'Why are these opportunities ignored?'

If the nature of the poverty trap is well understood, it can only be presumed that many jobs do not offer the flexibility necessary to take advantage of this particular anomaly, that changing jobs is itself costly, or that people take pride in having as good and as well-paid a job as possible. Each of these possibilities is realistic. If the tax and benefit system is not well understood, people will do a little more work or take a better job, and assume, not unreasonably, that they are worse off because a mistake has been made in calculating their take-home pay or benefits. On being assured that no mistake has been made,

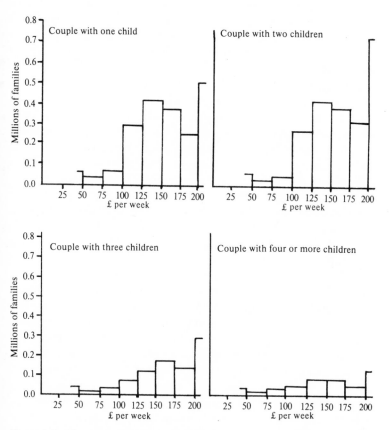

FIG. 4.4. The Distribution of Gross Weekly Income by Family Size: 1982.

Source: Family Expenditure Survey 1977, data uprated to November 1982.

bewilderment sets in. They may assume that they can reverse the situation, and do less work or return to their old job. But if they do not understand the system, they probably will not trust it to return the money they have lost, and so they simply stay where they are. Some people understand the system and exploit it; the number is probably small. A few others reject the chance of gain, for the reasons given. But we would judge that of the 400,000 who could be better off if they earned less, a large number do not understand the system. It is only because of its sheer complexity that many people do not play the system to their own financial advantage. This complexity cannot be claimed to be a merit of the system. On the contrary, it discredits it.

The extended poverty trap is a new concept. In particular it should be pointed out that the extended poverty trap is intended to be quite distinct from the poverty plateau, which is an extension of the poverty trap that some have described (see Parker, 1982). The poverty plateau extends not only over that range of earnings where marginal tax rates are in excess of 100 per cent, but also over where they are less than 100 per cent though still very high. (However, to describe all marginal tax rates over 40 per cent as very high, as Parker does, perhaps goes too far). This is an interesting concept, and one relevant to the discussion of the ways in which the poverty trap can be sprung.

Single-parent families

There are around three-quarters of a million single parents in Britain who do not receive widows' benefits. Some of these are in full-time work, but because they are typically women and womens' earnings are somewhat lower than those of men, a disproportionate number will find themselves in the poverty trap we have already described. It is unlikely that more than a handful of people in full-time work earn sufficiently little not to pay tax. Those with low earnings are most probably employed on a part-time basis. Single parents are not required to register for work in order to qualify for Supplementary Benefit, and can receive Supplementary Benefit as long as they work less than thirty hours a week. They will not qualify for Family Income Supplement, but do not pay tax. Yet they too face extraordinarily high marginal tax rates. This is because Supplementary Benefit is withdrawn as earnings increase.

The amount paid in Supplementary Benefit makes up the difference

between weekly requirements and weekly resources. Weekly requirements are given by the scale rates, which in 1982–3 are:

	Ordinary weekly rate	Long-term weekly rate
Single person	£25.70	£32.70
Couple	£41.70	£52.30
Non-householder aged		
18 or over	£20.55	£26.15
16–17	£15.80	£20.05
Child aged		
11–15	£13.15	
under 11	£ 8.75	

plus full rent and rates. Weekly resources consist of the earnings of both
partners less normal deductions (income tax, National Insurance contributions), reasonable work expenses, the first £4 of each partner's
weekly earnings, 50 per cent of earnings between £4 and £20 received
by single parents, and most social security benefits, including child
benefit. Supplementary Benefit is not paid to those with capital
resources exceeding £2,500.

The impact of the disregards is that the first £4 of earnings are
received in full, each additional £1 received between £4 and £20 is
taxed at 50 per cent, and the marginal tax rate on earnings over £20
is 100 per cent. This is so until the transition is made from part-time
work to full-time work, when, presuming full-time work is 'rewarded'
with earnings which attract income tax, the marginal tax rates for
single-parent families on low earnings are those faced by all other
working families in the traditional poverty trap. Thus for single-parent
families the poverty trap and extended poverty trap span a range of
earnings which is wider than that for a married couple with the same
number of children. The net income which will be received by a family
with two children when earnings are £20 a week will not be matched
again until earnings have increased, through working full time rather
than part time, by around £100 a week. The precise increase will
depend upon the children's ages and upon housing costs.

There are two reasons why single parents are given a concession in
respect of part-time work. First, it is recognized that many single
parents may not be available for full-time work, but perhaps can take

on a part-time job: this is to be encouraged because it enables single parents to make regular contact with other adults on a regular basis, and therefore performs an important social function. Second, the earnings from part-time work – mainly received by married women with husbands in full-time work – are usually taxed at a marginal rate of 30 per cent, 33.2 per cent, or 38.75 per cent. Without the concession, all but the trivial part-time earnings of single-parents receiving Supplementary Benefit, would be taxed at a marginal rate of 100 per cent. Taxing a band of earnings at 50 per cent brings the treatment of these two groups more into line.

Relieving the poverty trap for two-parent families with their head in full-time work will help solve the problem for single-parent families. They will then only fail to be rewarded for additional effort on a small band of earnings in excess of £20 a week; extending the 50 per cent tax rate to earnings in excess of £20 a week would reduce this band, but at the same time would increase the level of earnings at which it becomes worth-while accepting a full-time job.

The tax structure and the poverty trap

If low earners were taken out of tax, tax rates (including National Insurance contributions) reduced, means-testing restricted, withdrawal rates of benefits reduced, or low earners paid more, the poverty trap would be relieved and possibly eliminated. Are there any problems in changing the tax structure to achieve this? Raising the tax threshold so that families receiving Family Income Supplement do not pay tax is a popular option. However, the cost of this is astronomical. For a two-child family the 1982–3 qualifying level for Family Income Supplement of £91.50 a week is nearly twice the tax threshold of £47 a week; we estimate that a doubling of all tax allowances would take roughly half a million families out of tax (see Figure 4.4), including all poverty trap victims with one or two children. Then there will be a further 5 million or so single people, married women, and elderly. This increase in personal allowances, will benefit not only those taken out of tax but all taxpayers and would cost about £15 billion in lost tax revenue which must be raised elsewhere. Say the money has to come from an increase in the basic rate of tax, the most likely possibility. At the moment a one percentage point increase in the basic rate of tax raises about £1 billion. With an unchanged tax base a 50 per cent increase in the basic rate of tax, from 30 to 45 per cent, would pay for the required increase in personal allowances. However, the tax base would in fact be contracted, and the basic rate of tax would have to nearly double. And even then some families with more than two children would remain in the poverty trap.

A way of raising thresholds at lower cost is to increase them only for families with children, in other words reintroduce child tax allowances. The Child Poverty Action Group was the leading campaigner for their abolition, arguing that the funds released could be transferred to poor families with earnings below the tax threshold. But upon their abolition many low income families with children found that they entered tax, and were caught in the poverty trap. The campaign may have been misguided (see Bradshaw, 1980, for further discussion). Yet child tax allowances are still expensive, since, while they are not given to all taxpayers, they are given to all taxpayers with children, about one-third of all tax units. The cost saving is significant when compared with the option of increasing all personal allowances, but the overall cost is still large. If child tax allowances are to be large enough to take all families in the poverty trap out of tax they need to be (82.50 – 47) × 52 = £1,846 for the first child and 9 × 52 = £468 for each subsequent child. We would estimate this change to take only 700,000 taxpayers out of tax, to cost £2¼ billion, and therefore to require a basic rate of tax of only 35 per cent to finance. This would be a fairly modest increase; however, the reintroduction of child tax allowances would be a return to a complexity that tax administrators were relieved to be rid of.

The cost of taking low income families out of tax is clear. The high cost is a result of both the density of the income distribution at incomes just above the tax threshold and the fact that increasing tax allowances benefits all taxpayers. Hence it is not at all surprising that those low income families who need help to support their children or pay their rent also have to pay tax. And although it is often claimed that a system is ludicrous which requires those who earn less than they would receive if they were on Supplementary Benefit to pay tax, such a system, is in fact quite sensible. For if tax allowances were always equated with Supplementary Benefit scale rates, the incomes of the poor could only be increased by increasing the incomes of all taxpayers and, almost inevitably, by raising marginal tax rates by much more than would be necessary to pay for the increase in Supplementary Benefit alone. The view that the current arrangement 'is not necessarily irrational, but a possibly appropriate response to the difficult trade-offs

between equity, efficiency and incentives which are part of the problem
of formulating satisfactory tax schedules' (Kay and King, 1980,
p. 110), is quite correct.

If the first £2,000 or so of taxable income were taxed at a reduced
rate of say 20 per cent, many families receiving Family Income Supplement and paying tax would not be in the poverty trap because their
marginal tax rate would be 10 percentage points lower. In 1978 a
reduced rate band was reintroduced in Britain (reduced rates were
common before the late 1960s); when the basic tax rate was 34 per
cent, the first £750 of taxable income was taxed at 25 per cent. The
reduced rate band was intended to help the low-paid relative to those
on average earnings and/or in receipt of state benefits, bring Britain
into line with other countries which did not have such high initial rates
of tax, and to reduce the number of families facing marginal tax rates
in excess of 100 per cent.

Morris and Warren (1980) have argued that each of these attempts
to justify the reduced rate band was ill-conceived. Low income families
could have their relative position improved if the reduced rate band
were removed and the revenue raised used to increase personal allowances, maintaining their real value, or reduce the basic tax rate. Such
a change would also improve the position of those in work relative to
those out of work. The initial marginal tax rate in Britain is certainly
high by international standards, as shown in Table 4.4, but just because
Britain is different does not mean that it should change. High marginal
rates of tax worried many because of their disincentive effect. Yet
if the reduced rate band had not been there, a higher threshold would

TABLE 4.4

Starting Rates of Income Tax: 1982
(percentages)

United Kingdom	30
Belgium	21.6
Germany	18
Netherlands	16.3
Canada	15.5
Denmark	14.4
United States	12
France	7.2
Japan	7

Source: House of Commons Hansard (24 November 1982).

have taken some people out of tax, while a lower basic tax rate would have reduced the work disincentive for most. Some, but as it turns out not many, would have found that their marginal tax rate rose to the basic rate. Even if the whole of the revenue raised by the abolition of the reduced rate band had been used to raise tax thresholds, the average marginal tax rate would have fallen slightly.

Perhaps the most surprising indictment of the reduced rate band is that few recipients of Family Income Supplement faced a marginal tax rate of 25 per cent. In 1979–80, 3½ million taxpayers were estimated to be in the reduced rate band but only 10,000 were thought to be receiving Family Income Supplement. This is only about 15 per cent of families then in the poverty trap. The reduced rate band was mainly populated by married women in part-time work, juveniles, and the elderly.

Despite its apparent failure to achieve its stated objectives, and withdrawal in 1980, a reduced rate band still has supporters. Pond and Playford (1980) argue that the statistical basis of the estimation of the number of families receiving Family Income Supplement and in the reduced rate band is unreliable. Morris and Warren base their estimates on Family Expenditure Survey data, which record the existence of only 29 such families: the sampling fraction is thus only 1 in every 3,000. Using a Department of Health and Social Security sample of Family Income Supplement recipients – for which the sampling fraction is one in ten – Pond and Playford calculate that 49,000 paid tax at a marginal rate of 25 per cent in December 1979. However, Pond and Playford record earnings at the date Family Income Supplement is awarded, while Morris and Warren record earnings at the date families are interviewed for the FES. Thus the difference between these two estimates partly reflects the small sample of Family Income Supplement recipients in the FES, but the fact that they measure earnings differently is perhaps more important. And it is fairly clear that Pond and Playford have overestimated the number the reduced rate band took out of the poverty trap; evidence would appear to suggest that earnings do drift upwards after a Family Income Supplement award has been made.

Although the reduced rate band proved to be an unsuccessful attempt to reduce the number of families in the poverty trap, it need not have done. But to extend it so that most poverty trap victims are faced with a lower marginal tax rate would not be a cheap alternative. For example, in order to remove the poverty trap for all families with up to two children, the reduced rate band would have to extend up to an earnings level twice as great as the married man's allowance. If the reduced tax rate were 20 per cent, this option would cost £5¼ billion and the basic rate of tax would have to rise to over 40 per cent. The much higher basic tax rate is required because every taxpayer benefits from the reduced rate band. But still some families with three or more children would remain in the poverty trap.

Taking low income families out of tax through increased tax allowances, or reducing their marginal rates of income tax with a reduced rate band (or, as an alternative, a graduated structure of marginal tax rates), would not appear to offer any obvious hope of progress towards the springing of the poverty trap. The effect of the cut in the basic rate of income tax from 33 to 30 per cent in the 1979 Budget, following the election of the Conservative government, has in the following three years been swamped by a failure to index tax allowances, increases in National Insurance contributions and value added tax, and the abolition of the reduced rate band (Dilnot and Morris, 1982). The basic rate would have to be reduced to 21.5 per cent if the tax paid by a two-child family on average earnings were to be restored to its 1978-9 level (House of Commons Hansard, 23 November 1982). Tax cuts, although not of this magnitude, were the election promise. Even if these prove difficult to deliver, further tax increases are not on the agenda. For this reason it seems that either some retreat from the plethora of means tests or a reduction in benefit withdrawal rates which can be financed without higher marginal tax rates or the introduction of additional complexity into the tax and benefit systems, offer the most promising avenue to the eventual elimination of marginal tax rates in the region of 100 per cent. Unless of course there is scope for ensuring that low income families are paid enough not to need means-tested income assistance, and in particular Family Income Supplement.

The poverty trap would indeed be less of a problem if the low-paid earned more while pay levels generally remained unchanged. Therefore minimum wage legislation may be a solution. A figure of £100 a week is now widely quoted; it is about two-thirds of average male earnings. This would take all but larger families out of the poverty trap. However, it is a possibility that some families will be taken out of the poverty trap not because their earnings increase but because the principal earner loses his or her job. And perhaps more disturbingly, although minimum wage legislation is generally aimed at relieving poverty among working families, it seems that its success in this direction is likely to be extremely limited.

Low pay and minimum wage legislation

At the turn of this century the great majority of the poor were in full-time work; at the time of the Depression unemployment was the major cause of poverty; pensioners are now the most numerous among the poor. While unemployment has forced itself dramatically into the reckoning again, the problem of low-paid employment as an important cause of poverty now attracts little attention. The problem certainly exists, but is not seen as sufficiently serious to warrant treatment at source. Where low pay occurs, the social security system – Family Income Supplement and housing benefits – provides the necessary safety net, although we have seen that this form of support can be ineffectual and has a substantial cost, in the form of the poverty trap. Why is the subject of low pay treated so lightly? The existence of an independent Low Pay Unit which makes frequent references to 'the army of low paid' would seem to indicate that the contribution low pay makes to family poverty may be underestimated.

'Low pay' does not have an agreed definition. The bottom 10 per cent of the earnings distribution could be regarded as the low-paid, in which case low pay cannot be eliminated, although the relative position of the low-paid can be improved. Those receiving below a half or two-thirds of average male earnings could be treated as low-paid, and while the low-pay problem can in principle be eliminated, only redistribution can achieve this. General growth in earnings can help little. Alternatively, the net incomes of the low-paid and the benefits payable to those not in work could be compared. Low pay is then defined as pay below the gross income necessary to yield an income equivalent to that which would be received on Supplementary Benefit. Each of these has its proponents, but the second – where low pay is related to the average male earnings – would appear to attract the most supporters.

In April 1981 a minimum wage of £80 a week was about two-thirds of average male earnings. If the minimum wage had been set at this level, 30 per cent of employees – about 6¼ million – would have benefited; however, more than three-quarters of the beneficiaries would have been adult females and juveniles (this is based on unpublished research by C. Trinder of the National Institute of Economic and Social Research). Layard *et al*. (1978) and Berthoud and Brown (1981) have shown that in many cases where the head of a family worked in a low-paid occupation a working wife contributed substantially to family income; the epithet 'secondary' to describe the earnings of a working wife is often grossly misleading. The overlap between poverty and low pay is actually small; probably less than quarter of a million families fall into both groups. Thus while minimum wages may be supported on equity grounds, they could only have a limited impact on the poverty problem in Britain.

Even if a national minimum wage is desirable on equity grounds, equity gains have to be set against efficiency losses. The major efficiency loss is likely to take the form of increased unemployment amongst those who are supposed to benefit from the legislation. The economics is straightforward. In a competitive labour market, where wages reflect the value to firms of workers' skills, employers should react to the legislation by dismissing their now uneconomic employees, and substituting more skilled workers for some of those who have departed. The sectors where low pay is more prevalent – the distributive trades and services, for example – tend to be pretty competitive. It is therefore to be expected that there will be fewer jobs for those who it is intended should benefit from the legislation.

According to the dual labour market hypothesis others may be harmed. The labour market can be viewed as consisting of a primary sector, which is stable, structured, and highly unionized, and a secondary sector, with none of these characteristics. Low-paid workers are confined to the secondary sector. Any adverse impact of minimum wage legislation hits the secondary sector worst of all. But workers in the primary sector may also be affected. Employers may decide that they cannot afford to train young workers if they have to pay them the minimum wage. More young workers therefore have to compete in the secondary sector and the overall level of unemployment in the secondary sector is further increased. Minimum wage legislation may also create a pressure for customary differentials to be preserved; wages in both the primary and secondary sectors are bid up, and the relative position of the low-paid is ultimately no better than prior to the introduction of the minimum wage.

There is little empirical evidence on which to draw in order to determine the employment effects of minimum wage legislation. US studies tend to confirm that the federal minimum wage has reduced teenage employment, and to a lesser extent the employment of young adults – see Brown, Gilroy, and Kohen (1982). For Britain we have to rely on 'suggestive' evidence, but this is powerful. For example, since the mid-1960s, and in particular in the mid-1970s, the earnings of young men relative to older men have increased, and prior to 1976 this was accompanied by increasing unemployment amonst young men relative to older men. Up until the early 1970s, female employment, and most notably employment on a part-time basis, increased as women's earnings relative to those of men in general remained constant. In other words, women's earnings fell relative to those of young men. The supply of both types of labour was growing. But the 1970 Equal Pay Act, phased in between 1970 and 1975, changed this pattern, and as the relative earnings of women increased, so did female unemployment relative to male unemployment; while unemployment among young men fell relative to older men. These trends are described in more detail by Ermisch (1983). However, even these few observations make it difficult to believe that minimum wage legislation in Britain would not have adverse implications for the employment prospects of low-paid workers in general, and the young in particular.

5

UNEMPLOYMENT, SICKNESS, AND DISABILITY

Unemployment

At the beginning of 1983 there were over three million registered unemployed in Britain, and perhaps another half a million who were not registered – and therefore not included in the official unemployment count – but were none the less unemployed and seeking work. Unemployment can never be made to disappear; but much can be done to reduce its level to a point where unemployment no longer constitutes the most pressing social and economic problem facing Britain. It is the proper role of social security to guarantee that the unemployed are protected from the worst consequences of their misfortune. Yet it has been suggested that the social security system does more than this: indeed, it has been argued that benefits are so generous that not only are some of the unemployed not keen to return to work, but also some of the employed choose to become unemployed. Thus the high level of unemployment is in part attributed to over-generous benefits paid to the unemployed. This is not a new idea. Some inter-war observers blamed a significant part of the unemployment at that time on high benefits, a claim which has recently found some dubious statistical support (see Benjamin and Kochin, 1979, and the critique by Metcalf, Nickell, and Floros, 1982). If the social security system indeed provides a disincentive to work or seek work, it could hinder attempts to reduce the level of unemployment, with adverse repercussions for those unemployed who genuinely wish to work. To reduce unemployment requires a political will; but all the commitment in the world will be ineffectual if the unemployed include amongst their number many who have concluded that 'they are better off on the dole'.

It is clearly important that the relationship between the level of unemployment and the generosity of the benefit system is established. But the generosity of the system, no matter what its actual impact on unemployment, is also relevant. For if it is known that the system is generous and that it is rational to be unemployed, it is easily concluded that the opportunity to draw benefit will be seized, even though it is generally rejected. A characteristic of the system, and the exploitation of it by only a handful of people, brings into disrepute both that system and those who through no choice of their own have to depend upon it. The unemployed will find that not only is there not the political will to reduce unemployment, but that instead there is some pressure being exerted to reduce their benefits.

We intend to spend some time discovering how income received during unemployment compares with income when in work. Only then will we consider the impact of benefits on unemployment. But we begin by describing the social security benefits available to the unemployed.

Benefits for the unemployed

Unemployment benefit is paid following the loss of a job to those who satisfy the contribution conditions and are genuinely unemployed and available for work. It is not means-tested. An elaborate set of rules make up the work test. No benefit is paid for the first three days of unemployment – the 'waiting days' – and benefit only lasts for 52 weeks. Under the 'linked spells' rule, any spell of unemployment of two days or more (there cannot be only one day of unemployment for benefit purposes) can be treated as part of an earlier spell of two days or more if the two spells are not separated by a period of more than eight weeks. The 1982–3 benefit rates are:

Basic	£25.00
Increase for one dependent adult	£15.45
Increase for each dependent child	£ 0.30

Since July 1982 unemployment benefit has been taxable. The taxable part excludes the addition for children.

Earnings-related supplement has been discontinued. But for any spell of unemployment beginning before January 1982 (or subsequently

if it could be linked to a spell prior to that date), the supplement would
have been paid if earnings were sufficiently large. No supplement was
paid after June 1982. The supplement was paid from the 13th day of
unemployment for a period of 26 weeks. Reckonable earnings –
earnings on which Class 1 National Insurance contributions were paid
in the tax year preceding the calendar year in which a claim was
made – determined whether the supplement was paid, and the amount.
If reckonable earnings exceeded 50 times the lower earnings limit in
the relevant tax year, the supplement was paid. A claim in 1981, based
on earnings in the 1979–80 tax year when the lower earnings limit was
£19.50, would have resulted in a supplement of 33 per cent of
reckonable weekly earnings between £19.50 and £30.00, and 10 per
cent of reckonable weekly earnings between £30.00 and £135.00 if
reckonable earnings exceeded $19.50 \times 50 = £975$. Note that it is
possible for a payment of earnings-related supplement to reflect
earnings received 30 months previously. Unemployment benefit
plus earnings-related supplement was subject to an overriding limit
equal to 85 per cent of reckonable earnings, except when unemployment benefit itself exceeded this limit, in which case it was paid in
full.

Although earnings-related supplement is no longer paid it has been
necessary to describe it in some detail because, as we shall see, it has
played a prominent part in the 'why work?' story.

Supplementary Benefit, known as supplementary allowance when
received by the unemployed, can be paid in addition to unemployment
benefit, and is the sole form of income support for the unemployed
after 52 weeks of unemployment. The 1982-3 scale rates, together with
the way in which a Supplementary Benefit entitlement is determined,
are reported in Chapter 4. Supplementary Benefit paid to the
unemployed is taxable. The taxable part is whichever is the smaller of
the standard weekly amount of unemployment benefit *for a couple*
and the amount actually received. The *free school meals and free milk*
to which Supplementary Benefit recipients may be entitled are not
taxable.

While Supplementary Benefit includes the full cost of rent and rates,
unemployment benefit ignores housing costs. Recipients of unemployment benefit not receiving Supplementary Benefit are therefore entitled
to a *rent rebate or allowance and a rate rebate*.

Replacement rates

We are going to compare net incomes for those in work and those out of work. A convenient method of summarizing the relationship between them is through the computation of a replacement rate, which is the ratio of net income out of work to net income in work. Thus if N is net income and u indicates weeks of unemployment while $e = 52 - u$ indicates weeks of employment, we will define a long-term replacement rate as

$$\text{LTRR} = \frac{N(u = 52)}{N(e = 52)}.\tag{5.1}$$

Net income in work is computed as in Chapter 4, taking into account all the benefits to which a family is entitled as well as income tax and National Insurance contributions. Income out of work is computed in the light of the benefits available to the unemployed described in this chapter, again assuming that all entitlements are exercised. Table 5.1 illustrates this calculation for a one earner couple with two children

TABLE 5.1

Computing a Long-Term Replacement Rate
(One earner couple with two children aged four and six, £ a year)

	Employed whole year	Unemployed whole year
Gross earnings	5,200.00	
Income tax	− 826.50	
National Insurance contributions	− 455.00	
Child benefit	608.40	608.40
Unemployment benefit		2,134.60
Supplementary allowance		1,375.40
Rent and rate rebates	505.96	
Net income	5,032.86	4,118.40

LTRR = 4,118.40/5,032.86 = 81.8 per cent.

aged four and six, where the head could earn £100 a week. Rent is £15 a week and rates are £5 a week. It is assumed for the moment that benefits are *not* taxable, and free school meals and free milk have not been taken into account. It is straightforward to calculate that when the head is in work for a whole tax year, net income would be

£5,032.86. If the head is unemployed for that tax year, then net income would be £4,118.40, assuming benefit income does not change during the tax year. If this is the first year of unemployment, benefit income would be the sum of 11.70 × 52 = £608.40 child benefit, 41.05 × 52 = £2,134.60 unemployment benefit, and a supplementary allowance of £1,375.40 necessary to make total income up to [59.20 (the scale rate for a couple with two children aged below 11) + 20 (rent and rates)] × 52 = £4,118.40. The replacement rate is 81.8 per cent. Of course in any subsequent year of unbroken unemployment the amount which would have been received in benefits would take the form of Supplementary Benefit.

Replacement rates computed as in Table 5.1 vary from family to family. They depend upon a number of factors: earnings, housing costs, and the number of children and their age. Table 5.2 demonstrates that a reduction in earnings, an increase in rent, and the addition

TABLE 5.2

Variations in Long-Term Replacement Rates with Family Circumstances
(percentages)

	Earnings reduction of £20	A £5 increase in rent	Two additional children aged 11–15
Independent impact	84.3	82.7	92.0
Cumulative impact	84.3	87.0	93.3

of two older children, all increase the replacement rate, and the total impact of these changes is to increase the replacement rate from 81.8 per cent to 93.3 per cent. An earnings reduction increases the replacement rate simply because it reduces income in work without affecting income out of work. The increase in the replacement rate resulting from the rent increase, reflects the fact that while the Supplementary Benefit rent payment compensates for this in full only 60 per cent of the increase feeds through to the rent rebate. For an additional child aged 11-15 the Supplementary Benefit scale rate rises by £13.15. The qualifying level for Family Income Supplement rises by £9, and Family Income Supplement itself rises by £4.50. Child benefit for the additional child is £5.85. The needs allowances for rebates goes up by £11.40, and at earnings of £100 a week, rent and rate rebate increases by 23 per cent of $(11.40 - 4.50 - 5.85) = 24$p. The total increase in income while in work is £10.59, which is less than the addition to the scale rate. Hence the replacement rate rises. However, for additional children aged under 11 the Supplementary Benefit scale rate rises by only £8.75 and in our example the replacement rate would therefore be reduced. But at higher levels of earnings or with lower rent – both of which imply a lower replacement rate – this would not be so. It is worth noting that the cumulative impact of the three changes is not the sum of their independent impacts. The cumulative impact reflects the interaction of the various benefits.

Long-run replacement rates can rise above 100 per cent, but only for those families with very low earnings, many children, or high housing costs, or a combination of all three, since these characteristics increase benefit income relative to income when in work. This occurs because the social security system provides allowances for a dependent wife, for children, and for housing costs which are far greater than the tax allowance, child benefit, and rent and rate rebates provided for those in work.

A long-term replacement rate as computed above compares annual income when permanently employed with annual income when permanently unemployed. A comparison based on weekly income – which is the income concept many may use – will yield the identical result since both when employed and unemployed annual income is 52 times weekly income. However, a long-term replacement rate provides no guide as to the impact of working for part of the year and being unemployed for the remainder of the year. For this one needs a short-term replacement rate. Short-term replacement rates are different for the unemployed and the employed population. The specific details of their calculation are most fully explained for the employed population.

Short-term replacement rates for the employed and unemployed

To illustrate how a short-term replacement rate is computed we will assume that the decision period is a again a tax year and that benefits, which are not taxed, do not change in that year. The short-term replacement rate for an employed person faced with the possibility of u weeks unemployment is given by

$$\text{STRR (employed)} = \frac{N(u, e = 52-u)}{N(e = 52)}. \qquad (5.2)$$

In Table 5.3 we have recomputed the net income and then computed the short-term replacement rates for the family to which Table 5.1 refers, but on the basis that the head of the family is unemployed for part of the year. The replacement rate declines with additional weeks

TABLE 5.3

Short-Term Replacement Rates for the Employed
(£ a year)

| | Weeks Unemployment (u) | | |
	13	26	39
Gross earnings	3,900.00	2,600.00	1,300.00
Income tax	−436.50	−46.50	−
National Insurance contributions	−341.25	−227.50	−113.75
Child benefit	608.40	608.40	608.40
Unemployment benefit	533.65	1067.30	1600.95
Supplementary allowance	343.85	687.70	1031.55
Rent and rate rebate	379.47	252.98	126.49
Net income	4987.62	4942.38	4553.64
STRR (employed)	99.1%	98.2%	90.1%

of unemployment. Furthermore, as shown in Figure 5.1, the relationship between net income and weeks of unemployment is linear before and after a change in gradient. This pattern of short-term replacement rates emerges because of the relationship between the tax system and the benefit system.

Consider the case of a person working for a full year. If they were to be unemployed for a week they would lose their net wage income — after income tax and National Insurance contributions — and some of their rent allowance and rate rebate, but they would gain unemployment benefit and supplementary allowance. The difference between their losses and gains is modest; for our sample couple the figure is $(5,032.86-4,987.62 = 45.24) \div 13 = £3.48$. As long as the person pays tax this is the loss incurred for each additional week of unemployment. This is much lower than the average weekly loss involved in not working for a long time, $(5,032.86-4,118.40 = 914.46) \div 52 = £17.59$, which is reflected by the dotted line in Figure 5.1. But once earnings fall below £2,445, in the 27th week of unemployment, income tax is no longer paid, and earnings are only liable to National Insurance contributions. The loss attached to an additional week's unemployment increases by £30, the tax which would have been paid on foregone earnings, i.e. to (4,553.64–4,118.40 = 435.24) ÷ 13 = £33.48, somewhat in excess of £17.59. Hence the kink in Figure 5.1 at 27 week's unemployment. It is worth emphasizing that the relationship between net income and weeks of unemployment shown in Figure 5.1 is unique to the family to which it refers. The graph always has a downward kink when tax is no longer paid, but where this occurs will vary between single persons and married couples, and married couples with different mortgage commitments. The slopes of the graph will depend upon the benefits to which any individual or family is entitled.

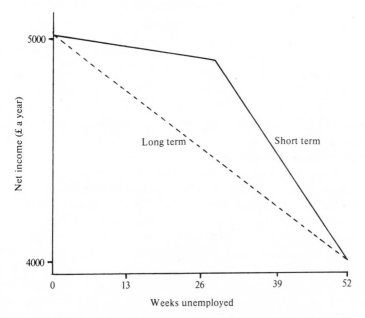

FIG. 5.1. The Relationship between Net Income and Weeks of Unemployment (One earner couple earning £100 a week with two children aged four and six).

We have noted that long-term replacement rates can be in excess of 100 per cent, and the conditions under which these emerge. Short-term replacement rates are more likely to exceed 100 per cent, given similar circumstances – low pay, a large family, and high housing costs – because in most cases short-term replacement rates substantially exceed long-term rates.

For an unemployed person faced with the possibility of e week's employment the short-term replacement rate is given by

$$\text{STRR (unemployed)} = \frac{N(u = 52)}{N(e, u = 52 - e)} \qquad (5.3)$$

and for our example family the rate is readily computed, for various weeks of employment, using the information in Tables 5.1 and 5.3. Table 5.4 reports the results. The replacement rate declines as the

TABLE 5.4

Short-Term Replacement Rates for the Unemployed
(percentages)

	Weeks employment (e)		
	13	26	39
STRR (unemployed)	90.0	83.3	82.6

number of weeks of employment increases: net income increases — as one moves across Figure 5.1 from right to left — and additional employment becomes more rewarding.

In computing long-term replacement rates there is no need to distinguish between annual income and weekly income. They both produce the same result since weekly income is constant through the year. With short-term replacement rates this is not so. In Britain income tax is levied on a cumulative pay-as-you-earn basis, and an attempt is made to guarantee that, on the assumption of unchanging circumstances, a taxpayer has always paid exactly the right amount of tax. Thus unemployment at the beginning of the tax year implies a lower tax bill in every week of work than that applying when working a whole year. Prior to the introduction of benefit taxation in July 1982, if unemployment occurred then at the end of the tax year there would be a tax rebate, although there may have been a delay before the rebate was received. Thirteen weeks unemployment, no matter when it occurs, leaves net income for the tax year the same; the replacement rate will be 99.1 per cent in our illustration. But the way in which tax is adjusted produces a replacement rate, when calculated on a weekly basis, which is lower than this figure if unemployment occurs at the beginning of the year and higher if it occurs at the end. The weekly perspective serves only to emphasize that the distribution of income receipts over the tax year depends upon when in the year unemployment occurs. The monetary costs and benefits of a spell of unemployment should ideally be measured over the period it takes for the full financial implications of that spell to work themselves out. Although this could be longer than a tax year, the information requirements become more demanding and the uncertainty attached to the estimated replacement rates more worrying as the time period lengthens. It seems sensible to truncate the calculation at the end of the tax year.

When the unemployed find that they would be little or no better off if they returned to work, or the employed discover that they would be little or no worse off if they were unemployed – either long-term or short-term, and after allowing for work expenses – they are widely referred to as being in the unemployment trap. Strictly speaking, only those facing replacement rates in excess of 100 per cent (or 95 per cent say, after allowing for some excess of work expenses over the costs of searching for a job) will find themselves in the unemployment trap. When we come to discuss the relief of the poverty trap through a reduction in benefit withdrawal rates, we will have to address the issue of how high marginal tax rates can be without them hitting the poverty plateau, where the disincentive effects usually associated with the poverty trap start to emerge, or creating disbelief in the eyes of detached observers. Similarly, it seems unlikely that those facing replacement rates of 100 per cent or a little higher are in a significantly different position to those facing replacement rates a little below 100 per cent. The point where adverse disincentive effects set in or incredulity develops is of course difficult to gauge. Many commentators take 80 per cent as a bench-mark; if a large number of families face replacement rates in excess of 80 per cent, this is judged to be harmful from an efficiency point of view.

The incidence of high replacement rates

The range of replacement rates is quite large and it is interesting to know whether the highest replacement rates, those in excess of 80 per cent, affect large numbers of the employed and unemployed populations. Using Family Expenditure Survey data, Kay, Morris, and Warren (1980) investigated this. They calculated replacement rates for a tax year, 1980–1, and considered the impact on their net income if the employed were to take four weeks unemployment from the date they were interviewed and the unemployed were to accept four weeks employment from the date they were interviewed. However, the STRR formulas cannot be computed by simply assuming either that $u = 4$ in (5.2), or that $e = 4$ in (5.3). Take the case of an employed man interviewed say in June. We know how much he earns, and given his family and housing circumstances we can calculate what he would receive if he were unemployed for four weeks. However, we are interested in comparing how much he would get over the tax year if he were unemployed for the next four weeks with how much he would get if he remained in employment for the rest of the tax year. Both of these sums would depend upon whether he has been unemployed previously in the tax year. The short-term replacement rate is given by

$$\text{STRR* (employed)} = \frac{N(u, e = 52 - u^* - u)}{N(e = 52 - u^*)} \tag{5.4}$$

where u^* is the number of weeks of previous unemployment and u is the number of additional weeks of unemployment. Similarly for the unemployed we will have

$$\text{STRR* (unemployed)} = \frac{N(u = 52 - e^*)}{N(e, u = 52 - e^* - e)} \tag{5.5}$$

where e^* is the number of weeks of previous employment and e is the number of additional weeks of employment. It is best to think of STRR as an *average* short-term replacement rate and STRR* as a *marginal* short-term replacement rate.

The Kay, Morris, and Warren (1980) short-term replacement rates are of the second type, marginal short-term replacement rates, reflecting the fact that offers of additional unemployment or employment will have financial consequences which depend upon past experience. Their results are reported in Table 5.5. For the employed population the average long-term replacement rate was 53 per cent and only 7 per cent of the employed faced a rate of 80 per cent or greater. In 1980–1 some unemployed were eligible for earnings-related supplement, which raised the average value of the marginal short-term replacement rate from 66 to 71 per cent. Excluding the supplement from the calculations, 22 per cent of the working population faced marginal short-term replacement rates in excess of 80 per cent, while including the supplement this figure rose to 28 per cent.

For the unemployed population, the average long-term replacement rate was higher and the average marginal short-term replacement rates

TABLE 5.5

The Incidence of High Replacement Rates: 1980–1
(percentages)

Replacement rate	Working population Additional unemployment			Unemployed population Additional work		
	Including supplement	Excluding supplement	Long-term	Including supplement	Excluding supplement	Long-term
Above 80	28	22	7	20	14	22
Above 100	5	4	2	2	1	1
Average	71	66	53	65	62	68

Source: Derived from Kay, Morris, and Warren (1980).

lower than for the working population. A larger proportion of the unemployed, 22 per cent, faced a long-term replacement rate in excess of 80 per cent, while smaller proportions, 20 per cent including and 14 per cent excluding earnings-related supplement, faced a short-term marginal replacement rate in excess of 80 per cent. Very few of the employed or unemployed could be better off in unemployment than in employment.

An earnings-related supplement clearly has an impact on the level and distribution of replacement rates. But this impact is less than the relatively generous formula by which it is computed would at first suggest. There is a perfectly good explanation. When Atkinson and Flemming (1978) concluded that in 1977 very few unemployed families would have been worse off if they had returned to work, part of the reason for this was that when they examined the incomes of the unemployed they found that only one in six received earnings-related supplement; the remainder were not entitled to it because they had been unemployed, less than two weeks or more than 28 weeks, had been low-paid, or had worked only intermittently in the previous tax year (see also Creedy and Disney, 1981). This will have been the case in 1980–1 as well.

Kay, Morris, and Warren take account of many of the complications ignored in the computation of our illustrative replacement rates: 60 per cent of wives of working men and 30 per cent of wives of unemployed men have full-time or part-time jobs; benefit levels usually change every November, and in November 1980 short-term benefits were cut in real terms; Family Income Supplement is paid for a year even if the family head becomes unemployed for a short period. Replacement rates are affected by these, and numerous other factors. Yet if those people interviewed for the FES were asked to calculate their own replacement rates it seems unlikely that the vast majority would produce answers close to our crude illustrative figures, let alone the precise estimates of Kay, Morris, and Warren. There are likely to be two sources of difference. First, respondents may not be aware of all the benefits they are entitled to, both when in work and out of work. A study of the characteristics of those unemployed with high replacement rates, carried out by economists at the Department of Health and Social Security (Davies *et al.*, 1982) – a study, incidentally, which revealed high rates to be most likely amongst those people who were low-paid or who had many children, although not so likely amongst those who faced simply high housing costs – reported that the take-up of means-tested benefits by unemployed men when in work is staggeringly low. The figures are: 12 per cent for Family Income Supplement; 39 per cent for free school meals; and 16 per cent for rebates available for local authority tenants. Second, the unemployed may not know what wage they would be offered with a job.

It is assumed by Kay, Morris, and Warren that all benefits are taken up, and that the unemployed will receive the same wage as in their last job, or the average wage of an unskilled engineering worker where previous earnings are unknown. Both of these are defensible assumptions. Clearly some people volunteer for unemployment rather than employment, and they are likely to be aware of their entitlements. The full take-up approach reveals the potential number of people who could benefit from doing the costing exercise that some probably do undertake very carefully. It therefore describes the disincentives created by the system, but provides no guide as to how individuals respond to them. Non-take-up serves to indicate that either not everybody does the calculations, or they do so in some ignorance of the social security system. Naturally it is perceived replacement rates which affect the decision to become unemployed, and actual replacement rates which affect the decision to return to work. In attempting to assess whether the 'better off on the dole' story is fact or fiction take-up of benefits should not be ignored. It is also pointless to try and guess what the unemployed would earn if they were to return to work; but the last wage received must provide a reliable guide, in most cases, to what they could reasonably expect.

The Kay, Morris, and Warren approach is not, however, devoid of problems. There is one particular element which is worrying. If one is concerned with incentives, computing a marginal short-term replacement rate for a tax year is not an appropriate economic calculation. Certainly, how much better or worse off a person is as a result of a short spell of employment or unemployment depends upon what happened in the past. But it does not follow that past income should be included in the replacement rate; since past income is unaffected by either future employment or future unemployment there is no case for doing so. Most economic calculations are forward-looking rather than backward-looking, and the computation of marginal short-term replacement rates should reflect this practice.

The taxation of benefits

Both in our illustrative calculations of replacement rates using current benefit levels and in the Kay, Morris, and Warren work, benefits are untaxed. The failure to tax benefits, together with the availability of earnings-related supplement, largely explains why, as Table 5.5 indicates, a significant proportion of the employed population faced short-term replacement rates in excess of 80 per cent in 1980–1: the financial penalties incurred if the fully-employed sought to be unemployed for part of the year were small and, for some, such actions were financially advantageous. Table 5.5 also suggests that the abolition of earnings-related supplement will have reduced replacement rates, and therefore the numbers facing high replacement rates. Taxing the benefits which replace earnings, as earned income, which has been done since July 1982, will have further reduced short-term replacement rates.

It is interesting to take a little time to consider why benefits have not been taxed in the past. In fact in 1948, when the National Insurance scheme was introduced, they were taxed, but taxation was abandoned almost immediately because of the administrative problems it presented to the Inland Revenue. And the Inland Revenue have been the principal opponents to its reintroduction. It is a requirement of the cumulative pay-as-you-earn tax system that when an individual changes jobs his new employer is immediately informed of earnings and tax paid in the current tax year so that he can deduct the correct amount of income tax. Benefit taxation under this system requires that a government department becomes the 'employer' of the unemployed, and it has been estimated that to perform this role many extra civil servants would be required. In the end benefit taxation could only be achieved through a limited retreat from cumulation in the case of those with a broken employment record. Tax refunds will be made at the end of the tax year, while tax which is owed will be collected in a subsequent tax year.

To examine the impact of abolishing earnings-related supplement, Kay, Morris, and Warren simply ignored the supplement and recomputed their 1980-1 replacement rates. They also recomputed their 1980-1 replacement rates with benefit taxation; although they assumed that all unemployment benefit and supplementary allowance would be taxed in full, which is not the case, their results provide a guide to the likely impact of benefit taxation. They are summarized in Table 5.6. The average marginal short-term replacement rate is significantly

TABLE 5.6

The Incidence of High Short-Term Replacement Rates with Benefit Taxation
(percentages)

Replacement rate	Working population Additional unemployment excluding supplement
Above 80	7
Above 100	1
Average	56

Source: Derived from Kay, Morris, and Warren (1980).

reduced, and the proportion of the population facing a replacement rate over 80 per cent falls dramatically from 28 to 7 per cent. Thus while in the second half of the 1960s and throughout the 1970s short-term replacement rates may well have exceeded 80 per cent for one quarter of the working population, only a minority are now in this position. It is far from obvious that high replacement rates have ever been a serious problem, in the sense that they are responsible for creating unemployment. If they ever were, it is now most unlikely that they continue to be so. We now turn to the evidence on the relationship between benefits and unemployment.

Benefits and incentives
That generous benefits should induce unemployment is a straightforward prediction of the same 'supply side' economic analysis which

contends that the punitive taxation of the highly-paid prior to the 1979 Budget blunted their incentive to exploit fully their supposedly valuable talents. Workers have a reservation wage, and will not work if they are paid less than their reservation wage. If the reservation wage is an increasing function of unemployment benefits then with an unchanged distribution of jobs and wage offers, more generous benefits should lead to increased voluntary unemployment.

This story is seriously incomplete. We have seen that unemployment benefits are paid subject to a work test which requires that the unemployed are available for work and actively seeking employment — and the policing of this provision is keen — while there are only restricted benefits for those who either leave a job of their own accord or are dismissed for misconduct. Thus the freedom to choose to remain unemployed or begin a brief spell of unemployment is in principle limited. But for those who carefully 'cost themselves for unemployment', these measures are unlikely to be a serious practical impediment. Nevertheless, there is the possibility, which the simple theory ignores, that any non-financial benefits from working will influence the number of such people. While still recognizing that the primary benefits from work are financial, a House of Lords Select Committee pointed out that, 'It also helps the worker to find a place in society, to interact with others, to contribute to personal identity, to lessen anxiety and to structure the passage of time. ... there has grown up a widespread belief that work is essential not only to survival but also to self-fulfilment' (House of Lords Select Committee, 1982, par. 2.4). The non-financial benefits may therefore be substantial; although it could be argued that the theory also ignores the benefits of the additional leisure achieved by the unemployed, and that these compensate for the loss of the pecuniary benefits which are gained from work. However, any suggestion that these two non-financial items are offsetting is totally unjustifiable.

What happens on the demand side may also bear upon the predictive ability of the model. Unemployment can only be viewed as being related to the benefit regime if acceptable job offers would be forthcoming in the absence of benefits. If the demand for labour is low there may be few offers around to be turned down by the unemployed; and if demand is buoyant wage offers may be so generous that benefits are irrelevant. It is also possible that an offer refused by one worker will be taken up by another, who is involuntary unemployed. Generous benefits may simply change the composition of the unemployed, but not its overall level. Demand conditions may also affect the decision of someone as to whether to leave work, if he or she anticipates that it will be difficult to return to work on the terms at which he or she left.

How much benefit-induced unemployment is there? There are two different types of evidence, time-series and cross-section. Figure 5.2 gives us evidence of the first type; it shows that both the benefit-

FIG 5.2. The Benefit–Income Ratio and Unemployment Rate 1950–81

Notes: (1) The benefit–income ratio is calculated for a married couple where the husband receives the average net earnings of adult male manual workers in manufacturing and certain other industries (1948–72) or the average earnings of adult males in all occupations (1973–81). (2) The unemployment rate refers to males (excluding school-leavers and adult students) in Great Britain.

Sources: DHSS, *Social Security Statistics.* Department of Employment, *British Labour Statistics 1886–1968. Department of Employment Gazette.*

income ratio and the unemployment rate have generally increased since 1948, although during the 1970s the benefit-income ratio fell while unemployment increased. Note the large increase in the benefit-income ratio in 1966 when earnings-related supplement was introduced. Maki and Spindler (1975) investigated the extent to which variations in the unemployment rate between 1948 and 1972 were explained by variations in the benefit–income ratio when labour market conditions are controlled for. They paid particular attention to the impact of the introduction of earnings-related supplement, and concluded that the unemployment rate was 30 per cent higher after the supplement was brought in than it would have been if the supplement had not been introduced.

This conclusion has been widely criticized. Perhaps the most damaging criticism is the fact that the result is sensitive to the specification of the benefit variable. Maki and Spindler use the benefit-income ratio for a couple with two children where the husband receives the average male manual earnings in the manufacturing industry. However, we have discovered that the replacement rate is very sensitive to earnings and household characteristics, and that those facing the highest replacement rates are not families with two children where the husband receives the average male manual earnings in manufacturing industry.

The cross-section evidence attempts to explain the duration of unemployment in terms of the benefit–income ratio, personal characteristics (age, qualifications, employment history), and local labour market conditions. There are many studies using such evidence, and fairly typical is that by Nickell (1979) based on the sample of unemployed in the General Household Survey. His conclusion, more or less shared by the other studies, is that the duration of unemployment is likely to be longer the higher the benefit–income ratio. But the impact is small. However, these studies have their limitations. They are concerned only with the flow *out* of unemployment, and little can be inferred about the effect of the benefit–income ratio on total unemployment; it is assumed that all benefits are taken up in full; and the replacement rate used is always the long-term one. Only Atkinson *et al.* (1982) have experimented with alternative specifications of the replacement rate variable — of which there are more than we have any need to consider — in a similar exercise, and as with the time-series studies it turns out that the results of cross-section analyses are sensitive to the specification of the replacement rate.

Overall the evidence is difficult to assess; one can find the answer one wants, and each view can be defended by those who want to adopt the position supported by a particular set of econometric results. The results of continuing research in this area are eagerly awaited.

Unemployment benefit policy

'Let us take supply-side theory at its face value, however modest that may be. It holds that the work habits of people are tied irrevocably to their income, though in a curiously perverse way. The poor do not work because they have too much income; the rich do not work because they do not have enough income. You expand and revitalize the economy by giving the poor less, the rich more' (J. K. Galbraith, quoted in the *Guardian* newspaper, 18 February 1982).

This strategy has been exactly that followed in Britain in the 1980s: the abolition of earnings-related supplement, the real cut in unemployment benefit in the 1980 Budget, supposedly a prelude to the taxation of benefits (and which was expected to be restored to avoid 'double taxation'), and the taxation of benefits from 1982, have served to reduce the short-term replacement rates. The aim has been to eliminate adverse incentives from the system, and these measures may have done this. But we can be no clearer about what has happened to incentives at the lower end of the distribution than we are about the impact on incentives of the cuts in higher rates of income tax in the 1979 Budget.

Attention in this chapter has so far been focused on high replacement rates. Unemployment benefits exist to help the unemployed maintain an adequate standard of living, and possibly to protect customary living standards over a short period of unemployment or smooth the transition from employment to a sustained period of unemployment. Income maintenance, in the sense of preventing poverty, is provided by flat-rate unemployment benefit and short-term Supplementary Benefit. The real cut in unemployment benefit and the abolition of earnings-related supplement should not have increased the number of unemployed who are poor, if Supplementary Benefit – which has been preserved in real terms – is claimed. The taxation of benefits only affects the income of the unemployed once they have returned to work. But we have noted that many of the unemployed will be poor simply because they do not claim Supplementary Benefit. The way to alleviate poverty amongst the unemployed is to reduce dependence on means-tested Supplementary Benefit; there can be little justification for any extension of means tests for the unemployed, indeed there is much to commend a reduction in their use.

Those unemployed for more than a year *have* to rely on Supplementary Benefit, and no matter how long they are unemployed they receive only the short-term rate. There is substantial pressure for the long-term unemployed to be paid the long-term Supplementary Benefit rate after one year on Supplementary Benefit. The rationale for the two Supplementary Benefit rates is that in the first year claimants can draw on savings and the need to replace clothing and durable goods is minimal. After a year this is less likely to be the case. This rationale rests rather uneasily in the company of a pernicious savings rule, officially viewed as a generous concession, which in 1982-3 precludes those with over £2,500 in assets (other than a house and reasonable personal possessions) from receiving Supplementary Benefit, although is not ruled out by it. And if it has any force for those not required to register for work why should it not be similarly forceful in the case of those who are? The case for treating these two groups equally is widely recognized, but extending long-term benefit is felt to be too costly, over £200 million in 1981 (SSAC, 1982). Yet in terms of total social security expenditure this figure is modest, and if there is to be a distinction between short-term and long-term Supplementary Benefit rates, the claims of the long-term unemployed to the latter should be conceded.

Furthermore, taxation of unemployment benefits is expected to raise £450 million the 1983-4 tax year, and there must be a case for using some of this revenue to increase the incomes of the long-term unemployed.

When it was available earnings-related supplement supplied an element of short-term income continuity; if it had still existed the average amount would have been about £12 at the end of 1982, when unemployment benefit for a couple was £40.45. Income replacement, i.e. relating benefit to earnings for a short period, has now been rejected. There were good reasons for discontinuing earnings-related supplement. In particular, the way in which entitlement was determined made ineligibility extremely common, as a result of the linked-spells rule. The most serious problem with earnings-related supplement was that many failed to benefit from it, although it was abolished primarily because it was too generous to others.

While it must be admitted, for reasons already given, that very high replacement rates should be avoided, this does not imply that there is not a case for a modest earnings-related supplement from which anyone becoming unemployed can benefit. We have seen that it is justifiable for the state to provide cover for those contingencies the private market ignores, and unemployment is such a contingency. But when there is pressure to reduce the resources devoted to social security, and because poverty relief is a more immediate objective of the social security system, earnings-related unemployment benefit should perhaps, for the moment, be attached a relatively low priority.

Sickness

An employee who is sick and unable to attend work for four days or more, and satisfies the contribution conditions, is at least in the first part of 1983, entitled to *sickness benefit*, which is paid at the same rate as unemployment benefit. Sickness benefit too was augmented by an earnings-related supplement before its abolition. Periods of sickness separated by eight weeks or less are linked in order to determine benefit entitlement, and sickness benefit is paid for a maximum of 28 weeks.

Most employees do not rely on state benefits when they are sick. Over 80 per cent of employees are covered by occupational sick pay schemes, under which it is common practice for sickness benefit to be made up to the employee's normal earnings. While occupational sick pay is taxable, sickness benefit is not: thus many employees will be better off when they are sick. A one earner couple with two children earning £100 a week will, ignoring housing benefits, have a net income of £87.06. In a week of sickness this will increase to £102.96. Do employees take advantage of these sick pay provisions? Certainly the three waiting days may have deterred those who simply fancied a paid day at the races. And prior to June 1982 the method of claiming sickness benefit, which required that a sick note be obtained from a doctor, would have discouraged some. But the determined malingerer who asserted that he was 'under the weather' was unlkely to be subjected to a detailed medical examination by an overworked GP. Since June 1982 employees have been able to declare that they are sick without seeing a doctor, and can receive sickness benefit for up to a week. This procedure – known as self-certification – has been described by some as a 'lead-swinger's charter', although since it is difficult to judge whether the sick note system was widely abused, and given that self-certification will be monitored, this claim should not be attached great significance.

Most spells of sickness – around 90 per cent – last less than eight weeks, and very few indeed extend beyond 28 weeks. But if they do a claimant moves on to *invalidity benefit*, itself a non-contributory benefit but one which is only paid to those who qualified for sickness benefit. In effect it is contributory. Invalidity benefit has two components, an *invalidity pension* at a 1982-3 basic rate of £31.45 with additions for adult dependants of £18.85, and for children of £7.95, plus an *invalidity allowance* which depends upon the age at the onset of sickness: if less than 40, £6.90; if between 40 and 49, £4.40; and from 50 to pension age, £2.20. *Non-contributory invalidity pension* is available after 28 weeks of sickness to those who do not qualify for sickness benefit; they move to it from Supplementary Benefit, and because the pension is small a recipient may still qualify for Supplementary Benefit.

Statutory Sick Pay

Self-certification was the first stage in a radical revision of state benefits for initial sickness. As a consequence of the 1982 Social Security and Housing Benefits Bill, in June 1983 the Employers' Statutory Sick Pay Scheme is effective. This scheme places the responsibility for paying initial state sick pay in the hands of employers. An employer will decide whether an employee should receive sick pay – relying on self-certification or if in doubt requiring further medical evidence of sickness – and records of employee sickness must be kept for possible examination by Department of Health and Social Security inspectors.

For periods of sickness of more than three days but less than eight weeks (after eight weeks, sickness benefit is paid under the conditions outlined above), statutory sick pay is equal to:

Average earnings over last eight weeks	Statutory sick pay
Up to £29.50	None
£29.50 to £44.99	£25.00
£45.00 to £59.99	£31.00
Above £60.00	£37.00

Employers deduct payments of statutory sick pay before making payments of National Insurance contributions and pay-as-you-earn income tax to the Inland Revenue.

The principal reasons for changing the sick pay arrangements are to recover through taxation those benefits not needed by employees covered by occupational sick pay schemes, and to ease the administrative burden on the Department of Health and Social Security, which handles 10 million claims for sickness benefit every year. Reference has also been made to the fact that payments by employers during periods of initial sickness are common overseas. Statutory sick pay will be subject to both income tax and National Insurance contributions, leaving the employee who receives his full earnings during sickness no better or worse off than if he were not sick. He would be worse off than under the current arrangements, but this is perfectly justified. However, in some industries, like manufacturing, and among manual workers, occupational sick pay coverage is patchy. Combined with the absence of any allowances for dependants in the statutory sick pay rates, it would appear that a significant proportion of the work-force will not be adequately covered, and that there will be a greater reliance on Supplementary Benefit than at present (see O'Higgins, 1981). Note also that part-time workers, those on short time, and job sharers are likely to be excluded from the scheme altogether.

The scheme will save the Department of Health and Social Security £400 million in administrative costs in 1983/4 (SSAC, 1982). But employers will pay more. The administrative burden is shifted to them, and where firms are responsible for doing similar work for the government — say in collecting and paying valued added tax — the compliance costs are often immense (see Kay and King, 1980). Furthermore, because National Insurance contributions are charged to statutory sick pay, and statutory sick pay rates will often be below sickness benefit entitlements, the employer must pay more. Table 5.7 demonstrates this, for the case where occupational sick pay makes up earnings in full. If the employer runs an occupational pension scheme, contributions to this will also increase. Naturally the additional tax payments and National Insurance contributions should be added to the administrative cost savings of the state. These are the direct financial consequences of the new scheme.

The new scheme shifts both the responsibility for and some of the costs of initial sick pay provision from the state to employers. This privatization of social welfare is viewed by some as damaging to the principles which have governed social policy in Britain, and in particular the idea that the state should be solely responsible for providing a guaranteed minimum income. However, O'Higgins (1981) has said that the change should be viewed as a substitution of state regulation for state provision and has argued that it allows sick pay to escape cuts in public expenditure. This is a special case of a general argument which says that some privatization will allow social welfare expenditure to increase while that part met by the government falls in absolute terms (see Judge, 1980a). Since the private market has the potential, and is willing, to provide income during initial sickness, further calls for reduced public expenditure may well result in the new scheme being short-lived, and workplace provision become a statutory requirement.

TABLE 5.7

Gross Labour Costs Under Alternative Sick Pay Arrangements:
June 1983
(Married man with two children, £ a week)

	With sickness benefit	With statutory sick pay
Normal gross earnings	100.00	100.00
Sickness benefit/Statutory sick pay	−41.05	−37.00
Occupational sick pay	58.95	63.00
Employer's National Insurance contribution	7.19	12.20
Gross labour cost	66.14	75.20

Increase in gross labour cost = £9.06.

However, privatization does raise problems which cannot be ignored. For example, those with justifiably poor attendance records — mainly the chronically sick and disabled — may find it difficult to secure or retain employment, or employers may attempt, in a covert manner, to discriminate in favour of those employees with few absences through sickness. On the other hand, since employers do have to bear more of the cost of initial sickness, they may attempt, in so far as they are able, to reduce the incidence of genuine sickness — by means of preventive medicine and health education programmes — and to improve working conditions so that there is less need to use sickness as an excuse for absenteeism.

Disability and industrial injury

The scheme of benefits for those injured at work is quite separate from other parts of the social security system, and from the tort system, where employees suffering personal injury may take legal action against negligent employers. Where the main scheme offers equivalent benefits, the industrial injuries benefits are higher and they also contain a compensatory element, there being no contribution conditions and the largest benefits going to those who suffer the most. This reflects what has been termed an 'industrial preference', whereby those injured at work are judged more deserving than other social security beneficiaries. The principal benefits are *injury benefit* and *industrial disablement benefit*.

Injury benefit is the equivalent of sickness benefit in the main social security scheme; only those who are prevented from working qualify. The standard rate in 1982-3 is £27.75 (with a reduced rate for a claimant aged under 18), £2.75 more than sickness benefit, although the additions for dependants are identical. Unlike sickness benefit, the benefit period includes periods of temporary recovery. Injury benefit is tax-free and is paid for 26 weeks, after which a claimant who satisfies the contribution conditions can switch to sickness benefit and then to invalidity benefit. However, *industrial disablement benefit* may be payable. This is compensation for any lasting, although not necessarily permanent, disabilities, even if the claimant is still capable of working. When disability is only slight, compensation takes the form of a lump-sum gratuity. A pension is paid to the more severely disabled. Disability is elaborately differentiated – loss of the top joint of the little finger is 5 per cent disability, loss of a big toe is 14 per cent disability, loss of a hand is 60 per cent disability, and loss of one leg and the other foot is 100 per cent disability. A disablement pension of £53.60 is paid for a 100 per cent disability; with a lesser disability there is a pro rata reduction. *Disablement gratuity* is paid if the degree of disablement is less than 20 per cent, and it too depends upon the precise degree of disablement. Recipients of industrial disablement benefit may be entitled to one or more of the following weekly allowances: unemployability supplement; special hardship allowance; constant attendance allowance; exceptionally severe disablement allowance; and hospital treatment allowance. Constant attendance allowance is only for those with a 100 per cent disablement, and the maximum payment is £43 in 1982-3; if disablement is likely to be permanent, an exceptionally severe disablement allowance of £21.50 will also be paid.

With effect from June 1983, injury benefit is also abolished and the injured will initially be entitled to statutory sick pay, after which they will move on to sickness benefit, the contribution condition being waived, and then invalidity benefit. Invalidity benefit will be paid in addition to the other benefits received from the industrial injuries scheme.

The benefits to the disabled who do not qualify for industrial injury benefits are far more limited and modest. *Attendance allowance* is paid to the severely mentally or physically disabled who require regular nursing care. It is paid at a lower rate, in 1982–3, of £17.50 if care is needed only either at night or during the day and at a higher rate of £26.25 if care is needed around the clock. *Invalid care allowance* is a benefit for those who care for the disabled and cannot work in consequence. There are increases for dependants. *Mobility allowance* is paid to those disabled who cannot, or virtually cannot, walk. It is £18.30. Both invalid care allowance and mobility allowance are taxable.

Industrial preference

The impact of the industrial preference is most clearly demonstrated by looking at a simple example. Take the case of a single man aged below 40 and with a 100 per cent disablement. Table 5.8 shows how

TABLE 5.8

The Impact of Industrial Preference: 1982–3
(£ a week)

Injured in a non-industrial accident	
Attendance allowance	26.25
Mobility allowance	18.30
Invalidity pension	31.45
Invalidity allowance	6.90
Total state income	82.90
Injured in an industrial accident	
100 per cent disablement benefit	53.60
Constant attendance allowance	43.00
Exceptionally severe disablement allowance	21.50
Mobility allowance	18.30
Invalidity pension	31.45
Invalidity allowance	6.90
Total state income	174.75

Difference in state income = £91.85.

state income is made up in the event of disablement resulting from both non-industrial and industrial accidents. The benefits received by the man injured at work are over twice those received by the one whose disablement has another cause. And this is not the most stark of the examples which could have been constructed.

Beveridge supported the industrial preference; it was essential compensation for taking the risk of working in dangerous industries. The Industrial Injuries Advisory Council recently reaffirmed this view. There were also some other less important defences. And a recent inquiry into the system of compensation for personal injury, the Pearson Commission (1978), recommended that the industrial preference be strengthened, industrial injury benefits being enhanced to provide a much higher degree of earnings replacement than achieved at the time. The arguments against the industrial preference are numerous. The most persuasive is that providing compensation for the cause of a disability rather than the disability itself is inequitable and administratively wasteful. The recent government White Paper on the subject (DHSS, 1981), published in the International Year of Disabled People, contains indications that there is some official sympathy with this view. However, only minor tinkers with the existing scheme are proposed, with the promise of a more detailed review, and an examination of the feasibility of a comprehensive disability income scheme, when sufficient resources are released.

A comprehensive disability income scheme

The Disability Alliance are the principal proponents of a comprehensive scheme of assistance for the disabled, irrespective of the cause of disablement. Their scheme – alternative variants have been suggested by other disability organizations – has three components. A tax-free disablement allowance would be paid to any disabled person, the rate varying with the degree of disablement. The rates would reflect those prevailing in the industrial injuries scheme. This would be the compensatory element of the scheme, designed to reflect that the disabled are relatively disadvantaged by virtue of their disability, even if in all other respects they achieve the economic and social status of the able-bodied. Those unable to work full time would receive an additional invalidity pension, again non-contributory, which would be set at, or preferably above, the long-term Supplementary Benefit level. Part-time work should be permitted, and not discouraged through a punitive earnings test as at present. Lastly, there would be a series of special allowances, much along the lines of the existing supplements to industrial disablement benefit.

The comprehensive disability income scheme would cover some 2 million disabled people. According to Wilson (1981) such a scheme would have cost £1.6 billion in 1978-9, and in 1982-3 this would probably be around £2 billion. This is an expensive proposal — about two-thirds of the cost of child benefits — but the Disability Alliance do not underestimate how ambitious it is. They suggest that if limited funds are available then only one-tenth of this sum would be needed to implement the scheme for the most severely disabled, numbering some 80,000. This smaller sum, equal to the cost of extending the long-term Supplementary Benefit rate to all the unemployed who have been on Supplementary Benefit for a year, should not be difficult to secure, and would be a sensible and valuable first step towards a clearly much-needed rationalization of disability benefits.

6

RETIREMENT PENSIONS

THE development of social security pension provision in Britain has already been described. In 1948 the National Insurance scheme was introduced: this paid flat-rate benefits on retirement, financed by flat-rate contributions. Rising costs – due to enhanced real benefits, declining labour market participation of those over pension age, and adverse demographic changes – led firstly to increased flat-rate contributions, and when these reached levels which began to place an unacceptable burden on those with low incomes, the contribution base was gradually modified so that an increasing proportion of it was related to earnings; this process was completed in 1975 when all contributions became earnings-related. A very limited earnings-related element to pensions was introduced in 1961, mainly to disguise the purely revenue-raising intent of earnings-related contributions.

Despite these modifications, state pensions appeared to fail the retired in two ways. First, their interaction with the Supplementary Benefit scheme not only created a high incidence of poverty among the retired but also acted as a deterrent to developments which might relieve it. We have seen that a large number of studies in the 1960s and 1970s revealed the retired to be the largest distinctive group among those living in poverty, and that being over retirement age confers a high probability of being poor. In this work, and more generally, the poverty line has been based on the Supplementary Benefit rate, and the flat-rate retirement pension has never deviated greatly from this. However, the Supplementary Benefit rate can be augmented by a rent and rates payment, so that any pensioner relying solely on a National Insurance pension would normally be entitled to Supplementary Benefit, referred to as supplementary pension. But while the National Insurance pension was earned by contributions, the supplementary pension was means-tested. The stigmatizing effect of the means test effectively prevented many pensioners from claiming the supplement.

Secondly, the coverage of occupational pension arrangements has increased rapidly since 1948. About one-half of the work-force are now members of an occupational pension scheme, coverage being somewhat better in the public sector than the private sector, in non-manual jobs than manual jobs, and among men than women. This rapid development has been stimulated by the existence of tax advantages for schemes which receive Inland Revenue approval. Such approval implies that employers' contributions are not a taxable benefit to their employees and indeed attract expense relief, that employees' contributions are tax-deductible, that the pension fund itself is tax-exempt, and that the pension resulting is taxed as earned income. These benefits are sufficiently substantial that schemes operating without approval are virtually unknown. The principal condition for approval is that pensions do not exceed two-thirds of final salary, and the majority of schemes pay full pensions of half to two-thirds (near) final salary.

Thus in the late 1960s and early 1970s there was a marked occupational division in pension provision: half the work-force, mainly public sector employees and non-manual males employed in the private sector, were well catered for by occupational pension arrangements, while the remainder had to be satisfied with the National Insurance scheme. There was therefore considerable pressure placed upon the state to establish a scheme which would enable those who were not members of occupational pension schemes to receive pensions comparable with those who were. At the same time, concern was being expressed about two aspects of occupational pension arrangements in Britain, aspects which remain a source of some antagonism. First, public sector occupational pension schemes operating on a pay-as-you-go basis have generous indexation provisions, while most funded schemes, including all those in the private sector, although they have increased pensions to take account of inflation, do not even offer a commitment to partial indexation. The principal reason given for the failure to index has been the absence of indexed investments with which to hedge indexed liabilities. But at the same time, indexation of either assets or liabilities was generally disapproved of — because indexation institutionalized inflation, and reduced the incentive to make it go away — which may in part explain why today, despite the widespread availability of index-linked government securities, indexed pensions are hardly any more common. Second, private occupational pension schemes have always treated people who change jobs in an unfavourable way. It used to be the common practice to refund a departing employee's contributions, often without interest; the preservation legislation contained in the 1975 Social Security Act provided some protection for those with more than five years' service after 1975, who can no longer be paid contributions refunds on the basis of that service. They must have a pension preserved in the scheme they are leaving, or an equivalent pension purchased in the scheme of their new employer. But because preserved pensions are typically based on completed service and the salary at the date of leaving, which is less than final salary, job changers forfeit pension rights. Like a contribution refund, this arrangement is clearly advantageous to the schemes, and in particular to those members who do not change jobs; equally clearly, it is inequitable, both between stayers and leavers, and between private and public sector employees. Furthermore, it was widely believed, and there is now evidence in support of this belief, that these arrangements impede labour mobility (see McCormick and Hughes, 1982). Hence there was a call for measures to reduce the gap between public sector and private sector occupational pension provision, by providing some indexation of earnings-related pensions and improving the arrangements for the transferability and preservation of pension rights.

With the passing of the 1975 Social Security Pensions Act, the structure of retirement pension provision in Britain was changed with effect from April 1978. The complex State Earnings Related Pension Scheme it introduced, has at its heart a partnership between the state and the occupational pension sector that is designed to overcome the failings of the previous arrangements.

The State Earnings Related Pension Scheme

Full members of the new state scheme will receive both a basic pension which is flat-rate, and an additional pension which is earnings-related. The basic pension paid to a single pensioner is in 1982-3 £32.85 per week. A male pensioner whose wife is not entitled to a pension in her own right receives an additional flat-rate pension of about 60 per cent of the single rate, giving a pension for a couple of £52.55 per week. Current practice requires that flat-rate pensions in payment are increased at least in line with prices. Men and women have equal pension status, except that pensions are paid to women aged 60 and over and men aged 65 and over.

To qualify for a basic pension a person must have been a member of the scheme for at least 90 per cent of their working life, including time spent in the previous National Insurance scheme. In general, membership is concomitant with the payment of National Insurance contributions. However, there are exceptions. The sick, the unemployed, and people remaining at home to look after children, the sick and the elderly are credited with National Insurance contributions (they do not actually have to pay them) sufficient to maintain full membership of the scheme.

Additional pension is based on qualifying earnings, which are earnings above the lower earnings limit but below the upper earnings limit. The current limits have been reported in Chapter 2. Qualifying earnings are calculated in the following way. Take somebody who enters the scheme on 1 January 1983 aged 16, and works until retirement 49 years later in 2032. Earnings actually received in each year are denoted $E_1, E_2, E_3, \ldots, E_{48}, E_{49}$. A record of these is kept. Over these 49 years, earnings in general increase, and an index of earnings $I_1, I_2, I_3, \ldots, I_{48}, I_{49}$ captures this. Revalued earnings are given by $E^*_1 = E_1 I_{49}/I_1$, $E^*_2 = E_2 I_{49}/I_2$, etc. Some of the figures so produced will exceed the upper earnings limit operating in January 2032, and these will be truncated at that level. The level of the basic pension in January 2032 is subtracted from the remaining figures to yield qualifying earnings. A full additional pension is equal to 25 per cent of the average of the best twenty years' qualifying earnings. This will be referred to as a SERPS pension. Pensions in payment are to be indexed directly to prices. Pension ages are the same as those for the basic pension, but the qualifying condition is far less stringent. Any full year of employment can be included in the best twenty, and thereby earn some SERPS pension, but the pension fraction is reduced by the new scheme's accrual rate on qualifying membership, 1.25 per cent (25 per cent ÷ 20), for each year of membership less than twenty. Clearly full SERPS entitlements, that is a pension based on twenty years' earnings, will not have been earned until 1998. For persons retiring in the interim a SERPS pension is therefore earned at a rate of 1.25 per cent of average qualifying earnings for each year of membership.

Not all employees are full members of the new scheme. As pointed out above, occupational pension coverage in Britain is fairly widespread. Occupational pension schemes can choose to contract-out of the new scheme. In doing so they relinquish their members' claims to a full SERPS pension. There are two principal conditions to be met if a scheme is to contract out. First, it must provide a guaranteed minimum pension (GMP), which is equivalent to the SERPS pension. However, this equivalence is only rough. The major reason for this is that it is not very satisfactory to apply the best twenty years rule in respect of employees who change jobs, since an employer would not know whether he, or some other employer, was liable in respect of a particular year of service until the employee retired. Hence the GMP is based on average lifetime qualifying earnings. An employer's obligation to index until retirement the GMPs of employees with more than five years' service, is limited to 8.5 per cent per annum, or 5 per cent on payment of a limited revaluation premium. There is also a facility for an employer to be completely relieved of any obligation to an employee with less than five years' service. Second, the occupational pension scheme must provide a pension based on either average revalued salary or final salary, and which accrues at a rate of at least 1.25 per cent for each year of qualifying service.

The state's commitment to contracted-out employees extends beyond the basic pension. The state also makes up the difference between employees' SERPS entitlement and GMP, and provides indexation payments sufficient to preserve the real value of their SERPS pension. Thus the difference between total state pension payments made to a person as a full member of the new scheme and as a contracted-out member is potentially much less than the SERPS pension.

The new scheme is operated on a pay-as-you-go basis, financed partly by National Insurance contributions levied on both employees and employers and partly by a transfer from general revenue. The 1982–3 contribution rates were reported in Chapter 2. A contracted-out scheme receives a contracting-out rebate of 7 per cent of qualifying earnings which is split between 2.5 per cent to employees and 4.5 per cent to employers. This rebate is to be progressively reduced to 3.75 per cent, reflecting the fact that GMPs accrue at well above the ultimate rate in the early years of the scheme.

It is perhaps worth pointing out that National Insurance contributions, which, offsetting the surcharge against the Exchequer contribution, amount to 20.95 per cent for full members of the new scheme, pay for more than retirement pensions. They finance a wide range of predominantly flat-rate National Insurance benefits, and include a 1.9 per cent contribution to the redundancy fund and the

National Health Service. However National Insurance contributions mainly pay for retirement pensions: the finance of retirement pensions being paid in the early 1980s would alone require a contribution rate of about 14.5 per cent of earnings below the upper earnings limit.

Under the previous National Insurance scheme, married women who paid the full National Insurance contribution received reduced pension, and could opt to pay a reduced National Insurance contribution and forgo their pension rights. As part of the move towards equal pension status for women, the married woman's option is to be phased out. However, the precise way in which this will be achieved, without adversely affecting the expectations of many married women currently in the labour force, remains a matter of some uncertainty.

Pensions for both widows and widowers are provided under SERPS. A woman inherits her husband's pension if she is over 50 when he dies, and a fraction of it if she is over 40. It does not matter whether the husband is working or retired at the time of his death. A man inherits his wife's pension if they are both over retirement age when she dies. Inherited pensions are received in addition to any pension paid to widows and widowers in their own right, except that there is an upper limit to total pension receipts with the maximum being that which any individual could have earned for himself or herself.

At the moment very little SERPS pension is paid, and so current National Insurance contributions do not reflect the additional costs in the future of the pension commitments implied by the new scheme. Nor did the government ever attempt to measure these costs. Yet the scheme is extremely generous, and the implied 'gradually increasing transfer of income and therefore of claims on resources from the economically active section of the community to those who have retired' (DHSS, 1974), is largely attributable to the new provisions. This raises two questions, which are closely related. Firstly, how much will the new scheme cost, and will the cost be within the capacity of the nation to support it? Secondly, does the scheme overcome the weaknesses of previous arrangements, and does it try to do so in the most effective way?

The cost of SERPS

The analysis contained in this and the next section draws heavily on Hemming and Kay (1982). In that paper we treated SERPS as a self-contained earnings-related pension scheme, financing pensions based on qualifying earnings by contributions levied on the same base. Because SERPS is a pay-as-you-go scheme its costs are determined by two factors, the number of workers relative to the number of pensioners and the provisions of the scheme.

Assume that the population has reached steady state, that is the number of births has been at replacement level indefinitely and mortality rates have remained constant at those experienced in the recent past. This would imply that there would be 3.22 people of working age per person of retirement age: 3.22 is the 'dependency ratio'. Of course, in the real world demographic changes ensure that this figure will sometimes be too high and at other times too low: the British population will never reach steady state, but the steady state calculation is a bench-mark providing an estimate of costs when demographic developments have been neither particularly beneficial nor particularly harmful. Assume that SERPS is fully mature, that is each member has spent all his or her working life in the scheme, and that it pays pensions based on an average lifetime's, and not the best twenty years', revalued earnings, with pensions in payment indexed in line with earnings. Then, if mortality can be taken to be independent of all individual characteristics (for example income and social class) except age and sex, and allowing for the fact that the average qualifying earnings of men exceed those of women, the mature scheme in steady state could be financed with a contribution rate of 6.3 per cent of qualifying earnings.

However, pensions are not determined by average lifetime qualifying earnings but by qualifying earnings in the best twenty working years. Because they are in education, are sick or unemployed, or are at home looking after dependents, many people of working age are not actually working: the 'support ratio' is less than the 'dependency ratio', in steady state it is 2.69. If the number of years of work does not fall below twenty, periods out of work do not affect SERPS entitlements but do reduce the contribution base. It is assumed that all men and women will complete twenty years in the work-force. In the case of women this may appear somewhat implausible. Yet recent research suggests that family responsibilities are unlikely to cause more than only a few women to work less than twenty years (see Joshi, 1982). At recently experienced participation rates, and assuming 5 per cent unemployment, the steady-state contribution rate rises to 9.8 per cent of qualifying earnings. It is almost certain that the average of the best twenty years' revalued earnings will exceed average lifetime revalued earnings, though the size of the difference is conjectural. Hemming and Kay (1982), using cross-section data, estimate it to be 18 per cent for men and 17 per cent for women, but confidently believe these to be underestimates; Creedy (1982), using simulated cohort data, gets a figure closer to 33 per cent but there are various reasons why this should be an overestimate, though not necessarily a large one. On the basis of the first estimates, the full effect of the best twenty years rule would be to raise the steady state contribution rate to 11.5 per cent of qualifying earnings.

SERPS provides pensions for widows and widowers. Widower's pensions have virtually no additional cost, but because a husband's pension is paid until the later of his or his wife's death, and women tend to be younger than their husbands and live longer, widows' pensions are quite costly. Indeed they add another 1.9 per cent to the cost of SERPS, bringing the total contribution rate to 13.4 per cent of qualifying earnings.

Given that retirement pensions currently require a contribution rate of 14.5 per cent, an additional 13.4 per cent to finance SERPS is quite alarming. However, for a number of reasons these two figures cannot be added together. Firstly, National Insurance contributions are levied not on qualifying earnings but on all earnings below the upper earnings limit: the contribution base is in fact some 27 per cent larger than the benefit base, and this implies that the steady state cost of SERPS, expressed as a National Insurance contribution, would be 10.6 per cent. Secondly, the support ratio is currently 2.76, slightly more favourable than in steady state: the steady state National Insurance contribution necessary to meet basic pensions would be 14.9 per cent. Thirdly, pensions indexation is more complex than we have described. There are two elements to this additional complexity. We assume that everything is indexed to earnings. The basic pension is in fact indexed to prices, and therefore so are the earnings limits, while the qualifying earnings which fall within these limits are indexed to earnings. Clearly the pension base increases faster than the earnings index if the earnings index outstrips the price index, which is indeed the most likely occurrence. This mismatch of indices clearly implies that we *underestimate* the costs of SERPS. But pensions in payment are only linked to prices, in which case we *overestimate* the costs of SERPS. This alone would suggest that our estimated contribution rate of 10.6 per cent should be nearer 8.0 per cent. However, allowing for the offsetting underestimate the reduction would probably be less than

1 per cent. We are going to ignore this: the indexation arrangements have no apparent rationale, and the 1982–3 situation is the result of a change from earnings to price indexation in 1980 motivated purely by the desire to achieve an immediate reduction in social security expenditure. It is difficult to believe that the indexation formula will not be changed again, and therefore assuming a single index, which we have specified as an earnings index but could equally well be a price index or any other 'inflation' index without affecting our conclusions, seems the sensible course.

In steady state, pension provision will require a contribution rate of 25.5 per cent of earnings below the upper earnings limit, 14.9 per cent to pay for basic pensions, which are fixed relative to earnings, and 10.6 per cent to pay for SERPS. But we have said that steady state will never be achieved, and alternative demographic structures, some less and some more favourable, would imply contribution rates spread around the steady state level. Indeed over the next fifty years the support ratio will at times be above and below 2.69: the large post-war birth cohort is currently in the labour force and the support ratio is high, but by 2030 the cohort will be retired and with no equally spectacular increase in the number of births in the next twenty or thirty years the support ratio can be expected to fall substantially. Also over the next fifty years SERPS will steadily approach maturity. Demographic development and this maturing process together determine the future evolution of pension costs.

Projections of the support ratio require that an assumption is made about the fertility rate – the number of children to be born to each woman – and we will assume that this remains at 2.1: the support ratio will therefore change as shown in Figure 6.1. (A fertility rate of 2.1 is little above that of 1.8 recently experienced in Britain.) But the fertility rate rose during the late 1970s and official population projections of the Office of Population Censuses and Surveys (see OPCS, 1980) tend to assume that it will level out at 2.1, which is replacement level. The picture which emerges is one where the support ratio will gradually improve, reaching a maximum of 3.08 in 2006, but it then falls and is only 2.40 in 2033. If the fertility rate were to remain at 1.8 the support ratio would be 2.04 in 2033. These projections allow for some moderate mortality improvement: support ratios tend to be relatively insensitive to those changes in mortality which one can regard as reasonably likely. However, if death from cancer were eliminated then the impact of mortality change would easily dominate that of even wildly optimistic changes in fertility.

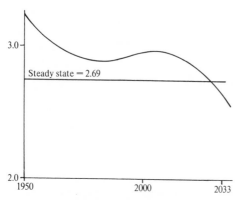

FIG. 6.1. The Support Ratio: 1951–2033 and in Steady State

Source: Ermisch (1981).

Any prediction of the buildup of SERPS entitlements is speculative, and the combined effect on pension costs of our speculation and the population projections is shown in Table 6.1. The pattern is fairly clear. For the rest of this century the growth in pensions costs is low: favourable demographic trends reduce the cost of providing basic pensions and this is sufficient to compensate for the additional costs of low SERPS entitlements. But when early next century demographic trends become unfavourable, basic pensions begin to cost more, and the emerging cost of SERPS cannot be obscured as before. Yet even Table 6.1 does not tell the whole story, since it ignores the cost of contracting-out.

Contracting-Out

Contracting-out does not affect an employee's level of pension: it simply implies that part of his state pension entitlement, the GMP, will be paid by his occupational pension scheme. In return for relieving the state of part of its pension obligations a rebate of National Insurance contributions is paid. Through allowing contracting-out the state can be viewed as attempting to fund part of its pension

TABLE 6.1

The Changing Costs of State Pensions
(expressed as percentage of contribution base)

	1991	2001	2011	2023	2033	Steady state
Support ratio	2.87	3.03	2.99	2.66	2.40	2.69
Cost of basic pension	13.9	13.2	13.4	15.0	16.7	14.9
Percentage of final SERPS liability reached	20	45	65	80	90	100
Cost of SERPS	2.0	4.2	6.2	8.5	10.6	10.6
Cost of state pensions	15.9	17.4	19.6	23.5	27.3	25.5

Source: own calculations based on Hemming and Kay (1982).

commitments by investing in occupational pension schemes: the state forgoes contribution income now, by paying rebates, and the occupational pension schemes will meet part of its pension bill. Conversely, occupational pension schemes are simply borrowing from the state, and investing contribution rebates along with their other income. Contracting-out is therefore more than a simple transfer between the state and occupational pension schemes. It is a gamble. Either party can be better off: the state is better off if it can meet its pension commitments with lower National Insurance contributions, because rebates are below the contribution rate required to finance GMPs on a pay-as-you-go basis; while the occupational pension schemes are better off if contribution rebates are greater than the sums necessary to finance GMPs through funding.

Remember that the GMPs of employees must be increased in line with average earnings, and that there is no indexation of GMPs after retirement. The cost of funding a GMP therefore depends upon both the rate of investment returns and the rate of earnings growth, and the difference between them, the real rate of return. Table 6.2 presents estimates of the cost of funding a GMP at various levels of real rate of return and rate of earnings growth. Low real rates of return increase the cost of providing a GMP — because investment is less profitable relative to the scheme's indexation commitment — and high rates of earnings growth reduce the cost — because the value of GMPs in payment is eroded. If all the combinations of real rates of return and rates of earnings growth are reasonably possible, the range of costs lies between 1.3 per cent and 9.2 per cent of qualifying earnings. However, it seems

TABLE 6.2

The Cost of Funding a GMP
(as a percentage of qualifying earnings)

Real rate of return (relative to earnings, percentage)	Rate of earnings growth (percentage)				
	4	8	12	16	20
+ 2	2.6	2.1	1.7	1.5	1.3
+ 1	3.5	2.8	2.2	1.9	1.6
0	5.0	3.7	3.0	2.5	2.2
− 1	6.7	4.9	3.9	3.3	2.7
− 2	9.2	6.6	5.0	4.0	3.4

Source: Hemming and Kay (1981).

likely that the higher the rate of earnings growth the lower will be the real rate of return. The most likely range of costs is 2.6 per cent to 3.4 per cent, and our best point estimate would be 3.0 per cent.

This figure has to be compared with the contribution rebate, but not the 1982–3 rebate of 7 per cent. In the first years of the new scheme GMPs are being earned at nearly twice their ultimate rate, because those whose working careers began before 1978 can obtain full pensions in what remains of their working lifetime so long as they work for twenty years. Occupational pension schemes will initially be providing GMPs on more generous terms than when the scheme matures. The contribution rebate has therefore to be higher than in the long run to reflect this, and it will progressively fall to 3.75 per cent at a rate of about 0.5 per cent every five years. But even the rebate of 3.75 per cent does not reflect the money available to provide GMPs. National Insurance contributions are not tax deductible but occupational pension contributions are. If the 3.75 per cent rebate is split between employees and employers as at present, the final rebate is nearer 4.75 per cent.

Comparing this figure with those in Table 6.2 it is clear that the rebate is generous, although not as generous as occupational pension schemes, faced by lower real rates of return but higher rates of earnings growth than they probably expected, had anticipated. Providing GMPs could only cost more than 4.75 per cent if real rates of return were negative and rates of earnings growth low, which is not very likely. At 12 per cent earnings growth, the state is in fact making a real rate of return of a little more than −2 per cent on its contracting-out investment.

Contracting-out costs the state money, but exactly how much it costs depends not only on the real rate of return on its investment but also on the size of that investment. Only a half of all employees are contracted-out, which is nearly all occupational pension scheme members, but the contracted-out tend to have higher earnings. The contracted-out still receive considerable earnings-related pensions from the state: it makes up the difference between the average of the best twenty years' qualifying earnings and average lifetime qualifying earnings, provides indexation after retirement, and pays a substantial part of the generous pensions for widows. It seems unlikely that many more than a quarter of SERPS entitlements of contracted-out employees will be met from GMPs, and these constitute about an eighth of total SERPS entitlements. In steady state the contribution rate under funding is 50 per cent higher at a real rate of return of -2 per cent than the contribution rate required under pay-as-you-go (see Hemming and Kay, 1984, for further details). This implies that in steady state the contribution rate would be some 2/3 per cent $(0.125 \times 10.6 \times 0.5 = 0.66)$ higher at a real rate of return of -2 per cent to reflect the cost of contracting out. The impact of contracting-out is adverse but small, and given the range of error attached to this cost estimate it is probably best not to include it explicitly in the estimate of the long-run cost of SERPS and instead just keep in mind the qualitative result.

The implication of this conclusion is that in the long run contribution rebates will be only slightly in excess of the GMPs being paid by the occupational pension schemes. But at the outset of the scheme no GMPs had been earned, and there was therefore nothing to offset the contribution rebates. At that time National Insurance contributions had to be increased by 3.5 per cent, and this reflected the cost of the rebates. As GMPs become payable, and the rebate falls, so the cost of contracting-out will decline. The impact of contracting-out on total pension costs is shown in Table 6.3.

The new state pension scheme will ultimately cost around twice as much as the scheme which preceded it. In 1978 the level of personal taxation in Britain was a third of the way down the Organization for Economic Co-operation and Development league table (see OECD, 1980, Table 30), with income tax and employee's National Insurance contributions taking about 25 per cent of the average industrial earnings of a typical family. If everything else remained unaffected the doubling of the cost of state pensions would raise this figure to about

RETIREMENT PENSIONS

135

30 per cent, moving Britain up the table somewhat, but still leaving her behind the Scandinavian countries and the Netherlands. However, the pressures of demographic changes will be experienced by all these OECD countries, in some cases to a much greater degree than in Britain, and most will face higher social security 'taxes' than at present (see Rosa, 1982). An international perspective would appear to suggest that state pensions in general, and SERPS in particular, are unlikely to impose an unsustainable burden on the working population. But it may none the less be one that is widely regarded as being too high; and even if acceptable, it need not be the case that the current pension arrangements are the most desirable. The fact that it took more than a quarter of a century to reform the system of state pensions, and that the new scheme has bipartisan or even tripartisan political support, does not imply the absence of a case for either reviewing the provisions of the scheme or abandoning it altogether, before it has any marked influence on pension expectations.

TABLE 6.3

The Changing Costs of State Pensions with Contracting-Out
(expressed as a percentage of contribution base)

	1991	2001	2011	2023	2033	Steady state
Cost of SERPS	4.5	5.7	6.7	8.5	10.1	10.6
Cost of state pensions	19.4	18.9	20.1	23.5	26.8	25.5

Source: Own calculations based on Hemming and Kay (1982).

Pension reform

The central principle governing state pension provisions in Britain as presently organized is that it should be the state's responsibility to guarantee a minimum pension and that the state and private sector should in partnership provide earnings-related pensions. If this principle is acceptable, there still remains much in the detail of the current arrangements which is unsatisfactory, and which contributes substantially to their significant cost.

Although it is commonly agreed that the differential pension age for men and women is anomalous, it was introduced as an attempted solution to genuine problems. Married women tend to be younger than their husbands and could not claim a pension even though their husbands had reached retirement age, and single women would often stay at home caring for sick or elderly parents and forsake marriage or a working career but received little financial support. Yet clearly an earlier pension age could not provide a solution to these problems, and it ultimately had to be defended in terms of the labour market discrimination against women (see DHSS, 1974).

Equalization of pension ages is widely called for: some have suggested that this should be at 60, but this would be expensive; others have recommended 65, but this is felt to be unfair to those women who have made irreversible decisions on the basis of retirement at 60. The solution to this problem is likely to take the form of flexible pension ages and compensatory pension adjustments for both men and women. Such a scheme has recently been proposed by the House of Commons Social Services Committee (1982). No matter how long change takes, and ten to fifteen years is suggested for the Social Services Committee scheme to be phased in, what is clear is that there is no obvious reason why a newly-introduced scheme should persist with the differential retirement age.

The inheritability provisions of the new scheme are designed to make sure that women with poor earnings records can receive reasonable pensions as widows. But to grant widows pensions based on both their own and their husbands' earnings records does far more than this, and the justification for letting a widow be treated both as a dependent of her husband and an individual, is extremely elusive, if indeed one exists.

The best twenty years rule is the major source of unpredictability in the whole scheme: 'How large will SERPS pensions be?' and 'Who will get the largest SERPS pensions?' While the size of pensions may be difficult to guess, it is very clear which group benefits most from the scheme. Their longevity (to which we do not object, nor which do we wish to penalize), the differential pension age, the inheritability provisions, and the best twenty years rule, together imply that women get four times as much benefit per pound of contribution as men. While it is clear that women have been at a great disadvantage in previous state pension schemes, sensible reform clearly does not involve reversing the balance of sexual advantage. If pension age were equalized at 65, widows received pensions based on their own or their husbands' earnings records, whichever is most favourable, and SERPS pensions were related to average revalued lifetime earnings, as with GMPs, women could not complain about unfair treatment, and the details of the scheme would be more sensible. Furthermore, for the cost conscious, these seemingly peripheral changes would reduce the long-run costs of SERPS by half (see Hemming and Kay, 1982).

At the beginning of this chapter we suggested that the new scheme was a response to a number of problems: poverty among retirement pensioners, the incomplete coverage of occupational pension schemes, and certain inadequacies of occupational pension schemes in the private sector. How far does the new scheme go towards overcoming these problems? Unfortunately the answer is not very far. It will certainly perpetuate poverty; SERPS offers little or nothing to those with low earnings, who have only the basic pension to rely on. This is the same basic pension which leaves so many pensioners below the poverty line today. Poverty is relieved by raising basic pensions to a level which guarantees an adequate standard of living for all pensioners, and not through elaborate earnings-related schemes. Indeed, it is interesting to note that if the basic pension were raised to 30 per cent of average male gross earnings, an increase of one-third, this could be achieved at half the long-run cost of SERPS. In other words, such a change could be financed by the removal of those unjustifiable provisions of the scheme which were just outlined.

Certainly earnings-related pensions are available to those disenfranchised by the occupational sector, although SERPS pensions, while ambitious by the standards of state provision, are modest relative to occupational pensions which can be received. And clearly the indexation provisions of SERPS and the contracting-out conditions guarantee a moderate degree of protection against adversities for which some occupational schemes have failed to provide. But equally the new scheme may lead to many people being over-provided with pensions — they are forced to save far more than they want to — and it has protected the occupational schemes from realities they probably do not wish to admit the existence of, and almost definitely do not want to face up to.

Thus this may well be the time to ask fundamental questions about pension provision in Britain. We have said that effective poverty relief can be achieved by a shift of resources from earnings-related to basic pensions. But the case for the state provision of any earnings-related pensions at all rests on uneasy foundations, and it is not clear that the objectives the state wishes to achieve cannot be met in other ways. We believe there to be preferable alternatives.

The British tax system strongly favours the compulsory collective provision for retirement, and the growth of occupational pension schemes is a response to this incentive. At the same time, the development of private markets in indexed securities, which would be an attractive form of saving for individuals planning for retirement, has not transpired, and nominal rather than real investment income has attracted high rates of tax. In a reformed pension system the bias towards collective action could be removed. Furthermore, the private sector could be given an enlarged role, as the sole provider of earnings-related pensions. Existing occupational schemes would probably be the major part of the private sector, offering the final-salary based pensions they do at the moment, but with their most obvious weaknesses removed. Scheme membership should be voluntary, and instead of offering potentially large pensions and then, through the maltreatment of job leavers and the failure to index preserved pensions and pensions in payment, relieving themselves of the obligation to pay them, schemes must be required to make a pension promise which has a much higher probability of being fulfilled. This requires a significant degree of indexation, and indexed securities simplify the task of meeting indexed obligations, although this may have to be paid for by pension levels starting lower.

Occupational pension schemes can be augmented by a flourishing market in individual or small group plans which are tailored to the requirements of each particular case. Membership of these schemes should attract all the tax advantages of the existing occupational schemes. Thus the trend towards the substitution of collective provision and social security for private saving will be reversed; the government has already gone some way towards this, through the introduction of a limited quantity of indexed securities and the substitution of a tax on real capital gains for one on nominal capital gains. But in our opinion this freeing of the capital market is only part of desirable reform of the pension system. The private sector must improve its product: if it does, it can be assured of continued operation with a degree of state intervention no greater than that currently exercised in other areas of contract law. The state is then free to concentrate on the role only it can play, that of providing adequate basic pensions. If it becomes necessary for the state to have to involve itself deeply in the operation of the private sector, by monitoring its behaviour and intervening where pension rights are threatened, then there would appear to be little alternative to the state taking over the responsibility for earnings-related pension provision. The state can readily supply much of what the private sector is apparently unwilling to provide. But in the first instance the onus should be placed upon the private sector to adjust to new and quite reasonable demands made of it.

A reformed pension system, operating along the lines we suggest, would almost certainly involve a shift from pay-as-you-go towards funding. Contrary to popular belief this will only reduce the burden of pension provision if smaller pensions are promised; the way in which they are financed is of no consequence. But funding does have an obvious advantage, and the discussion earlier in this chapter emphasizes this advantage's importance. Funding forces those who make pension promises to contemplate the financial provisions which ought to be made to meet them at the time the promise is made. Our assessment of SERPS reveals little evidence of a careful assessment of pension requirements against future costs, but instead a ready willingness to buy off interested pressure groups – women, occupational pension schemes – with vague promises of future public expenditure. A move to further funding may also affect the levels of saving and investment.

Saving and investment

If a fully-funded social security pension scheme, earning the market rate of interest, were introduced, then in principle it would be a perfect substitute for other forms of retirement saving. Therefore introducing a funded social security pension system would leave aggregate saving and investment unaffected. If individual perceptions were sufficiently sophisticated, the introduction of an unfunded scheme would have the same impact: anticipating the social security pension, people would save less in other forms. Current contributions would be lower than under funding, but future contributions would inevitably have to rise. Individuals, perceiving that their current net income is being enhanced at the expense of their own and their children's future net income, would increase their saving by an offsetting amount. In practice, however, it is hard to take this ultra-rational model seriously. It seems reasonable to conclude, therefore, that in the absence of any offsetting influences the substitution of pay-as-you-go for funding depresses the levels of saving and investment.

However, there is a potential offset. In the absence of a social security pension scheme some individuals might have worked until they were physically incapable of continuing. Compulsory membership of a pension scheme on the other hand may induce many people to plan an earlier and longer retirement, and to increase their saving. In the standard life-cycle model of saving behaviour, in which individuals plan to leave the world having consumed their lifetime resources, the conflicting influences of saving replacement and induced retirement lead to the conclusion that the saving response to membership of an unfunded pension scheme is theoretically indeterminate. However, induced retirement should not depend upon whether pensions are funded, and our confident expectation must be that funding will be associated with higher levels of saving and investment.

There is a celebrated, and hotly disputed, result for the US which suggests that social security pensions considerably depress private saving (see Feldstein, 1974). But critics have argued that the time-series data on which this result is based include a period when coverage was expanding rapidly; that contributors failed to take account of inevitable cost increases; that the impact of social security cannot be separated from other influences on saving; that allowing for inter-generational transfers completely mitigates the result; and that the result is explained wholly by computing error. Little purpose would be served by attempting to resolve the debate here; the best assessment of the evidence is to be found in Danziger, Haveman, and Plotnick (1981). On the other hand, it is true that post-war UK data reveal no evidence that social security pensions have depressed saving (the latest and most sophisticated study is Browning, 1982). However, the UK data refer to a period when social security pension coverage was fairly stable, and only a flat-rate pension below the official poverty line was provided. The earnings-related scheme which will be maturing over the next fifty years may well have a more significant impact on saving and investment.

A fully-funded occupational pension scheme, again earning the market rate of interest, should in theory substitute for private retire-ment saving. Yet there is evidence that this is not the case; Green (1981) actually concludes that occupational pension scheme member-ship increases private saving. Hemming and Harvey (1983) tend to agree that members of occupational pension schemes save more. However, they argue that this should not be attributed to scheme membership *per se*, but to individual characteristics which lead high savers to seek out jobs with pensions. Since these characteristics are unobservable, this issue is difficult to resolve. But given the shared opinion that funding does not reduce private saving, any reform which involves substituting funding for pay-as-you-go can be expected to increase national saving and the level of investment.

The earnings rule and labour force participation

In the absence of social security retirement pensions, people would obviously plan to retire at different ages. The knowledge that a pension is available may induce many to retire at the official retirement age; for those not similarly tempted, work can be made to appear relatively unattractive. For the five years immediately following a male pensioner's sixty-fifth and a female pensioner's sixtieth birthday, pensions are subject to an earnings rule. Pensions are not affected by earnings up to £57 a week, but for every additional £1 earned between £57 and £61, the pension is reduced by 50p, and thereafter £1 in the pension is forfeited for each additional £1 earned. This is a clear disincentive to full participation in the labour force after the official retirement age. But the disincentive to work part time is less, and this is a popular option among younger pensioners, especially those without an occupational pension.

US studies have shown that participation decisions are affected by the availability of social security pensions and the operation of an earnings rule. It has been suggested that there are significant disincentive effects (see Clark and Spengler, 1980, for a review and critique of the evidence). A pre-SERPS study in Britain shows that both men's and women's participation decisions have responded to social security pensions and the earnings rule much as economic theory would predict (see Zabalza et al., 1979, and Zabalza et al., 1980). In general, the impact of the pensions is far greater than that of the earnings rule, and women are more responsive to financial incentives than men. We can expect SERPS to reduce participation in the workforce in the future because pensions will be significantly more generous once the new scheme has matured. This greater generosity is particularly evident for women. And as pension costs rise, it is possible that the earnings rule will be made more severe; the current government are pledged to phasing it out, although there has been little indication of any movement in this direction.

7

HOUSING BENEFITS

HOUSING is the largest item of household expenditure, 15 per cent on average in 1980 (Family Expenditure Survey, 1980), and for low income families it completely swamps all other expenditures. Instances where housing expenditure accounts for over 30 per cent of the family budget are not unusual. It is therefore important that the social security system makes some provision for helping low income families with their housing costs. Were the housing market fairly competitive then housing of a similar quality would cost much the same and social security benefits could include an allowance for housing reaching a minimal standard. If housing of this minimal standard was in demand the market would provide it; the additional cost of a better quality of housing would have to be met by those who wanted it. This is how Beveridge approached the problem of housing costs. But he realized that given the conditions of the housing market in the 1940s – in particular a chronic housing shortage accompanied by policies to prevent its unscrupulous exploitation – such a provision would be inadequate.

Housing costs in no way reflected the quality of the accommodation being paid for, and much hardship would inevitably result. However, the post-war reconstruction offered the prospect of a more sensible housing market in which high housing costs would be the outcome of a free choice. It was a prospect to which Beveridge attached some uncertainty, and he was aware that his design might have to be modified to reflect individual housing costs. This uncertainty was warranted; if anything the British housing market is in the 1980s in a bigger mess than forty years ago or at any time since. And the system of providing help with housing costs through social security has become far more complex than Beveridge could ever have envisaged.

The British housing market

The principal characteristic of the British housing market is the extent of government involvement. In addition to housing payments made through the social security system, amounting to about £1.6 billion in 1980-1, the government provides what might be termed general financial assistance. This takes the form of subsidies to local authorities, who are responsible for the provision of nearly all public housing, contributions from the rate fund, by means of which local authorities can subsidize public housing from rate receipts, a subsidized 'option' mortgage scheme, and the provision of tax relief on mortgage interest payments made by owner-occupiers, up to a maximum. This assistance cost a little more than £4 billion in 1980-1; over half went to owner-occupiers. Then there is indirect financial assistance, most obviously to private tenants who benefit from various forms of rent control and legislation governing security of tenure. But local authority tenants benefit from a rent pooling arrangement whereby rents are determined mainly by historic cost – the original cost of providing each house – averaged across that authority's housing stock. In both the private and public rented sector, gross rents, after allowing for all direct and indirect financial assistance, are held well below the economic cost of providing housing.

General and indirect financial assistance from the government is widely blamed for the most obvious shortcomings of the housing market. There are two. The first is the virtual absence of a private rented sector. Less than 15 per cent of the housing stock is neither public housing nor owner-occupied: this is vastly out of line with every other advanced western nation, and with Britain itself in the first quarter of this century, when over 90 per cent of the housing stock was privately rented. What has caused the demise of the private landlord? Certainly rent control, which has operated since 1915, when it was introduced as a temporary measure to prevent landlords from exploiting wartime shortages, has played a significant part. As new homes were slowly built, control was relaxed but only slightly. By the mid-1950s 'peanut' rents were still being paid, and many landlords had given up. Further decontrol followed; but this could not reverse the trend. Decontrolled homes were normally sold. The 1965 Rent Act introduced the 'fair rent', the aim being to set rent at a level to preserve the supply and standard of privately rented houses. This has been a qualified success; but it clearly came too late, and subsequently little has been done to repair the damage done by fifty years of ill-considered rent control.

Another reason for the decline of the private rented sector is the tax advantages which accrue to those who are not only the owner of a house, but also its occupier. A person in business as a landlord is in the same tax position as any other businessman: he obtains tax relief on interest payments but pays tax on the income from his investment, rent, and capital gains, when he sells a house for more than he paid for it. Owner-occupiers also get tax relief on mortgage interest payments, but they pay tax on neither imputed income – the rent they would otherwise have to pay – nor the capital gain when they sell their principal residence. Up until 1963 tax was paid on imputed income, but it was discontinued when the method of charging the tax – in relation to outdated rateable values – became unworkable.

Governments of all persuasions have felt it proper to encourage home ownership. It is regarded as the most satisfying form of tenure, and the one to which all aspire, and the Conservative government's 'right to buy' policy for sitting tenants of local authority houses is the clearest affirmation of this view. But the consequential decline of the private rented sector is damaging. Local authority housing and owner-occupation are the only realistic alternatives facing most people, yet there are important functions these two sectors fail to perform. The role of the private rented sector has been clearly expressed by Cullingworth: 'It caters particularly for the young, the student, the single and the mobile; it provides a stepping-stone to owner-occupancy or the public sector; and it provides the most easy "access" for newcomers to an area and those who require immediate accommodation. For those who are not able to afford to buy or who are unable to afford a mortgage, and those who are not "eligible" for council housing little alternative exists' (Cullingworth, 1979, p. 37). In effect, the decline of the private rented sector has removed much essential flexibility from the housing market.

The second major problem with the housing market relates to price variation. It is well known that there are wide differences in housing quality both within and between sectors. This is understandable and necessary, although the very low quality of some housing – in disrepair and lacking basic amenities – is certainly not desirable. However, there is also substantial variation in the price paid for housing of similar quality. Within each local authority, rents reflect the diversity (in terms of type of housing) and age distribution of that authority's housing stock; within the small private rented sector they reflect variations in discretionary 'fair rent' assessments.

For the owner-occupied sector the issue is more complex. It is first
necessary to define the price of housing. This is unambiguous, but not
generally appreciated. The first element in the price of housing is the
income forgone by having housing equity (the market value of a house,
V, less mortgage debt M) tied up in a home rather than investing that
money in some other asset which would yield an after-tax rate of
return $(1-t)r$, where t is the personal tax rate. The second element is
the interest paid on the mortgage, which being tax deductible is
$(1-t)iM$. History suggests that the market value of houses rises over
time, and this is a gain. If market values increase at the inflation rate
Π, this gain is given by ΠV, a third element which can be offset against
the first two. We ignore maintenance costs. Then the price of owner-
occupied housing (P) is given by

$$P = (1-t)r(V-M) + (1-t)iM - \Pi V \qquad (7.1)$$

which can also be written

$$P = (1-t)rV + (1-t)(i-r)M - \Pi V. \qquad (7.1a)$$

The price of housing, given the market value, depends upon
individual tax rates, interest rates, and mortgage debt. All other things
being equal, it is clear from (7.1) that the price is lowest for those who
by virtue of the fact that they earn most have the highest marginal tax
rates. From (7.1a), at a given tax rate the price is lowest for those with
the smallest mortgages if i exceeds r, while if r exceeds i the price is
lowest for those with the largest mortgages. The interest on borrowing
from a building society is generally less than the interest which can be
earned on fairly secure investments elsewhere, say in the bond market,
so that r typically exceeds i.

King (1980) has examined the price variation which results from the
different methods of pricing used in each sector. His data come from
the FES for 1973/4, and are for England and Wales only. The pattern
is clear. Excluding furnished rental housing, there is no extreme price
variation between sectors: the average price paid in the most expensive
sector — local authority housing — is less than 25 per cent greater than
that paid in the least expensive — unfurnished private rental. Furnished
rental housing is twice as expensive as local authority housing. Within
sectors there is marked variation, particularly in the private rental
sector. But this is less so in the local authority sector, and there appears

to be little price variation amongst owner-occupiers. However, overall, that is both across and within sectors, King's conclusion seems unavoidable: 'the single most important feature of the UK housing market is the sheer diversity of prices paid by different households' (King, 1980, p. 140).

As we stated in the introduction to this chapter, it is because of this price variation that a system of helping low income families with their housing costs has to be somewhat removed from the pristine simplicity of the scheme Beveridge, and many other people, might apply in an ideal world.

Assistance with housing costs prior to April 1983

We have seen in our earlier discussions that there are four types of transfer designed to help those with low incomes meet their housing costs. These are rent rebates for council tenants, rent allowances for private tenants, rate rebates for both tenants and owner-occupiers, and the housing payments made under the Supplementary Benefit scheme. In 1980-1 housing assistance was extended to 6½ million households at a cost of £1.6 billion. A breakdown of this expenditure is shown in Table 7.1. Since 1979, income-related assistance has become increasingly important as with real increases in local authority rents more families have been drawn into the rebate scheme. In earlier chapters the calculation of housing benefits has been described in detail; we will not repeat this. But it is worth providing just a brief reminder of the systems. Rebates and allowances can be received by

TABLE 7.1

Income-Related Assistance with Housing Costs: 1980–1
(£ million)

Rent rebates[a]	317
Rent allowances[a]	48
Rate rebates[b]	235
Supplementary Benefit housing payments[c]	1,040
Total	1,640

Sources: [a] The Government's Expenditure Plans 1982-3 to 1984-5, Cmnd. 8494.
[b] Supplied by the Department of the Environment.
[c] Supplied by the Department of Health and Social Security.

anyone not claiming Supplementary Benefit. A family whose gross weekly income is equal to their needs allowance, which depends on family composition (non-dependants are assumed to contribute towards housing costs), will receive 60 per cent of their rent and/or 60 per cent of their rates. If income is below the needs allowance, the rent rebate or allowance is increased by 25 per cent of the difference and the rate rebate by 8 per cent of the difference. If income is above the needs allowance, the rent rebate or allowance is reduced by 17 per cent of the difference and the rate rebate by 6 per cent of the difference. These are referred to as the 'tapers'. Recipients of Supplementary Benefit have their rent, rates, and, if they are owner-occupiers, the interest due on their mortgage (but not capital repayments) met in full if their income is below the Supplementary Benefit scale rates, or only in part if their income is above the scale rate but they receive Supplementary Benefit by virtue of their housing costs.

This system of support has developed in a piecemeal fashion: the Supplementary Benefit scheme has operated since 1948; rent rebates and allowances were first available in the 1930s, most local authorities developed their schemes in the 1950s and 1960s, and a national scheme was introduced in 1972; rate rebates were introduced in 1966. We have noted that the take-up of rebates and allowances is low, and that when they are received they contribute considerably both to the poverty trap faced by the families of low income workers, and the unemployment trap. But there is another, equally serious, problem. David Donnison, former chairman of the Supplementary Benefits Commission, has described some of the interests and work of the Commission thus:

Housing costs and subsidies, it soon became clear, lay at the heart of some of the most chaotic tangles in the supplementary benefit system. There must be something wrong with arrangements which seemed to cause more work and were the source of more mistakes than any other feature of the scheme. I began to understand why prominent members of the Government's Advisory Committee on Rent Rebates and Rent Allowances had privately pressed me to look into these questions. In an attempt to sort things out as best we could for our own customers the Commission had already asked social security staff to go through about one million files to check whether claimants were getting the right benefits. That laborious exercise eventually transferred 90,000 claimants from supplementary benefits, paid through the Department of Health and Social Security, to rate rebates and rent rebates or allowances paid by local housing authorities. But we believe there were another 270,000 people – about three times as many – drawing these housing rebates and allowances who would have been better off with Social Security benefits (Donnison, 1981, p. 4–5).

The 'better off' problem arises from the complexity and incomprehensibility of the system of housing benefits. It is best demonstrated with an example, shown in Table 7.2. We consider the case of a pensioner couple, since it is pensioners who make up the majority of those households which are estimated to be on the wrong benefit. A

TABLE 7.2

The 'Better Off' Problem: 1982-3
(Pensioner couple, £ a week)

State pension only : £15 rent	
Retirement pension	52.55
Rent rebate	11.11
Income	63.66
Income on Supplementary Benefit[a]	67.30
State pension and occupational pension of £12 : £15 rent	
Retirement pension	52.55
Occupational pension	12.00
Income tax[b]	– 0.36
Rent rebate	8.40
Income	72.59
Income on Supplementary Benefit	67.30
State pension and occupational pension of £5 : £15 rent	
Retirement pension	52.55
Occupational pension	5.00
Rent rebate	9.86
Income	67.41
Income on Supplementary Benefit	67.30
State pension and occupational pension of £5 : £16 rent	
Retirement pension	52.55
Occupational pension	5.00
Rent rebate	10.46
Income	68.01
Income on Supplementary Benefit	68.30

Notes: [a] Excluding any special additions.
[b] Taking account of the age allowance of £850.

pensioner couple receiving only the state retirement pension and a rent rebate in respect of their £15 rent would be better off on Supplementary Benefit. That many of the retired who receive a full pension fail to realize that they may still be entitled to Supplementary Benefit is not particularly surprising. Where a moderate occupational pension of say £12 a week is received, it is better to claim the rent rebate. And it remains so even if the occupational pension is small, say £5 a week. But the gain is marginal, only 11p. However, as rent goes up the rent rebate increases by 60p in the pound while the Supplementary Benefit housing payment would increase by a pound in the pound. Therefore if rent rose by £1 the balance of advantage would change, and this pensioner couple would be 29p better off on Supplementary Benefit than when receiving the rent rebate. In cases like this the decision as to which system is the 'best buy' is one which can only be taken with expert advice. This is especially true when the special heating, dietary, and other costs which can be provided for in Supplementary Benefit payments, and also passport benefits, are taken into account. More often than not it will be an uninspired guess.

The source of the better off problem is the fact that the system of housing benefits is in fact two quite separate systems which overlap. It is the overlap, where there exists a choice of which system to go with, that creates confusion. Any sensible reform would eliminate this. Reform would also be directed at other shortcomings. Most importantly, the rebate and allowance scheme is not applied uniformly across local authorities: for example, some check information about savings, non-dependants, and housing costs more carefully than others. The same claimant could be awarded a different rebate or allowance by two or more local authorities.

Donnison has for some time advocated a unified housing benefit scheme; 'a single income related housing benefit to replace the confusion and injustice of our present arrangements. Such a scheme would replace rent rebates, rent allowances, rate rebates, and the rent element of supplementary benefit; and would ideally extend to the owner-occupier' (Donnison, 1979, p. 2). The scheme Donnison had in mind would meet 100 per cent of housing costs for those on Supplementary Benefit and others in similar financial circumstances, but assistance is then reduced as income rises. The scheme would be operated by local authorities, with whom claimants apparently prefer to deal, but according to a set of rules applying nationally. At the same time as he was voicing these ideas, the government were working on an integrated housing benefit scheme. When the plans were announced in March 1981 in a consultation paper (D.o.E, 1981), they were widely criticized. Yet Donnison described them as, 'in a somewhat battered form the unified housing benefit which the Supplementary Benefits Commission have been seeking all these years' (Donnison, 1981, p. 11).

The new housing benefit scheme

The government consultation paper stated very clearly the objectives of reform. A new housing benefit scheme should be easier for claimants to understand, thereby improving the chances that benefits when due are received; it should treat equally those in the same financial circumstances; it should not impose large losses on current beneficiaries; it should be more streamlined in administration; and it should have no net cost. The 1982 Social Security and Housing Benefits Act introduced a new housing benefit scheme – there is no reference to it being unified – which began in part in November 1982, and operated fully from April 1983.

The new scheme is administered by the Department of Health and Social Security, almost totally through local authorities. A family previously receiving a rebate or allowance would notice only minor alterations to the scheme they face. Needs allowances will remain at their November 1982 levels, except that there is an additional allowance of 75p for pensioners. The tapers are different. For rent rebates and allowances, instead of being 25 per cent when income is below the need's allowance and 17 per cent when income is above the needs allowance, they become 25 per cent and 21 per cent respectively, except in the case of pensioners, for where they become 50 per cent and 21 per cent. Instead of 8 per cent and 6 per cent for rate rebates, the tapers for non-pensioners become 8 per cent and 7 per cent respectively, and for pensioners 20 per cent and 7 per cent. The impact of the change in the tapers is that those with income above their needs allowance will have to pay a larger proportion of their rent themselves and some will lose any rebate or allowance previously received. As a transitional arrangement these losses are to be limited to 75p. Additional help for those paying very high rates will continue on a discretionary basis.

Families previously receiving housing payments as part of the Supplementary Benefit scheme can be divided into two groups. Some receive Supplementary Benefit in excess of their housing costs. Since

November 1982, council tenants have had their rent and rates paid direct — they are credited with having paid their rent and rates — a practice which had previously been adopted by many local authorities when tenants had been in rent arrears. Other tenants receive 100 per cent rebates and allowances; owner-occupiers receive 100 per cent rate rebates but have to claim help with mortgage repayments directly from the Department of Health and Social Security. Supplementary Benefit will no longer be paid to those who only have part and not all of their housing costs met. They switch to rebates and allowances. About 200,000 families are 'floated-off' Supplementary Benefit. Some — about 75,000 households — will find themselves better off on rebates and allowances; others — mainly pensioners, despite the 50 per cent taper below the needs allowance — will be made worse off. They will be eligible for 'topping-up' payments of Supplementary Benefit.

The extension of 'rent direct' to all local authority tenants on Supplementary Benefit has attracted some criticism. It is said to remove flexibility in budgeting for those with low incomes who would previously have delayed paying their rent in order to meet large periodic bills, for example fuel bills. Although this difficulty is inherent in any practical unified scheme, it will clearly present considerable problems for some families. Already some low income families have been forced to cut fuel consumption to a level which endangers their health, or have run up considerable fuel debts and have had their gas and electricity disconnected. 'Fuel' poverty is discussed in some detail by Berthoud and Brown (1981). They note that it is a problem for which rising oil prices, attempts to maintain parity between the charges for alternative fuels, and the practice of installing central heating in local authority houses, are largely responsible. Rent direct may soon have to be added to this list. It is also claimed that rent direct is undignified, given that it was previously only resorted to if tenants were in rent arrears, although since rent direct will be more widely used this argument could become increasingly invalid.

Fiegehen and McGwire (1982) have tried to determine who the gainers and the losers in the scheme will be, and the extent of their gains and losses. The gainers will be pensioners, who benefit from the increased taper below the needs allowance and the increased needs allowance. These include 650,000 tenants, with an average gain of £1.31 a week, and 400,000 owner-occupiers, with an average gain of 40p a week. 230,000 further pensioners will find that they receive 100 per cent rebates and allowances when they themselves previously paid part of their housing costs. 2 million households will lose as a result of the increased tapers above the needs allowance; 300,000 will lose rebate or allowance altogether. About 40 per cent of the losers would be. pensioners, with an average loss of 50p a week if they are tenants and 16p a week if they are owner-occupiers. The losses for non-pensioners will be greater; for tenants 84p a week if they were not limited to 75p, and for owner-occupiers 28p a week. Overall the new scheme involves a transfer of funds to poor pensioners which is paid for mainly by non-pensioner tenants, and by tenants with incomes in excess of their needs allowance in general. Owner-occupiers, who make few demands on the current scheme of rebates and allowances, pay relatively little.

In only a very limited respect will the new scheme fulfil the objectives of a reformed housing benefit scheme outlined earlier. There is some administrative unification, in that local authorities take over the administration of nearly all housing benefits; their work-load is thus increased, but the administrative costs of Supplementary Benefit will be reduced. However, any savings are in the first instance to be used to compensate losers from the scheme. This modest unification does not involve any change in overall expenditure on housing benefits. But it is difficult to argue that with the new and additional tapers, the introduction of its topping-up arrangements, and the possible need for more claimants to deal with two offices, the system of housing benefits has become any more coherent or easy to understand. For those in work the poverty trap deepens – because the withdrawal rate above the needs allowance increases – and the unemployment trap is made more severe for the same reason. And the topping up provision actually means that the 'better off' problem remains, although in a slightly diminished and different form to that previously. People who believe that they have a Supplementary Benefit entitlement may go to their local Department of Health and Social Security benefit office; if they discover that they are right, but that their housing costs will take the form of a 100 per cent rebate from the local authority, then they will be told. They will also be informed that they are entitled to a topping-up payment. However, if they go to the local authority for their assessment there is no guarantee that the local authority will do the calculation necessary to determine whether a topping-up payment is due. Total income assistance may depend upon which office is attended first.

Clearly the new scheme has ranked the administrative savings and the pegging of expenditure at current levels as the principal objectives of housing benefit reform. While this is easy to understand it is difficult to defend. The new scheme fails on what most of those concerned with the weaknesses of the current social security system believe to be the main advantages claimed of it, its transparency and fairness; neither has been much improved, if at all. On the basis of this assessment it is difficult to understand the favourable reception Donnison gave the new scheme. It is in no way the unified housing benefit scheme he described; and while the details of the new scheme can be modified to reduce the severity of the problems mentioned above (see Lansley, 1982), housing benefit reform must still remain firmly on the agenda. Any serious unified housing benefit scheme must be a prime contender. Only if the housing market were fundamentally reformed might such a scheme prove inappropriate.

Reform of the housing market

In a reformed market, housing costs should not vary for a given quality of housing in a particular locality. In principle this uniformity is fairly easy to achieve. Owner-occupiers would continue to receive tax relief on mortgage interest payments, but would be taxed on their real imputed income and capital gains. It is readily confirmed that if the opportunity cost of capital r and the mortgage interest rate i were equal, the rate of imputation were the real opportunity cost of capital, and nominal capital gains were taxed at the same rate as income, (7.1) would become

$$P = (1-t)r(V-M) + (1-t)rM - (1-t)\,\Pi V + t(r-\Pi)V$$
$$= (r-\Pi)V \tag{7.2}$$

and then the price of housing is simply the market value of a house V multiplied by the real interest rate $(r-\Pi)$. P is independent of marginal tax rates and mortgage debt.

If all controls in the private rented sector were dispensed with, landlords would not be discriminated against, and rental housing as an investment should increase in attractiveness. Under the assumptions made above, rents will be determined by (7.2). And local authority rents could be fixed in exactly the same way, since the market value of the local authority housing stock can be inferred from the market values of equivalent houses in the private sector. Under this new regime, house prices would adjust naturally, taking account of both the extent

to which the tax advantage of owner-occupied housing had previously
been capitalized into house prices – house prices are higher than they
would be if imputed income and capital gains were taxed – and the
increase in the supply of private rented accommodation. Prices stabilize
when the housing market is in equilibrium: supply and demand is
equated in each sector.

To varying degrees, housing market reform along these lines has been
proposed. Grey, Hepworth, and Odling-Smee (1981) have suggested
the introduction of 'economic pricing' which under the assumptions
made above is exactly the reform package suggested above. King and
Atkinson (1980) support a plan which goes part of the way towards
economic pricing, imposing a tax on nominal imputed income but not
on capital gains. Again under the assumptions made above the price of
owner-occupied housing is that given by (7.2). Rents in the local
authority sector are set as a fraction of the economic price of the
local authority housing stock in the country as a whole – national rent
pooling is substituted for the more limited rent pooling currently
favoured. King and Atkinson do not discuss the private rented sector.

In the above comparison of reforms it has been assumed that the
rates of income tax and capital gains tax are identical, which is not
typically the case. Nominal capital gains have until very recently been
taxed at a rate of 30 per cent although the effective rate was much
lower; in *The Economist* (12 June 1982) a figure of only 5.5 per cent
is reported. The average marginal rate of income tax of taxpayers in
general is only a little above 30 per cent, although that of landlords is
probably higher. If nominal capital gains are taxed at an effective rate
c then (7.2) becomes

$$P = (r-\Pi)V - (t-c)\Pi V \qquad (7.3)$$

which is identical to (7.2) if $t = c$.

A weakness with these approaches to housing market reform
concerns the definition of imputed income. Owner-occupiers are no
more than landlords renting to themselves, and their imputed income
should really be the rent they would charge if they were competitive
landlords. This is also the rent which would be charged by local
authorities for similar houses. Ermisch (1982) shows that a competitive
landlord would charge a rent

$$R = (r-\Pi)V - \{(t-c)/(1-t)\}\Pi V \qquad (7.4)$$

and the price of owner-occupied housing would be

$$P = (1-t)r(V-M) + (1-t)rM - (1-c)\Pi V + t(r-\Pi)V - t\{(t-c)/(1-t)\}\Pi V$$
$$= (r-\Pi)V - \{(t-c)/(1-t)\}\Pi V$$

which is simply (7.4), so that $P = R$. The price of owner-occupied housing is therefore less than indicated by (7.2), as implied by the King and Atkinson approach, or (7.3), as implied by the Grey, Hepworth, and Odling-Smee approach. If capital gains are taxed at the income tax rate, (7.4), like (7.3), reduces to (7.2). However, the current practice is to tax real capital gains. This changes the price formulae, but not the way in which they are derived.

The attraction of the Ermisch proposal is that it starts from the first principles of price determination in competitive markets, and it implies that owner-occupiers and landlords will be treated equally while local authority tenants would pay market rent. However, even the King and Atkinson proposals, if implemented, would introduce a semblance of logic into the UK housing market which has so far been lacking. And since the complex system of housing assistance that we currently have is designed to work in a confused housing market, housing market reform would naturally offer the opportunity for reforming housing assistance.

We have said that Beveridge recommended that in a perfectly functioning housing market the only form of housing assistance should be an addition to social security benefits to pay for housing at the minimally acceptable standard. This would be a fixed sum dependent only on family composition, say C. In a perfect market this is all King and Atkinson would provide. However to the extent that the market remains imperfect, or that the transition to a perfect market takes a long time – and people still pay different amounts for housing of similar quality – a housing allowance $A = \lambda(R-C)$ would be paid, where R is rent and $\lambda < 1$, subject to a maximum. They argue that means-testing has failed many in need of help with their housing costs – mainly non-claimants – and that it creates the poverty trap. They therefore reject income-related assistance. Grey, Hepworth, and Odling-Smee, on the other hand, support income-related assistance even with a perfectly functioning market. They do not consider the role it plays. Under their scheme all households would receive a housing allowance which increases with the price paid for housing and falls as income rises. The housing allowance substitutes for all other forms of financial assistance. It is a mixture of the King–Atkinson housing allowance and the current system of housing benefits. However, in a perfect market it is difficult to see the need for the cost-related element. It serves no apparent purpose when the market provides exactly the housing people are willing to pay for; however, if the consumption of good quality housing – and the consequent improvement of the housing stock – is to be encouraged then there clearly is a case for an income-related benefit. This would perhaps take the form of the sum C paid to all those in similar circumstances as social security beneficiaries – and only paid if they spend at least C on housing – which is then progressively withdrawn as income increases.

When the market is imperfect, income-related assistance plays a different role. The King and Atkinson housing allowance would be a satisfactory housing benefit but for the following problems. First, rent may be correlated with income, and a scheme which pays the largest benefits to those with the highest rents will also pay them to those with the highest incomes. Second, any particular level of rent is paid by households with widely ranging income, and no account is therefore taken of capacity to pay when determining housing benefit. And general income redistribution measures cannot do this either, since they take no account of rent. Income-related housing assistance cannot be abandoned. But equally the existing system leaves much to be desired.

Unified housing benefit

From the description offered by Donnison of a unified housing benefit scheme it would appear that the principal feature of such a scheme is that the net rent payment – rent less housing benefit – is a smooth function of income. We use the term 'rent', but mean rent, rates, and possibly all or part of owner-occupiers' mortgage repayments. The new housing benefit scheme, like its predecessor, does not possess this characteristic. Figure 7.1 demonstrates the problem. The kinked line, RR, represents the rent and rate rebate component of the new housing benefit scheme, ignoring the different tapers for pensioners. At a fixed rent, net rent will increase as income increases, as the variable income-related component of the rebate or allowance is withdrawn. Full rent is paid to Supplementary Benefit recipients. But for those ineligible for Supplementary Benefit, net rent would not necessarily reach zero when income reached Supplementary Benefit level. Indeed it would be a fluke if it did. For a one earner couple with two children, rent would have to be exactly £20.30. Only by chance – if the combination of rent and family composition is right – will the two coincide. With a unified housing benefit scheme net rent would always reach zero at the Supplementary Benefit level.

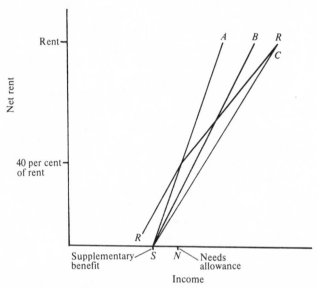

FIG. 7.1. Alternative Single-Taper Housing Benefit Schemes.

Goss and Lansley (1981) have proposed a simple linear or single-taper housing benefit scheme; in Figure 7.1 we show three single-taper schemes *A*, *B*, and *C*. Of the three tapers, *A* is greater than *B*, and *B* is greater than *C*. Any family with an income below Supplementary Benefit level has its housing costs met in full, and as income rises above this level the housing benefit is withdrawn at a rate given by the chosen taper. Scheme *A* is simply driven through the existing scheme, guaranteeing that those paying 40 per cent of their housing costs will continue to do so. Everybody paying less than 40 per cent of their housing costs, except Supplementary Benefit recipients, will gain and those paying more than 40 per cent of their housing costs will lose. To reduce the number of losers the taper will have to be reduced – there are fewer losers under scheme *B* and none at all under scheme *C*. As far as we know a single-taper scheme has not been costed. But predictable problems cannot be avoided.

If there are to be no losers the scheme could be much too costly; and if the scheme is to be introduced at zero cost there may be many, some large, losers. The critics of the new housing benefit scheme have agreed almost unanimously that more money must be put into housing benefits. Changes in structure which involve some people losing more than trivial amounts are ruled out; however this attitude could be a barrier to reform even occurring. It should come as no surprise that a system which has developed haphazardly should distribute the benefits in a way very different to that which emerges from a reformed system designed from first principles. Clearly no one wants to take so much money off people that they suffer an intolerable reduction in their standard of living. But housing benefits are not the only source of income for those of limited means, and if a change in the system of housing benefits would create additional poverty, then measures can be taken to prevent this happening. The brief to produce a distribution of housing benefits such that there are few, and only tiny, losses is a strait-jacket which should not be placed upon feasible reform.

If losers are permitted, but the zero cost constraint must be binding, the taper will have to be a little higher than those presently used. This could have implications for the poverty trap. If Family Income Supplement were to persist in its current form the higher marginal tax rates implied for low-income families would be a serious objection to any increase in the taper. However, it is our view that desirable reform of the social security system involves the abolition of Family Income Supplement, and its replacement with a means of helping low income working families which imposes an additional marginal tax rate substantially below 50 per cent. The crucial objection to the single-taper scheme in particular is that housing benefit is independent of housing expenditure. If gross rent is given by R, net rent by NR, income by Y, the Supplementary Benefit scale rate by S, and the taper by β, the simple linear housing benefit scheme implies that

$$
\begin{aligned}
NR &= 0 & Y &\leqslant S & (7.5)\\
&= \beta(Y-S) & Y &> S\\
&= R & Y &> S+R/\beta
\end{aligned}
$$

and rent does not appear in this formula for benefit recipients. It has been argued that there are no barriers to the quality of accommodation that people choose because the marginal cost of housing is zero. This is currently the situation for those who have their housing costs met in full from Supplementary Benefit. Few people have criticized this provision, presumably because hardly anybody actually takes advantage of it, and he or she would find it difficult to do so if he or she wanted to. Most live in local authority houses, the only alternative is another local authority house, and few people are going to move to higher cost, higher quality housing in another local authority. However, we have seen that housing benefits are paid to those with quite high earnings, and if this bizarre incentive does exist it will be at these higher earnings levels.

In Figure 7.1 the net rent was measured on the vertical axis. Now if this was the proportion of rent instead, then the scheme becomes

$$
\begin{aligned}
NR/R &= 0 & Y &\leq S \\
&= \beta^*(Y-S) & Y &> S \\
&= 1 & Y &> S+1/\beta^*
\end{aligned}
$$

or

$$
\begin{aligned}
NR &= 0 & Y &\leq S \\
&= \beta^*(Y-S)R & Y &> S \\
&= R & Y &> S+1/\beta^*.
\end{aligned} \tag{7.6}
$$

With this scheme, at a given income net rent increases with rent; it might be called a 'rent-proportional-taper' scheme. This affects those earning just more than Supplementary Benefit only a little since Y is close to S. As income rises a greater proportion of any higher rent has to be met. Given that β^* is set by specifying the income at which unified housing benefit is to run out, and if this is Y^* then $\beta^* = 1/(Y^*-S)$, it is clear that as income approaches Y^* nearly all of any increase in rent has to be paid for. Those on higher earnings therefore have little to gain from seeking higher quality, higher rent accommodation they do not really require.

However, a problem may arise with this scheme. It relates to the taper. As income goes up, net rent rises by β^*R. For a one earner, two child family with a rent of £20, housing benefit currently runs out when earnings reach about £140 a week. The corresponding Supplementary Benefit scale rate is about £60. If the new scheme is to stop paying benefit at the same point as the current scheme then $\beta^* = 1/80$

and the taper would be 25 per cent. A zero cost scheme would have a taper closer to 35 per cent. In themselves these rates are not alarming, they create no poverty trap problem in the absence of Family Income Supplement. But as rents get higher so the taper increases correspondingly. If there are working families paying very high rents out of low incomes – probably renting local authority houses in the more exclusive London boroughs or living in decontrolled privately rented accommodation – it is conceivable that they might have to face tapers of 70 or 80 per cent under this scheme.

The purpose of unification is to ensure that those who share the same financial circumstances receive identical housing benefit, as equity demands; both the single-taper scheme and the rent-proportional-taper scheme guarantee this. But the former, although only a moderate taper is a possibility, meets any additional rent incurred, while the latter, although it forces part of any additional rent to fall upon the household, implies a taper which is potentially very large. The current scheme, because of its different tapers above and below the needs allowance, has neither of these weaknesses, but fails to satisfy the equity principle. Is there scope for combining the strengths of the unified schemes suggested above and the existing rebate scheme without having to take on board their weaknesses? Hemming and Hills (1983) have devised a dual-taper scheme which seems to do this. It is a significant modification of a scheme – which was neither designed nor recognized to have this property – suggested by Bradshaw and Bradley (1979).

The dual-taper scheme is illustrated in Figure 7.2. Rent is met in full if income is below S, the Supplementary Benefit scale rate. Housing benefit is then paid according to the more generous of two single-taper schedules. The first, which will be appropriate to those with lower incomes, will imply that net rent is

$$NR_L = \beta_1 (Y-S) \qquad (7.7)$$

exactly as under the single-taper scheme. The second, which will be appropriate to those with higher incomes, will imply that net rent is

$$NR_H = \alpha R + \beta_2 (Y-S) \qquad (7.8)$$

and so housing benefit is cost-related as under the rent-proportional-taper scheme, with the proportion α of any additional rent having to be paid by the claimant. There is a switch from NR_L to NR_H at

$$\hat{Y} = S + \alpha R/(\beta_1 - \beta_2) \tag{7.9}$$

and benefit runs out at

$$Y^* = S + (1-\alpha)R/\beta_2 \tag{7.10}$$

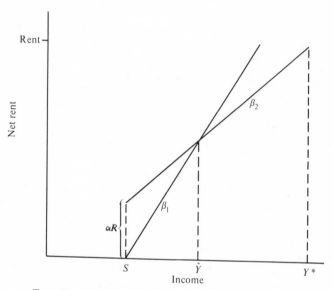

FIG. 7.2. The Dual-Taper Housing Benefit Scheme.

It is therefore a simple matter to determine which schedule applies. For example, if $\alpha = 0.3$, $\beta_1 = 0.25$, and $\beta_2 = 0.1$ then $\hat{Y} = S + 2R$ and $Y^* = S + 7R$. If income is S or less then rent is met in full; if income exceeds S but not $S + 2R$ then net rent is NR_L; if income exceeds $S + 2R$ but not $S + 7R$ then net rent is NR_H; and if income exceeds $S + 7R$ then no housing benefit is paid. If $\beta_1 = 0.25$ and $\beta_2 = \alpha = 0.16\dot{6}$ (i.e. 1/6) the financial impact of the existing scheme will be more or less replicated.

The single-taper and rent-proportional-taper housing benefit schemes offer many advantages compared to the existing arrangements. Unification is not only horizontally equitable, but it also produces a system of housing benefits which is uncomplicated, and which should therefore be widely understood, as well as straightforward to administer. It is difficult to think of problems inherent in the previous and latest arrangements which would not be swept away. Yet the case for introducing a proper unified housing benefit scheme cannot be upheld on these grounds alone. We have seen that both of these schemes bring with them their own problems. The single-taper scheme allows more expensive housing to be consumed at no additional cost. While we might confidently believe that the limited scope for moving 'up-market' rules this out in all but a few cases, the need to maintain a credible social security system has been repeatedly emphasized. A housing benefit scheme which permits such activities – not only the single-taper scheme but also any other scheme which shares this feature – especially at incomes which are difficult to describe as low, is not an attractive proposition. A unified housing benefit scheme will only be taken seriously if it is in part cost-related. The rent-proportional-taper scheme is, but it can impose unacceptably high marginal tax rates on those with high rents.

The dual-taper scheme satisfies the principal objective of unification; at the same time those with higher incomes are forced to contribute part of any additional rent incurred and the kink in the taper provides the flexibility to limit marginal tax rates without imposing massive additional cost. However, the full cost implications of the many variants of this scheme – which follow from the exact choice of α, β_1, and β_2 – like the cost implications of alternative single-taper and rent-proportional-taper schemes, remain to be worked out. The case for a proper unified housing benefit scheme is difficult to dispute. But the exact form unification should take will depend upon the strengths and weaknesses of each scheme, and on how much they are likely to cost. If – as seems likely – a single-taper scheme or a rent-proportional-taper scheme is only feasible at some considerable cost or when it is made far more complex, then the best alternative must be to think about achieving the objectives of unification while maintaining some of the main features of the existing scheme. The dual-taper scheme does this, and rather neatly.

8

SOCIAL SECURITY REFORM

A loose framework for analysis of the social security system was described in Chapter 1. This required us to investigate the ability of the system to attack poverty and to combine with the tax system in order to achieve society's wider equity objectives without imposing high marginal tax rates which blunt incentives. On the basis of our analysis it is difficult to believe that the British social security system is a success which cannot be greatly improved upon.

The most desirable feature of a social security system is that it be capable of relieving poverty. Poverty would be far more extensive in Britain if there were no social security system, and when assessed in terms of the reduction in poverty it achieves, social security in Britain is successful. But government survey data reveal that in 1971 there were still about 2½ million people who were poor by official standards, and this could be a massive underestimate. Two-thirds of the poor were in receipt of social security benefits, and the majority of these were retirement pensioners. However, with over three times as many unemployed at the beginning of 1983 as in 1971 unemployment must have become a major cause of poverty. It is clearly very difficult to guess how many poor there are in 1982. To suggest that the number is larger than 2½ million is to play ridiculously safe; to suggest a number nearly twice as large is not in the least outrageous. How could the current arrangements fail so many?

The staggering complexity of the social security system is one of its features which it would be impossible to disguise. Nowhere is this more obvious than with the system of means-tested benefits. New means-tested benefits have been introduced when they were felt to be necessary — for example, Family Income Supplement and housing benefits — with little regard to their relationship to existing means-tested benefits. We have noted in Chapters 2 and 4 that the means tests differ both in the way in which they assess income and determine needs, and in the period over which benefit entitlement extends. The current muddle is expensive to administer and a deterrent to claiming. Furthermore, the process of means-testing – still with its cap-in-hand connotations – is claimed to be undignified, and this too reduces take-up.

Our wider concept of equity requires that social security does not impose unreasonable constraints upon a tax and benefit system which is designed to be a vertically and horizontally equitable means of redistributing income. There are numerous features of the current system which are patently inequitable: the failure to pay the long-term Supplementary Benefit rate to the long-term unemployed; the industrial preference in determining disablement benefits; and the favourable treatment of women under SERPS. These are the most blatant examples of horizontal inequities. The tax and benefit system redistributes from the rich to the poor, and if all benefits were taken up it would be more redistributive. If there were fewer horizontal inequities it might be more redistributive still. Whether it would then be redistributive enough is a different question, which we are not going to tackle. We only note that the existing social security system need not provide a barrier to further redistribution.

The tax system and the social security system have developed quite independently; there has been little regard for the interaction between the two systems. And nor would we expect there to be, when one is the responsibility of the biggest collecting Civil Service department – the Inland Revenue – and the other is mainly the responsibility of the biggest spending department – the Department of Health and Social Security. But the two systems do combine to produce an outcome which is clearly nonsensical. Low income households ought to be better off if they do more work or take a better-paid job, it is desirable that such courses of action are followed, yet it is frequently the case that when these opportunities arise they are not profitable, and it would be understandable if they were rejected. The poverty trap is a serious flaw in the system of income maintenance.

The related unemployment trap is now less of a problem than it was a few years ago, in the sense that the abolition of earnings-related supplement, the taxation of benefits, and the 5 per cent reduction in the real level of unemployment benefits in 1980 has reduced the number of families facing high replacement rates. However, we have also argued that while the 'better off on the dole' or 'why work?' syndrome is a widely publicized implication of the social security system, it is one with only the most slender basis in fact. Nevertheless, there remain maybe 7 per cent of working families and a slightly larger percentage of unemployed families facing short-term or long-term replacement rates in excess of 80 per cent.

We begin our discussion of social security reform by considering proposals for 'root and branch' reform of the system. These fall into two groups. At the moment some social security benefits are purely contingency benefits – child benefit, the retirement pension, sickness benefit, unemployment benefit, and disablement benefit – while others are purely income-related – Supplementary Benefit, Family Income Supplement, and housing benefit. The two groups of proposals begin by suggesting a move either towards the predominant use of contingency benefits – 'Back to Beveridge' schemes – or towards the use of income-related benefits alone – integrated tax and benefit schemes – but we will see that the proponents of each cannot afford to discard useful information provided by the other, the first concerning income and the second concerning status. These schemes are only serious practical propositions if there is some retreat from their purest form.

'Back to Beveridge' schemes

We have emphasized that the current social security system is in many respects very different to the one Beveridge envisaged. The 'Back to Beveridge' proponents call for a return to the basic characteristics of the original Beveridge plan. This would involve marked improvements in National Insurance benefits, and less reliance on means-tested benefits. Such an approach was first recommended by Atkinson (1969), and has since been adopted by the Child Poverty Action Group (see Lister, 1975), the Meade Committee (1978), and some others; Atkinson was an adviser to the first, a temporary member of the second, and probably the principal influence on most of the latter.

There are six main elements to a 'Back to Beveridge' scheme. First, a minimum acceptable standard of living is specified; this is the long-term Supplementary Benefit scale rate. Second, all National Insurance benefits and the tax thresholds would be set at Supplementary Benefit level, although there would be no payments for dependent children. Third, child benefit, which would be the sole means of child support, would be substantially increased and brought broadly into line with Supplementary Benefit provision for children, although not necessarily related to age. Fourth, a home responsibility allowance would be introduced for those who cannot work because they are committed to raising children or caring for the sick, disabled, or elderly, with the minimum acceptable level of support corresponding to that for children. Fifth, all benefits, except child benefit, would be taxed. And sixth, the contribution conditions for National Insurance benefits would be substantially relaxed, with increased use made of credited contributions.

Atkinson, the Child Poverty Action Group, the Meade Committee, and others who have recommended the 'Back to Beveridge' strategy differ in the particular characteristics of their preferred scheme but the basic package of reforms is shared. And it is a package which has much to commend it. Many of the weaknesses of the current social security system would be overcome. The raising of tax thresholds and the reliance on improved child benefits for child support means that those on low incomes would face lower marginal rates of tax, and the poverty trap would disappear; improving child support for those in work relative to those out of work will reduce replacement rates; if all National Insurance benefits are set at or above the poverty line, and these are more widely available, then poverty ought to be eliminated amongst pensioners, the unemployed, the sick, and the disabled; home responsibility payments should help single parents. As Beveridge intended, the safety net provided by means-tested Supplementary Benefit would be hardly used. And if, as we suggested in Chapter 4, low pay is to blame for very little poverty, there can be no more than a few poor. However, there are two fundamental difficulties.

The first concerns help with housing costs. We have seen in Chapter 7 that the British housing market is in disarray. This is why the system of help with housing costs is so complex: housing costs are themselves moderated through rent control and housing subsidies; Supplementary Benefit recipients are then compensated for their full housing expenditure; means-tested housing benefits are available to others. It is also hopelessly inadequate. We said that it would be simplest if all benefits could include an allowance for average housing costs, but this would be too generous for some, while others would be left with resources insufficient to meet their requirements. The reform of the system of housing benefits is a crucial element of any reform of the social security system. Yet the 'Back to Beveridge' camp tend only to admit the gravity of the problem, announce their lack of qualifications to deal with housing benefit reform, and offer their sympathy to those charged with this responsibility.

The second difficulty is cost. With 13 million children and 9 million pensioners, raising child benefit and pensions is very expensive; with 3 million unemployed and 2 million disabled people, raising other National Insurance benefits is also costly; paying a home responsibility allowance to all non-working women who are at home raising children, say 3½ million women, is as costly as an equivalent increase in the number of children; and all taxpayers benefit from increased tax thresholds. A huge increase in public expenditure and taxation would be required if the 'Back to Beveridge' plan were implemented. For example the Meade Committee proposals were estimated to cost up to £3.6 billion in 1976-7 (equivalent to £8 billion at 1982-3 benefit levels), to be met by an increase in the standard rate of tax (by 7 percentage points from 35 per cent to 42 per cent in 1976-7) and an expansion in the tax base following the proposed abolition of the married man's tax allowance. The Child Poverty Action Group proposals were more generous than those of the Meade Committee, and therefore more expensive. They favoured raising the additional revenue by abolishing the upper earnings limit for National Insurance contributions and the tax relief for occupational pension schemes.

On cost grounds alone it is difficult to be enthusiastic about the 'Back to Beveridge' scheme. Yet, as we have indicated, the idea which provides the foundation of the scheme – that if contingency benefits were more extensive, adequate, and always paid at their full rate there would be far less means-testing, and we would therefore have an effective system of poverty relief – seems to be a good one. It is therefore perhaps unfortunate that those who have promoted the scheme also tend to be those who favour a massive redistribution to the poor, and that discussion of the merits of a change in the structure of social security cannot be separated from discussion of how much money ought to be transferred from the rich to the poor under such a change.

Linear integration

The British income tax system was described in Chapter 4. Under this system a taxpayer with gross income Y pays

$$T(Y) = t(Y-A) \tag{8.1}$$

in tax, where t is the marginal tax rate and A the appropriate tax allowance. (We will ignore higher tax rates.) Only those for whom Y exceeds A are taxpayers; if A is equal to or exceeds Y no tax is paid. Those with gross income of A or below receive no automatic payment to boost their income, but they might be entitled to social security. Low income alone is not a sufficient condition to establish a benefit entitlement. The full integration of taxes with benefits would change all this. We can rewrite (8.1) as

$$T(Y) = -tA + tY \qquad (8.2)$$

and it is easily seen that net income is

$$N(Y) = tA + (1-t)Y. \qquad (8.3)$$

Every taxpayer receives a lump sum tA and then pays tax on all other income. But if A is equal to or in excess of Y then $N(Y) = Y$. Full integration would see (8.3) applied at all levels of gross income, and if there were no other sources of income then net income would still be tA. This is the minimum income guaranteed under the integrated system, which we will henceforth denote M; it would reflect different family circumstances. Thus (8.3) can be written

$$N(Y) = M + (1-t)Y \qquad (8.4)$$

which is the basic formula for an integrated linear tax and benefit system. Figure 8.1 makes it clear that this system is a logical extension of the current British tax system, extending what happens to the right of the point A on the Y axis to the left of that point.

There have been a number of proposals describing how such an integration might be achieved. With a *negative income tax scheme* the existing system is extended in the most direct manner. Those with incomes below the tax threshold are regarded as having a negative tax liability, and would receive an addition to their income, equal to $t(A-Y)$, from the Inland Revenue. With a *social dividend scheme* all income tax allowances would be abolished and all income would be subject to tax. But an untaxed social dividend S would be paid to all families. And with a *universal tax credit scheme* all income would again be taxable, but the taxpayer would be given a tax credit C, which can be offset against tax liability, and which can be refunded to those whose tax liability is so small that they cannot fully benefit from it.

If those outside the tax system receive the minimum income implied by the negative income tax scheme or the tax credit, and M, S, and C are all set at the same level, it is clear that with a single tax rate these schemes are all identical and are no more than different ways of implementing (8.4). And given our discussion of the weaknesses of the current social security system at the beginning of this chapter, comprehensive schemes for income maintenance of this type are obviously attractive: because they are simple, they are easy to understand, and, because they deliver benefits automatically, they are capable of achieving poverty relief while preserving the dignity of the needy. But they have a crucial drawback — their cost.

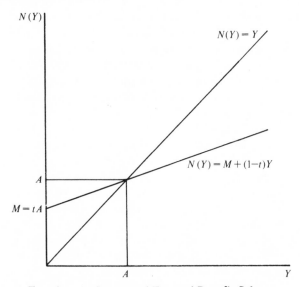

FIG. 8.1. An Integrated Tax and Benefit Scheme.

Take the case of the social dividend scheme, which was originally proposed for Britain by Lady Rhys Williams in 1942, and which has since been taken up by others. The scheme involved the abolition of all social security benefits and the payment of a social dividend to all men, women, and children. In attempting to cost such a scheme Atkinson (1969) assumed that social dividends would be at the prevailing Supplementary Benefit scale rates with an allowance for average housing expenditure (additional housing assistance would be needed if the relief of poverty were to be fully achieved). If the scheme were financed by a proportional tax this is relatively straightforward to compute. The total tax revenue which has to be collected is increased because the total value of social dividend payments has to be included, but is reduced because all other social security benefits are discontinued. Income below the tax threshold has to be included in the tax base. For 1967 Atkinson estimated that the tax rate required to finance the scheme would be 52 per cent. Other estimates for the late 1960s are similar, and the most recent estimates are of much the same magnitude (the Meade Committee, 1978, suggest 55 per cent). It was suggested earlier in this book that reforms involving the imposition of such high marginal tax rates on all taxpayers would not be popular. Naturally revenue could be raised in other ways. Brown and Dawson (1969) suggested that alternative personal taxes – value added tax, or a wealth tax – could be used. But in terms of their incentive effects there is little to choose between income tax and value added tax, and wealth taxes may not involve disincentives to work, but could introduce disincentives to save. Alternatively, it was suggested to the Treasury and Civil Service Committee (1982, Evidence from H. Parker), that an ambitious social dividend scheme replacing not only all social security benefits, except Supplementary Benefit and housing benefits, but also grants for education and training, could be financed with a basic rate of tax of 50 per cent. The principal source of the reduction in the tax rate as compared with those calculated by Atkinson and Meade, is an increase in the tax base which results from the abolition of all forms of tax relief and tax exemptions, for example those concerning mortgage interest, occupational pension schemes, and life insurance contributions, and the married man's allowance. If the tax base cannot be enlarged in this way, there is little scope for reducing the tax rate without damaging the scheme.

Let $\bar{Y}$ be the average level of gross income in society and $\bar{G}$ the average cost of public goods and services provided. With the simplest social dividend scheme, where every member of society receives the same social dividend, S,

$$S + \bar{G} = t\bar{Y}$$

as the average benefit must equal the average tax payment. It then follows that

$$\bar{Y} = (S+\bar{G})/t \tag{8.5}$$

which is the fundamental equation describing the trade-off between the social dividend, the tax rate, and other forms of government expenditure. A similar, though more complicated, 'trade-off' equation can be derived for the case where the social dividend is paid to families, and varies with family size. The tax rate can only be reduced if the social dividend is correspondingly reduced, in other words by not achieving the full relief of poverty through this system, or if funds are released by cutting back other public programmes. The nature of the trade-off can be complicated further. High marginal tax rates may affect the amount of work which is done. The implication of this is that taxable income, and specifically $\overline{Y}$ in (8.5), is a function of the tax rate, t.

If the tax rate is zero or 100 per cent then it seems reasonable to assert that there can be no social dividend: in the first case no revenue will be raised no matter how much work is done, while in the second case no work will be done. It therefore follows that the social dividend is related to the tax rate as shown in Figure 8.2. There is little point in

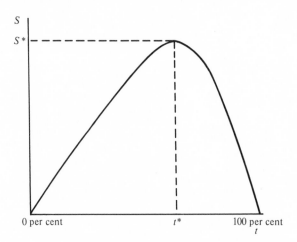

FIG. 8.2. The Trade-Off between the Social Dividend and the Marginal Tax Rate.

setting the tax rate above t^*: any level of S can always be supported at a lower tax rate. If one was only interested in equity considerations the tax rate would be t^* and the social dividend would be at its maximum possible level S^*. It is not obvious how high t^* would be in practice. But if this level is regarded as too high from an efficiency point of view the social dividend would have to be less than S^*. How much less will depend upon the weight which policy-makers attach to equity and efficiency objectives.

Modified integrated schemes

Fully integrated linear tax and benefit systems turn out to be only superficially attractive; they are costly and inflexible. They are costly because they provide benefits for everybody when only relatively few people are in need; and in order to guarantee that poverty is fully relieved the poor are left with net incomes above the poverty line and even some of the non-poor have their net incomes enhanced. While part of the additional cost of such schemes is that benefits are now paid to all of those who are entitled to receive them, a substantial part must be attributed to the extravagant manner in which this is achieved. They are inflexible because this cost cannot be reduced without adopting a more modest equity objective. Thus in Figure 8.3, SS represents a

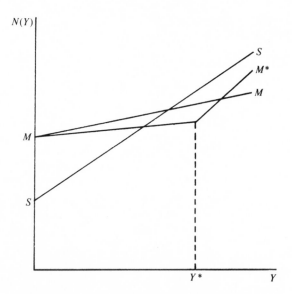

FIG. 8.3. A Two-Rate Social Dividend Scheme.

'feasible' social dividend scheme, in the sense that the marginal tax rate which is paid by everybody cannot be raised any further. However the social dividend this supports is below the poverty standard M. To finance a social dividend of M the marginal tax rate would have to rise to an unacceptable level, as given by the scheme MM. However, it is possible to introduce additional flexibility which will permit the relief of poverty while the bulk of the working population are not saddled with punitive taxation at the margin. This is achieved by having multiple tax rates.

In a two-rate modified social dividend scheme, income up to a limit Y^* is taxed at one rate, and income above Y^* is taxed at a lower rate. MM^* in Figure 8.3 represents one such scheme. Collard (1980) has provided a neat 'do-it-yourself tool kit for the construction of a two-rate modified social dividend scheme', which takes the form of a simple diagram. It shows how if a full social dividend scheme would require a tax rate of 55 per cent, and if the lower rate cannot exceed 40 per cent (there would be no National Insurance scheme, so this would be about the current level of taxation), then the tax rate that needs to be levied on lower incomes rises with the width of the initial band, Y^*. The greater the proportion of total income which is below Y^* the lower will be this tax rate. For example, if 30 per cent of income is in the initial band, as assumed in Meade (1978), the tax rate will be 90 per cent. If 40 per cent of income is in the initial band the tax rate drops to 78 per cent. With a given lower rate of tax there is a straight trade-off between the higher tax rate and the number of people it affects. Unless, of course, modified schemes can have more than two rates. For example, it may be desirable to reduce the tax rate faced by the poorest by exposing the very rich to a higher rate as well, and the feasible combination of rates is easily computed. However, the scope for reducing the lower tax rate is limited. If current higher rate tax-payers were taxed at 75 per cent then the tax rate on the initial band could itself only be reduced to 75 per cent when 40 per cent of income is in the initial band. This follows from the fact that there is only a small number of higher rate taxpayers.

The introduction of the second rate achieves a remarkable step forward. For with the basic social dividend scheme we postulated two objectives, the relief of poverty and the avoidance of adverse disincentive effects, but having fixed M to achieve the first we could not adjust t to achieve the second. This is a familiar impasse posed in 'the theory of economic policy'. By allowing there to be two rates we are free to vary any three of M, the two tax rates, and Y^*. We still have our initial two objectives, and because we now have three discretionary policy instruments we can add a third objective.

If a distinction is drawn between the disincentive effects on the low paid, of whom there are relatively few, and the disincentive effects on the work-force in general, and an attempt is made to minimize the latter, this leads to an interesting special case of the two-rate scheme, at the opposite extreme to the basic linear scheme outlined in the previous section. It emerges when the higher tax rate is exactly 100 per cent. This is the minimum income guarantee scheme which was once proposed by the Institute of Economic Affairs (IEA, 1970). The minimum income guarantee scheme is shown in Figure 8.4: the

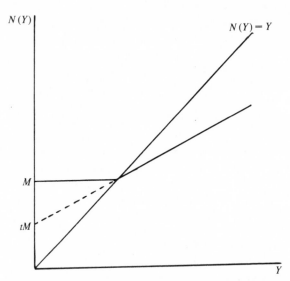

FIG. 8.4. The Minimum Income Guarantee Scheme.

important point to note is that if gross income is less than M, the guaranteed minimum, net income cannot exceed M. All additional income is paid in tax. If income exceeds M net income is

$$N(Y) = M + (1-t)(Y-M). \qquad (8.6)$$

Such a scheme 'institutionalizes' the poverty trap, since many low income working families will discover that they will be no better off (although not worse off) if they earn more. While the Institute of Economic Affairs felt that the disincentive effects of the scheme — because they would be isolated to those with low incomes, and only a few of them at that — were likely to be unimportant, its optimism did not find much favour, and the scheme has not been taken very seriously. This is perhaps not surprising. The extraordinarily high marginal tax rates in the poverty trap are implicit rates, and many of those in the trap will not know that they are there. With the minimum income guarantee scheme the 100 per cent marginal tax rate is quite explicit, and could possibly be much more damaging than implicit rates which are higher. But even if there is any truth in this argument there can be little merit in defending the current arrangements on the grounds that the marginal tax rates are not realized by many to be in excess of 100 per cent. The minimum income guarantee scheme, or any other reasonably transparent scheme with the same implications, must be preferable to the confusion it would replace. And it is far from obvious that such a scheme does not represent a desirable outcome to the problem of balancing the tax rates which will be faced at different levels of income.

An alternative to the two-rate scheme, again with the principal intention of achieving poverty elimination, automaticity, and administrative simplification, but with an acceptable marginal tax rate imposed upon the majority of the working population, is a two-tier scheme. Such a scheme was given serious consideration by the Meade Committee, although they ultimately came down in favour of the 'Back to Beveridge' model. The specific scheme contemplated was a two-tier social dividend, which would involve a modification of the basic social dividend scheme to take account of labour market status. Much of the extra cost of the basic scheme arises because the social dividend is paid in full to those in the work-force, all but a few of whom do not need it. Thus a high conditional social dividend is paid only to those who are prevented from working on a full-time basis; in other words those who would currently receive the principal contingency benefits. Everybody else is paid a lower unconditional social dividend.

Again Collard (1980) has produced the tool kit necessary to compute combinations of tax rate and unconditional social dividend given the conditional social dividend and the proportion of the population entitled to it. The Meade Committee, as an illustration, took the conditional social dividend to be 40 per cent of average earnings; if one-third of the population would be entitled to the conditional social dividend and the unconditional social dividend were half the conditional social dividend, the tax rate would be 42 per cent. Paying the same social dividend to everybody, at the conditional rate, would require a tax rate of 55 per cent. Therefore, as with the two-rate schemes, two-tier schemes turn out to be capable of achieving significant reductions in the standard rate of tax in comparison with the basic social dividend scheme. But while two-rate schemes necessarily levy very high tax rates on those with low incomes, two-tier schemes do not. Instead however they may not prove to be a reliable means of relieving poverty. For example, if the unconditional social dividend is set below the conditional dividend, and the former reflects the poverty standard, those who earn less than the difference between the two will remain poor. Using the figures quoted above, earnings must exceed 35 per cent of average earnings if poverty is to be avoided. There will therefore be an incentive for those with very low earnings to become unemployed; but perhaps, while we have been striving to avoid unemployment trap problems, the widespread rejection of full-time jobs which pay only a third of average earnings is not necessarily something to be regretted.

The two-tier scheme has been designed with the same aim as the two-rate scheme, to be less costly, and therefore not to require such a high standard rate of tax; but it is a very different proposition. The two-rate scheme is still an integrated scheme, although its mechanics are more complicated than those of the linear scheme. The two-tier scheme defines a different range of benefits, and then distinguishes between working and non-working beneficiaries to determine who gets which. This violates the underlying principle of integration, that only income is used to determine benefit entitlement. Any serious proposal for integration must inevitably be more modest in its intent than the purely linear or the two-rate schemes, and leave much of the structure of the existing social security system, and in particular the contingency benefits, untouched. The Conservative tax credit scheme proposed in 1972 and the more ambitious 'tax and benefit' scheme recently proposed by the Social Democrats are the most notable of only a few such examples.

The Conservative tax credit scheme

In October 1972 the Conservative government announced plans for a tax credit scheme (Inland Revenue, 1972), a proposal endorsed by the

Select Committee on Tax Credit (1973). Under the scheme all existing personal allowances were to be abolished, although most forms of tax relief – most notably relief on mortgage interest payments – would be retained, some in modified form. They would be replaced by weekly credits which would be offset against tax liability: if the value of credits exceeded the tax due, the difference would be paid as a cash sum. The standard rate of income tax would be 30 per cent, with surtax rates on higher incomes. The existing pay-as-you-earn system would be abolished and replaced by a non-cumulative assessment of income tax. In other words each week or month credits would be received and could be set against tax based on earnings in that period only. This differs from the cumulative tax system, where allowances unused in one week or month may be carried forward or backward in computing tax liability for another week or month. At the end of the tax year the right amount of tax has been paid. With income tax ultimately charged on annual income, non-cumulation may have required an adjustment at the end of the year. Of the existing social security system, family allowance and Family Income Supplement were to be abolished, National Insurance benefits would remain but become liable to tax, and Supplementary Benefit and other means-tested benefits would be retained as they were.

The following groups were to be included in the scheme: existing employees who paid tax, all main National Insurance beneficiaries, and most occupational pensioners. Roughly 10 per cent of the population would therefore have been excluded: the self-employed, low earners, and those receiving Supplementary Benefit but not National Insurance benefits, for example the long-term unemployed.

The scheme had numerous administrative intricacies – for example, the guarantee that some benefits would still be paid directly to the mother – which mercifully did not dominate the discussion of it. Rather this discussion concentrated upon the scheme's distributional implications. At the proposed credit levels the scheme was going to benefit most retirement pensioners and many of the unemployed and sick, although the taxation of benefits would leave some worse off. Amongst the working population those receiving up to a little over half average earnings would have gained, the net gains increasing with family size and decreasing with earnings. Given the predominance of gainers, and the fact that the major gains went to middle income groups, in the form of increased 'tax allowances', the scheme appeared to be costly – at some £1.3 billion – and not particularly redistributional given the cost. And even then the net gains and their incidence were illusory. For beyond a statement that the anticipated growth of national income would release resources to be devoted to the relief of poverty, little indication was provided as to how this additional cost was to be met.

Therefore, in order to evaluate the distributional impact of the tax credit scheme some assumptions had to be made about methods of finance. For example, Atkinson (1973) considered three possibilities: that the scheme was financed by fiscal drag, not adjusting the credits in line with inflation; that the scheme was financed by an increase in value added tax; or that the scheme was financed by an increase in the standard rate of income tax. Atkinson concluded that the help given to low income families was likely to be very limited. The main gainers would have been those groups entitled to but not receiving existing means-tested benefits, who would benefit from the automatic payment of credits. Most others would have been largely unaffected.

The cost of introducing the 1972 scheme has been investigated ten years later by the Inland Revenue (Treasury and Civil Service Committee, 1982, Evidence from the Inland Revenue). Between 1972 and 1982 prices have risen by a factor of 3¾, implying that the cost of the scheme would now be at least £4.9 billion. However, the principal aim of the 1972 scheme was to replace Family Income Supplement and child benefit (then family allowance). Since 1972 we have seen that Family Income Supplement has become more generous in real terms and the real value of tax allowances has fallen. Thus more families receive Family Income Supplement, and each family receives more. This raises the cost of the tax credit scheme.

In the Inland Revenue calculations the credits would be £10 a week for a single person, £15 for a couple, £24 for the first child, and £9.35 for each subsequent child. The adult credits are roughly £1 more than those implied by the 1982-3 tax system, viz. $0.3(1,565 \div 52) = £9.03$ and $0.3(2,445 \div 52) = £14.11$ − see equation (8.3). The aged would get slightly higher credits, since the age allowance is also converted into a tax credit. With credits set at these levels no family receiving Family Income Supplement would be worse off as a result of the introduction of tax credits. Most support is required by those families with the highest earnings on which the maximum Family Income Supplement is obtained. For a two-child family the maximum Family Income Supplement payment is £23 in 1982-3, and the highest earnings level at which this can be obtained is $91.50 - (2 \times 23) = £45.50$; net income, ignoring housing benefits, would be 45.50 + 23 + 11.70 (child benefit) – 3.98 (National Insurance contributions) = £76.22. Under the tax credit scheme earnings would attract income tax of £13.65 and credits amounting to £48.35 would be received. Net income would be 45.50 – 13.65 + 48.35 – 3.98 = £76.22. It is easily checked that this equivalence emerges for families of different composition.

The overall cost of this scheme would be £8.1 billion with a margin of error of about 10 per cent. As with the 1972 scheme little attention is paid to the way in which the scheme would be financed. It is difficult to believe that the scheme could be financed by anything but an increase in the tax rate, and this in turn would require an increase in credits to guarantee that families receiving the maximum Family Income Supplement payment are not made worse off. It is therefore extremely difficult to guess the tax rate required to finance the scheme; only a careful calculation can reveal the answer. It would be surprising if it were not well in excess of 40 per cent.

The Social Democrats' Scheme

In a consultative document (Green Paper No. 11) with the evocative title 'Attacking Poverty' the Social Democratic Party announced their strategy in November 1982. The corner-stone of their programme would be a basic benefit which would be used to top up the incomes of people in work and recipients of National Insurance benefits, except for the disabled. It would replace Family Income Supplement, free school meals, existing housing benefits, and reduce dependence upon Supplementary Benefit.

For working families basic benefit would be made up of a family component, more generous to adults and less generous to children than the revamped 1972 scheme but child benefit would continue, with a £5 increase for the first child. In addition a component for housing costs, equal to 60 per cent of rent and rates or 30 per cent of mortgage interest, would be included. Basic benefit would be withdrawn at a rate of 45p for each pound earned if there were children and at a rate of 30p in the pound otherwise. The amount left is a credit to be set against the income tax charged at the basic rate on earned income less personal tax allowances. National Insurance contributions would continue to be paid at the current rates. Figure 8.5 shows how a one earner, two child family paying tax would be affected by the scheme in 1981–2.

Basic benefit would be the only form of income-related assistance for single-parent families; there would be a larger adult component, an age-related child component and all rent and rate payments would be included. Figure 8.5 also shows the impact of the scheme on a low income single-parent family. Basic benefit would also guarantee that the short-term unemployed and sick received incomes at the short-term Supplementary Benefit level — therefore replacing supplementary allowances — and that the long-term unemployed received incomes at the long-term Supplementary Benefit level, and would replace and enhance supplementary pensions.

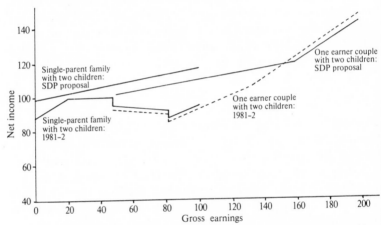

FIG. 8.5. The Effect of the Social Democrats' Scheme on Working Families: 1981–2 (£ a week).

In the absence of compensatory adjustments the net cost of the principal scheme — ignoring anything that might be provided for the disabled — would have been £6 billion in 1981-2, £4 billion for working families, £1 billion for pensioners and £½ billion both for single parents and the unemployed and sick. However, a 1.5 percentage point increase in the basic rate of income tax, to 31.5 per cent, the abolition of the married man's allowance and the age allowance — all allowed for in drawing Figure 8.5 — make the scheme self-financing. In an alternative scheme the £5 increase in child benefit for the first child would be transferred to the basic benefit, and hence become taxable at 76.5 per cent. This would save £1 billion, and the basic rate of tax could remain at 30 per cent if personal tax allowances were frozen in real terms for one year.

There would also be administrative changes. Basic benefit would be received by employees in their pay packet, the tax credit having been determined by local authorities. Claiming continues, but with only one means test. But in the long run, once the much heralded and equally much delayed computerization at the Inland Revenue has been completed, it should become possible for the administration of income tax and social security benefits to be unified. Administrative responsibility would rest with the Inland Revenue. The cumulative pay-as-you-earn system would be abandoned and replaced by a non-cumulative system which collects the information necessary to determine basic benefit on an annual tax return. From this return it would be possible to determine last year's tax liability and tax which will be collected in each week next year. If circumstances change the annual tax liability will not be the sum of each week's liability, and an end-year adjustment will be needed. Those not in work would receive basic benefit as a supplement to other social security benefits; the administrative arrangements would be determined by local authorities, and in the long term they too must complete an annual tax (and benefit?) return, to ensure that benefits are adjusted to reflect changes in circumstances. While, in general, annual tax returns create few problems, it is possible that changes in family composition and rent could create hardship if benefit entitlement is not adjusted more or less immediately. There may therefore have to be some flexibility to allow interim returns to be submitted. Naturally, the number of returns handled by the Inland Revenue will increase dramatically – at the moment not even all taxpayers are required to complete an annual return – but efficient computerization and the release of funds and staff from the Department of Health and Social Security and local authorities, whose administrative responsibilities would be drastically reduced, is expected to accommodate comfortably the extra work-load.

Despite the success this scheme would inevitably have in relieving poverty, eliminating the poverty trap, and achieving administrative simplification, it has a fundamental disadvantage. We saw earlier that the problem with two-rate social dividend schemes is establishing the combination of lower tax rate, higher tax rate, and range of income attracting the higher rate. The authors of the Social Democrats' report recognize the need to trade off these elements, and admittedly steer a middle course. Yet this course, instead of making it profitable for

½ million families to do less work — as is the case at present in the poverty trap and the extended poverty trap — makes it only marginally profitable for 5 million families to do additional work. Many families receiving above average earnings may still be entitled to basic benefit (see Figure 8.5). Essentially what the proposed scheme does is to replace a small poverty trap with a massive poverty plateau where marginal tax rates, taking into account National Insurance contributions, are in excess of 80 per cent.

Both the Conservative tax credit scheme and the Social Democrats' tax and benefit scheme have their greatest impact on working families. The former would replace Family Income Supplement and child benefit, and the latter would replace Family Income Supplement and housing benefits. Benefits provided under the new schemes would be paid through the tax system. Each scheme would eliminate the poverty trap and reduce claiming. However, the cost of so doing is still high. The Social Democrats' scheme has as one of its principal characteristics the one which makes fully integrated schemes so unpalatable; to preserve incentives for low income working families, they must face marginal tax rates of much less than 100 per cent, but then many families with high incomes must benefit from the scheme. The Conservative tax credit scheme achieves much the same outcome as that when Family Income Supplement is replaced with increased child benefit. Indeed this is a strategy which many believe to be a more straightforward way of eliminating the poverty trap and reducing claiming than that of helping working families through the integration of the tax and benefit systems. But to replace fully Family Income Supplement with child benefit is expensive.

Increasing child benefit

If Family Income Supplement were abolished the poverty trap would disappear, but all those families previously in receipt of this form of family support would be made worse off. They could be compensated by increased child benefit. To leave no family worse off in 1982-3 child benefit must be increased to £26.85 for the first child (the maximum Family Income Supplement payment for a one child family, £21, plus child benefit, £5.85), and £7.85 for each subsequent child (the maximum Family Income Supplement addition per child, £2, plus child benefit). Increasing child benefit would reverse the historical decline in the real value of child support in Britain, and by increasing income in work relative to that out of work (given the prevailing Supplementary Benefit scale rates for children) would reduce replacement rates, particularly the very highest which are faced by larger families. But this change would produce a structure of child benefit — with over three times as much being paid for the first child as for subsequent children — very different to that at present, and one which may not be felt to represent a sensible structure. The net cost of this change would have been £7¾ billion in 1982-3 (Treasury and Civil Service Committee, 1982, Evidence from the Department of Health and Social Security).

The structure of child benefit is the cause of some controversy. This mostly relates to the issue of age-relation. Supplementary Benefit child additions are age-related, to reflect the fact that older children cost more to maintain, and there have been calls to extend age-relation to child benefit for the same reason. This would be a mistake. It would be wrong in principle and in practice. Child benefit is designed not as a pure maintenance payment, but as a contribution to the total cost of raising children. Older children may cost more to maintain but younger children require more care if both parents work, and demand more of their time if one does not. Thus child benefit is not age-related. The practical objection is based upon the importance of a wife's earnings in determining whether families are likely to be poor (see Chapter 2). A mother's ability to work is in the main frustrated by the presence of a young child, and age-relation along the Supplementary Benefit lines would redistribute from the poorest to the better off. If there has to be age-relation the largest benefit should perhaps be paid in respect of one child under five say. Yet there is an alternative argument which suggests that it is the birth of the first child, when a mother has to give up work for the first time, which creates the greatest upheaval in family circumstances. A woman who wishes to look after her own children may only be able to return to work many years later, and often the skills she has to offer will have depreciated. Child benefit should therefore be highest for the first child to compensate for this. There is something in both of these arguments; however, judging their relative merit is an empirical issue, which can only be resolved through further research into the determinants of labour force participation amongst women with children. But for the moment, it is difficult to conclude that a much higher level of child benefit for the first child is necessarily a bizarre arrangement.

The cost of course would be a serious objection, and the substitution of child benefit for part of Family Income Supplement may be a more realistic and obtainable change. There are a number of alternatives. First, families could be floated off Family Income Supplement if the qualifying level were reduced as child benefit is increased. Thus if for each £1 increase in child benefit the qualifying level were reduced by £2 per child – and no passport benefits are lost – there would be no loss in income for any family but fewer families would be eligible for Family Income Supplement. Only a £5 increase in child benefit would float two-thirds of the families in the poverty trap off Family Income Supplement; this would be at a cost of £2¾ billion, after allowing for the fact that there is no additional cost in increasing child benefit for Supplementary Benefit recipients (Treasury and Civil Service Committee, 1982, Evidence from the Department of Health and Social Security). Compared to the £7¾ billion it would cost to eliminate the poverty trap through the abolition of Family Income Supplement, a more limited increase in child benefit is clearly a cost-effective method of elimination.

Second, increased child benefit could be matched by a reduction in the rates at which Family Income Supplement, or possibly housing benefits, are withdrawn as earnings increase. Again a £5 increase in child benefit combined with a halving of the Family Income Supplement tax rate on the first £20 of the difference between the qualifying level and gross weekly income would reduce the marginal tax rates faced by three-quarters of the families in the poverty trap from 105.25 per cent or 100.25 per cent to 88.5 per cent or 81 per cent (Treasury and Civil Service Committee, 1982, Evidence from the Department of Health and Social Security).

How would any increase in child benefit be paid for? The taxation of husband and wife has been the subject of a recent Green Paper (Inland Revenue, 1980) and much subsequent discussion. It is almost universally agreed that the married man's tax allowance – whereby a man gets an additional tax allowance if he is married – is an anachronism which cannot persist in a society which purports to treat men and women as equals (see Morris and Warren, 1981, for a discussion of the issues which arise in determining the proper tax treatment of husband and wife). In 1982-3 the married man's allowance, and the single parent's additional personal allowance will cost £3.6 billion, although £½ billion of this is spent in respect of married retirement pensioners. £3.1 billion would pay for an immediate increase in child benefit of £5.64. The married man's allowance is worth £5.06

to all of those who receive it. Taxpaying families with one child will be a little better off as a result of this change; taxpaying families with more than one child will be markedly better off; childless couples will be worse off. The redistribution of the married man's allowance in this way is supported by the majority of those who responded to the Green Paper, including the Social Security Advisory Committee (Kay and Sandler, 1982). Abolition of the married man's allowance would there- fore finance an increase in child benefit sufficiently large to achieve the partial alleviation of the poverty trap discussed above at the expense of childless couples. Other proposals for social security reform — 'Back to Beveridge', tax credit schemes, etc. — would exploit this source of finance. The indications at the moment are that while the government wants to abolish the married man's allowance they would prefer to replace it with a system of transferable allowances — part of the single person's allowance, probably about half, could be transferred by a wife to her husband when she is not in work — rather than to fund a benefit increase.

If we wish to achieve larger increases in child benefit there are three potential sources of finance. First, the marginal tax rate can be increased; allowing for the enlarged tax base which results from the abolition of the married man's allowance and the fact that any increase in the tax rate will bear upon some families who previously received Family Income Supplement, child benefit must be further increased to compensate for this, a four percentage point increase in the tax rate would be required if Family Income Supplement were to be dispensed with. Although this is a small increase, we would rule this out for the same reason that we rejected the abolition of the poverty trap through reform of income tax.

As an alternative, other forms of tax relief and tax exemption — in addition to the married man's allowance — could be abolished. It has been suggested by some that the age allowance — an additional tax allowance for pensioners withdrawn at higher earnings, and costing £½ billion — is a natural candidate. The reason that this money should at least in part be available to enhance the incomes of families, and not only pensioners, is that the age allowance benefits many non- pensioners. This occurs because interest on building society deposits have tax extracted at source at a rate which is a weighted average of the marginal tax rates faced by non-pensioners and pensioners (see Morris, 1981). More lucrative sources of funds, as some have realized, are the forms of relief for pension schemes, life assurance premiums, and mortgage interest payments, costing £3½ billion in 1982-3. However, we have argued elsewhere that mortgage interest relief would remain in a properly functioning housing market, although the required taxation of imputed income and capital gains might release an equivalent amount of money. But this is a long time off. Furthermore, the reform of the private pension system would see the tax advantages for retirement saving not withdrawn but instead extended to a wider range of savings instruments; this would cost money rather than save it, although the cost would be very small. Kay and King (1980) show that most personal saving already attracts favourable tax treatment, and therefore one would expect the main impact of extending tax relief to be a redistribution of saving from pensions and life assurance to other tax-advantaged categories.

The taxation of child benefit would provide a third source of funds. This would give the full benefit to those who do not pay tax, somewhat less to basic rate taxpayers, and relatively little to higher rate taxpayers. Unfortunately there are very few non-taxpayers and higher rate taxpayers affected, since most working families pay tax at the basic rate. In effect taxing child benefit is simply giving with one hand and taking with the other, a complete waste of time and money. Only if it were thought worth while introducing a more graduated structure of marginal tax rates to replace the basic rate band would taxing child benefits be worth considering. However, a desire to make sense of taxing child benefit cannot provide the justification for more graduated marginal tax rates. It is a feature of an optimal tax structure that the poor would face low marginal tax rates, for the very reason that we are attempting to move in this direction, namely to avoid disincentive affects. It is beyond the scope of our discussion to outline the issues involved in determining the remainder of an optimal tax structure, but the Meade Committee (1978) do so in a way which can be easily understood.

Constrained by the availability of funds it would appear that a partial replacement of Family Income Supplement by child benefit is all that is possible. A desire to reduce means-testing would suggest that this should take the form of floating families off Family Income Supplement. A £5 increase in child benefit seems feasible, leaving 40,000 families in receipt of Family Income Supplement and all facing marginal tax rates in excess of 100 per cent because there is no married man's or additional personal allowance. The reason it is so expensive to dispense completely with the supplement while compensating all of those who currently receive it for their losses is that large increases in child benefit are needed, particularly for the first child, to replace fully the largest Family Income Supplement payments. However, it is a feature of Family Income Supplement that there are numerous small payments and relatively few large payments. A half of all payments, and a slightly bigger share of large payments, are made to single-parent families (House of Commons Hansard, 8 April 1982). With only ½ million single-parent families it is relatively inexpensive to increase one-parent benefit. A £5 increase would cost about £125 million, and such an increase, over and above the increase in child benefit, would take many if not most single-parent families off Family Income Supplement. This suggests that there could be a combination of an increase in child benefit for the first or youngest child, an increase for all other children, and an increase in one-parent benefit which would leave relatively few and only modest losers if Family Income Supplement were abolished, even if funds are restricted to £3½ billion.

The advantages of completely abolishing Family Income Supplement are obvious. But because there will be some losers additional provisions will have to be made to guarantee them some compensation. The best they can sensibly be offered is a promise that they will be protected from poverty; to offer anything else would reintroduce the type of complication that reform is needed to eliminate. A simple way to achieve this promise is to extend the Supplementary Benefit scheme to those in work. No families will receive Family Income Supplement but some will qualify for Supplementary Benefit instead. There will be less means-testing and marginal tax rates on low incomes will fall, though some only to 100 per cent. If there is any problem with the idea of moving working families on to Supplementary Benefit it is the earnings rule which reduces benefit by a pound in the pound if earnings exceed £4. There is no financial reward to working if earnings do not exceed some minimum. What this minimum is for various families depends upon the level of child benefit, tax rates and personal allowances, and the structure of housing benefit, all of which are objects of reform. However, within the range of feasible alternatives it is difficult to produce a minimum level of earnings much in excess of £50 for a one earner, two child family, which is about a third of average earnings. There may be a disincentive to do part-time work, but it is unlikely that there is a serious disincentive to accept full-time work.

We have noted that both a social security system which relies mainly on contingency benefits and one which relies only on income-related benefits are impractical. Contingency benefits and income-related benefits must be combined. In discussing alternative proposals for reform above we have focused on working families, since it is generally accepted that those out of the work-force will rely mainly on contingency benefits. The proposals differ in their mix of the contingency and income-related benefits that working families should receive. Housing benefits are income-related. Under the Conservative tax credit scheme there would be no contingency benefits, and under the Social Democrats' scheme there would still be child benefit but a large income-related benefit as well. The alternative is to rely on child benefit to provide support for working families, with only a small income-related scheme for the very poorest. The income-related scheme is necessary because receipt of child benefit might not guarantee that working families would avoid poverty. If child benefit were generous enough to achieve this, and those who received contingency benefits did not need to claim Supplementary Benefit, we would simply have a more modest but still effective version of the 'Back to Beveridge' scheme.

A strategy of increasing child benefit combined with the extension of Supplementary Benefit to working families is really no more than a minimum income guarantee scheme of the type suggested by the Institute of Economic Affairs. Indeed since there was some ambiguity as to whether the negative tax payments under the IEA scheme would have been paid automatically by a new administrative agency or they would have had to be claimed from that agency, it is perhaps reasonable to claim that the suggested reforms amount to exactly those envisaged by the IEA, except that the scheme is administered using the existing means-testing machinery. However, there is no reason why, with the computerization of the tax system, there could not be administrative unification of the tax and benefit systems – as with the other schemes – and the consequent elimination of claiming altogether. If it presumed that a self-financing tax credit scheme would be linear, with presumably a high tax rate, then the Social Democrats' scheme, with its two rates, is a compromise between this and the minimum income guarantee scheme, trading off the tax rates on lower and higher incomes. This is exactly how we described the choice between fully integrated schemes earlier in the chapter. It is a choice which remains when objectives are more limited, and it must be faced even though extensive use may be made of contingency benefits to provide support for working families.

The future of social security

The British social security system is in need of major surgery. Having specified the objectives of the social security system some though not all of the problems which arise in planning a reformed system would be removed if the existing system could be assumed away. It is always easier to get where one plans to go by imagining that one can start from somewhere else. We have focused on strategies for reform which involve modifications to the current system designed to help it succeed where it currently fails. This approach is in the prevailing tradition of piecemeal reform.

It is often argued that piecemeal reform is largely responsible for the failings of the British social security system. This is not so. Much of the blame should be attached to uncoordinated and ill-considered reform, the failure to take account of the full implications of otherwise well-intentioned changes. With the piecemeal approach to reform the structure of the social security system is left more or less unaffected, but each component is examined to determine whether it successfully fulfils its own objectives, and whether it fits neatly into the overall design of a tax and benefit system which can meet society's equity and efficiency requirements.

In the course of this book we have considered many reforms, usually fairly broad strategies which were laced with specific detail where it served to clarify the nature of any particular reform. But if any of the reforms are attractive they cannot be implemented until the finer detail is worked out. We have deliberately ignored many of the intricacies which must be part of the social security system. If we had not it would have been all too easy to become bogged down in the minutiae of reform, to the exclusion of the broad strategies which should be our principal concern. Because of the wide variety and even peculiarity of some people's circumstances the detail of schemes is important, but if reform in any particular direction is agreed to be worth while then accommodating the detail should rarely if ever result in this opinion being changed. When discussion of detail dominates that of the value of a broad strategy it usually indicates that there is opposition to that strategy, and probably to the very idea of reform.

In this the final section of the book we are going to continue in this vein, mixing mainly the general with some specifics, and consider the direction in which the social security system might begin to head if there is any commitment to see the system reformed. We begin by looking at the main non-means-tested benefits for the retired, unemployed, sick, and disabled which will continue to provide help to the greatest number of people and to be the dominant element of social security expenditure. Our discussion in earlier chapters pointed to a number of desirable reforms.

It was concluded that the case for paying the long-term Supplementary Benefit rate to the long-term unemployed (for a year or more) is convincing, and that less than half of the saving from the taxation of benefits would be required to finance this provision. The linked-spells rule is also an anomaly which it is difficult to defend. It simply penalizes those who are not fortunate enough to hold on to a job for a significant period. The new arrangements for income support during initial sickness have not met with any significant disapproval, and if there is to be any diminution in the scope of the social security system this may indicate that sick pay is a natural candidate for privatization. This being so, it is clear that the statutory sick pay scheme is a hybrid scheme which is neither social security nor a substitute for occupational sick pay. But it is perhaps no more than a matter of time before privatization is completed, and the overall saving would be nearly double that effected by the statutory sick pay scheme. Benefits for the disabled are a mess, largely as a result of the industrial preference. Although the industrial preference has its supporters, we could find little to commend it. For this reason a start ought to be made towards the eventual introduction of a fully comprehensive disability income scheme. In the long term this requires a massive transfer of funds to the disabled. The minimum scheme suggested by the Disability Alliance to help the seriously disabled can easily be financed by the savings from benefit taxation – after increasing benefits for the long-term unemployed – or the savings resulting from the introduction of the statutory sick pay scheme. Then, in a sequence of steps, additional disabled can be brought into the scheme as funds become available. In adopting this approach to the reform of disablement benefits a deliberate effort will be needed to ensure that the disabled are not treated as a residual category of social security beneficiaries who will only be helped if there is enough money left over after all other plans are provided for. The past treatment of the disabled stands in stark contrast to that of retirement pensioners.

There are some who argue that the retired are pampered; perhaps a surprising claim given the extent of poverty in retirement. It is however fairly easy to see why such a view might be held. Retirement pensions have, in recent times, increased faster than other social security benefits, pensioners get a Christmas bonus, the earnings of retirement pensioners are relatively favourably treated; and there is now a generous earnings-related pension scheme which is going to place large demands on future public expenditure but has been left untouched by the recent retreat from earnings-related benefits. And even pensioners who are poor tend not to be very poor, and many will be better off than the supposedly non-poor. Pensioner poverty is assessed relative to the long-term Supplementary Benefit scale rates. However, many long-term sick and disabled can never qualify for long-term Supplementary Benefit, because their income makes them ineligible for the short-term rate. This is so even though their income is sufficiently low that they would otherwise qualify for long-term Supplementary Benefit. The reform of disability benefits is expected to be a gradual process. Under the Disability Alliance proposal those unable to work full time would receive a disability pension at least equal to the long-term Supplementary Benefit rate. In the interim, the sick or disabled who have been on a short-term benefit for a year, should, like the unemployed, be entitled to a benefit at the long-term Supplementary Benefit rate. This reform would not be costly, only £15–20 million (SSAC, 1982).

We have made specific proposals for the reform of retirement pensions. The most radical and contentious suggestion was that the new state earnings-related pension scheme should be discontinued. We believe it a fundamental principle that the state does not attempt to duplicate what the private sector can itself do well. The problem of course is that the private sector currently fails to provide for half the work-force. The responsibility for the provision of pensions above the state minimum can only be entrusted to a much improved private sector. Considerable antagonism to such proposals must surely be anticipated, mainly from those who have little faith in the private sector to effect necessary improvements. This may be justifiable agnosticism, and might in the end constitute an effective barrier to reform of this magnitude. Nevertheless, the new state scheme should not continue unamended; certain features are obviously anomalous, for example differential retirement ages, the inheritability provisions, and the best twenty years rule. And even if the private sector is not given an enlarged role, action is needed to improve the quality of many occupational pension schemes, particularly in respect to transferability, indexation, and solvency standards.

Many payments to the retired, unemployed, sick, and disabled are made from the National Insurance scheme. It has been suggested by some that even the 'Back to Beveridge' scheme 'may not be sufficiently close to the original spirit of Beveridge to warrant association with his name' (Judge, 1980b, p. 188). If this view has any force it must be even more warranted today, and if Beveridge's name should no longer be linked with the British social security system, this is perhaps the appropriate opportunity to ask whether any of the Beveridge legacy is worth preserving. In particular, does a separate National Insurance scheme still serve any useful purpose?

Beveridge laid great store by the insurance principle; indeed, it was the corner-stone of his plan. We have indicated that it is a justifiable although secondary purpose of governments to provide the insurance which individuals would or could not buy on the private market. The National Insurance scheme clearly provides insurance when the private market does not, as with unemployment insurance, for example, or where the private market is inaccessible or unreliable, as with pensions, and in as much as premiums are paid it is similar to a private insurance scheme. But there the similarity ends. With retirement annuities offered by insurance companies, premiums are related to the risk, i.e. life expectancy, they are accumulated in a fund and benefits are paid out of accumulated assets. None of these characteristics are features of the National Insurance scheme, and the implications of this are quite far-reaching. In particular, the payment of contributions may confer a right to benefits, but benefits can only be paid if contributions can continue to be extracted to finance them. Pay-as-you-go financing requires that the government has the power to do this, and that the work-force will comply by paying up. Note also that the scale of benefits is linked not to the contributions or investment returns but to the attitudes of the government of the day. If it is believed that 'insurance is what insurance does', then National Insurance may well be viewed by contributors as insurance; but if the National Insurance scheme is also expected to function like a private insurance arrangement then the analogy is wholly inappropriate.

If National Insurance and private insurance are viewed as being parallel arrangements, and the right to benefit is seen to be earned by making contributions, it is sometimes suggested that this is advantageous. Increases in contributions in order to improve benefits may not meet with the disfavour which would be associated with tax increases with the same purposes; the government may be reluctant to cut benefits; and taxpayers should display little antagonism towards benefit recipients. It is difficult to believe that the insurance principle would be widely defended on any of these grounds. National Insurance contributions are widely treated as a tax, and any belief that a tax increase can be recast as a National Insurance contribution and some-how will be regarded as more acceptable is misplaced. National Insurance benefits have not escaped cuts. Resentment against benefit recipients is difficult to gauge; but those who disapprove of paying benefits to the unemployed are unlikely to change their minds if the insurance principle were explained to them, and many others would perhaps happily accept an increase in income tax if they knew that better pensions and unemployment benefits would be paid as a result. There may be advantages in earmarked taxes − mainly so that people know what they are paying for − but the insurance principle appears to have outlived its usefulness, if it ever really had any. Indeed the only reason there can be for preserving it is one of historical continuity; in other words, because we have always had it.

Rejection of the insurance principle would lead quite naturally to other changes, all of which would be welcome. The distinction between contributory and non-contributory benefits would disappear, and the contribution conditions could be swept away, although they must be replaced by some other qualifying condition for benefits, probably based on residence. Income tax and National Insurance contributions could be fully integrated. The lower and upper earnings limits would be abolished, removing the very high marginal tax rate implied by the former and the local regressivity of the tax system resulting from the latter. Expenditure which is currently met from the National Insurance fund would be raised by increasing the marginal rate of income tax. We have said that earmarking may be advantageous, but if this is intended to result in a better understanding of how taxes are spent, it really only requires that each taxpayer receives a statement of expenditure on the different public programmes.

Employer National Insurance contributions could also be merged with the employee's income tax − on the grounds that these are shifted to employees anyway − although it is perhaps to be expected that this would be difficult to sell to employees. The revenue-neutral income tax rate would be about 39 per cent: if this were rounded up to 40 per cent this would yield a useful extra £1 billion. The revenue-neutral payroll tax, replacing both employer National Insurance contributions and the National Insurance surcharge would be 10 per cent; there seems little point in attempting to raise extra revenue, for example by setting the payroll tax rate at 12 per cent given that employer's National Insurance contributions are 12.2 per cent, at a time when there is pressure from industry to abolish the National Insurance surcharge of 2 per cent.

Unfortunately there is a complication, the State Earnings-Related Pension Scheme. There are two sources of complication. Firstly, because of the best twenty years rule, earnings records have to be kept to determine pensions; contribution and earnings records are currently kept together at a large and expensive computer installation in Newcastle. Earnings records could continue to be maintained as at present, although it might be preferable if income tax records could be used for this purpose. These records would also be needed if additional earnings-related benefits are introduced. The second complication is contracting-out. At the moment the contracted-out receive a rebate of National Insurance contributions, because part of their state pension, the GMP, will be paid by their employer, or employers. Perhaps the simplest way of replicating the current financial arrangements between the three parties to the contracting-out deal is for the state to pay a subsidy directly to private pension schemes who can then pass this on to employees. Abandoning SERPS would of course make these problems disappear, although they should have no influence upon a decision whether or not to follow this course of action.

There are currently too many people relying on means-tested Supplementary Benefit. However at the moment 85 per cent of Supplementary Benefit recipients are either retirement pensioners or unemployed. Most of the retired among these receive Supplementary Benefit by virtue of their housing costs. Under the new housing benefit scheme these households will be floated off Supplementary Benefit and on to rebates in the course of 1983. Some will continue to receive topping-up payments of Supplementary Benefit, although this would not be necessary with a unified housing benefit scheme. We have discussed a number of such schemes. However, the careful costing exercise which would indicate the most desirable structure for a unified housing benefit scheme has yet to be undertaken. We judge this a priority. It is likely that a unified housing benefit scheme combined with the setting of the retirement pension at or above the long-term Supplementary Benefit rate and the relaxation of the qualifying conditions would take all pensioners off Supplementary Benefit. Undeniably there are complications which could appear to be a barrier to this being achieved, for example the special additions, for heating or a special diet, which would raise pensioners' Supplementary Benefit entitlements. But this simply provides an example of how the detail can confuse the general issue. If it is desirable that pensioners should not need to claim Supplementary Benefit, or any other means-tested benefit, then we should aim to achieve this. It should not be beyond the wit of man to design a small scheme to meet special needs which is not in violation of this objective.

It is not so easy to take the unemployed off Supplementary Benefit. Short-term unemployment benefit for adults is below short-term Supplementary Benefit, but only by a small amount which can easily be made up. If the long-term unemployed were to receive unemployment benefit set at or above the long-term Supplementary Benefit rate, the unemployed without children will be taken off Supplementary Benefit. A problem arises with children. The Supplementary Benefit child additions exceed the sum of child benefit and the National Insurance child additions, so unemployed families with children would still be entitled to Supplementary Benefit by virtue of the fact that they have children. It is difficult to know whether this is likely to change. Certainly child benefit might be increased if Family Income Supplement is withdrawn, but it is uncertain as to by how much. However, there is also pressure to increase the Supplementary Benefit child additions. At face value they may not appear ungenerous, £8.75 for a child under 11, £13.15 for children aged 11–15, and £15.82 for children aged 16–17 in 1982-3. Yet Piachaud (1981) has shown that the minimal costs of raising children of different ages are in the range 14 per cent (for the youngest) to 21 per cent (for teenagers) higher than the additions to the scale rates. The National Foster Care Association recommend fostering allowances of more than double these rates. Piachaud's results suggest that the child addition should be of the order of £10, £15, and £20 respectively. Payments for children will probably remain greater under Supplementary Benefit; it would make sense to include in non-means-tested benefits an addition for children which makes up any difference between the Supplementary Benefit child additions and child benefit receipts.

Under the new statutory sick pay scheme there will be more sick people receiving Supplementary Benefit, although further privatization should reverse this. A comprehensive disability income scheme might eventually be introduced, and this should take the disabled – the third largest group of recipients – off Supplementary Benefit.

If contingency benefits were high enough most of those who currently receive Supplementary Benefit would not have to endure undignified means tests in order to claim their entitlement or suffer poverty because they cannot accept this intrusion. This platitudinous observation provides the basis of the above reforms. But if the Supplementary Benefit rates are to provide the bench-mark against which the levels of the contingency benefits are set, it then has to be asked whether the Supplementary Benefit rates themselves provide an adequate standard of living for those who receive the maximum payable under the scheme.

We have noted that the Supplementary Benefit child additions are inadequate, and it is widely felt that improving these is a priority. But are all Supplementary Benefit levels too low? Sinfield (1981) surveys the evidence on the standard of living of the unemployed living on Supplementary Benefit. The hardship revealed – lack of adequate clothing and bedding, days without a proper meal, etc. – is disturbing, as are its consequences – unpayable debts, illness, and marital breakdown – but this only demonstrates a link between unemployment and poverty. It provides a hint that Supplementary Benefit might be inadequate: but it is not proof. The impoverished life-style of some benefit recipients reflects a tangled tale of failure to claim, financial mismanagement, and inadequacy of benefits. Only careful research can reveal whether current benefit levels are sufficient to relieve the suffering that living in poverty entails. When further redistribution is politically unpopular it is only the results of this type of research that can justify a request that additional resources be devoted to social security with even a faint hope of being sympathetically received.

Benefit levels cannot be discussed without mention of indexation. The uprating of most benefits is quite rightly enshrined in legislation and the current practice, confused by a shambles of guesswork, short-falls, and claw-back (or 'correcting the overshoot' in official parlance), is to provide price indexation. This has more or less been extended to other benefits. However, the case for earnings indexation, so that benefit recipients share the fortunes – both favourable and unfavourable – of the working population who must pay for the benefits, is strong. And the way in which increases are implemented would be much simpler – both administratively, and for claimants to understand – if they were based not on forecasts but on the previous year's inflation or, preferably, earnings growth. If inflation were to begin rising rapidly more frequent upratings would be better than the current arrangements. But if these arrangements must be persisted with, the least one might reasonably hope for is the consistent treatment of overshoots and shortfalls, and the careful and explicit separation of benefit changes required to compensate for forecasting errors from planned adjustments in real benefit levels.

Apart from any change in the system of housing benefits the reforms mentioned above would leave working families unaffected. Since a unified housing benefit offers little hope of any reduction in benefit withdrawal rates, and may increase them, the poverty trap problem remains. We have devoted much of this chapter to discussing alternative strategies which would lead to the more sensible treatment of working families. Choices have to be made.

Reliance could be placed upon income-related benefits, in which case the choice to be made concerns the appropriate structure of tax rates; a linear scheme, a two-rate scheme, or a minimum income guarantee scheme? Each has its advantages and disadvantages. Alternatively contingency benefits – child benefit, and possibly a home responsibility payment for a non-working parent – could provide the sole means of support, in the spirit of the 'Back to Beveridge' scheme. However, a decision to mix contingency benefits and income-related benefits in an attempt to remove the worst excesses of the poverty trap has much to recommend it. This would be achieved by improving child benefit – although not necessarily with any commitment to compensate as many Family Income Supplement recipients as possible, an objective we, although not others, have used simply to illustrate the strategy of increasing child benefit – and then using Supplementary Benefit – and it is not at all fanciful to hope that this would be its primary use – to mop up any residual poverty among working families (cf. our discussion of housing benefit reform). The main attraction of this approach is that it is a relatively small change; incrementalism is often appealing to a government in office, as opposed to a political party with dreams of office, and nearly always appeals to adminis-trators. More radical changes – the administrative unification of the tax and benefit system which will remove the need to claim, another shift in the balance of contingency and income-related benefits, and maybe a change to a more progressive rate structure – can follow when it is felt that the time is right.

We cannot be sure that the poverty trap problem will be tackled at all. It, like many of the problems of the current social security system, has survived a long time. The reason is clear: 'The poverty trap is a big nonsense built from many small bricks. Reformers tend to think of one big solution, governments of restyling the brickwork. Neither talks the language of compromise, so the nonsense remains' (*The Economist*, 13 November 1982). We have described one such compromise which might be approved of by politicians, administrators, those who pressure for reform (as distinct from curtailment), and others who offer the informed and intelligent comment which should influence public attitudes toward the social security system. But we cannot know this, and nobody can justifiably claim to be in possession of the right answer. The resolution of all problems where the advantages and disadvantages of various actions have to be set against each other is properly placed in the hands of those who must accept the blame if their decision is unpopular. This is the fate of politicians and nobody else. But conscientious and successful politicians can only make important decisions if they are aware of the problems they are trying to solve, the alternative means of providing a solution, and the implications of each. The most important measure of the success of this book will be the awareness the reader has developed of these issues.

REFERENCES

BOOKS

Abel-Smith, B. and Townsend, P. (1965), *The Poor and the Poorest*, Occasional Papers on Social Administration, 17, Bell and Sons, London.

Atkinson, A. B. (1969), *Poverty in Britain and the Reform of Social Security*, Cambridge University Press, London.

Atkinson, A. B. (1973), *The Tax Credit Scheme and Redistribution of Income*, Institute for Fiscal Studies, London.

Atkinson, A. B. (1975), *The Economics of Inequality*, Oxford University Press, Oxford.

Beckerman, W. and Clark, S. (1982), *Poverty and Social Security in Britain Since 1961*, Oxford University Press for the Institute for Fiscal Studies, Oxford.

Berthoud, R. and Brown, J. (1981), *Poverty and the Development of Anti-Poverty Policy in the UK*, Heinemann for the Policy Studies Institute, London.

Brown, C. V. (1981), *Taxation and Labour Supply*, George Allen and Unwin, London.

Brown, C. V. and Dawson, D. A. (1969), *Personal Taxation, Incentives and Tax Reforms*, Political and Economic Planning, London.

Bruce, M. (1961), *The Coming of the Welfare State*, Batsford, London.

Clark, R. L. and Spengler, J. J. (1980), *The Economics of Individual and Population Aging*, Cambridge Surveys of Economic Literature, Cambridge University Press, Cambridge.

Creedy, J. (1982), *State Pensions in Britain*, Cambridge University Press for the National Institute of Economic and Social Research, Cambridge.

Cullingworth, J. B. (1979), *Essays on Housing Policy: The British Scene*, George Allen and Unwin, London.

Donnison, D. (1982), *The Politics of Poverty*, Martin Robertson, Oxford.

Ermisch, J. (1983), *The Political Economy of Demographic Change*, Heinemann Educational Books for the Policy Studies Institute, London.

Fiegehen, G., Lansley, P. S. and Smith, A. D. (1977), *Poverty and Progress in Britain, 1953–73*, Cambridge University Press for the National Institute of Economic and Social Research, Cambridge.

Field, F., Meacher, M. and Pond, C. (1977), *To Him Who Hath: A Study of Poverty and Taxation*, Penguin, London.

Franey, R. (1983), *Poor Law: The Mass Arrest of Homeless Claimants in Oxford*, Campaign for Single Homeless People (CHAR), London.

Grey, A., Hepworth, N. and Odling-Smee, J. (1981), *Housing Rents, Costs and Subsidies*, Chartered Institute of Public Finance and Accountancy, London.

Hemming, R. and Kay, J. A. (1984), *The Economic Basis of Pension Funding*, Oxford University Press for the Institute for Fiscal Studies, Oxford.

IEA (1970), Policies for Poverty, Institute of Economic Affairs, London.

Jackson, D. (1972), *Poverty*, Macmillan, London.

Kay, J. A. and King, M. A. (1980), *The British Tax System*, Oxford University Press, Oxford.

Kincaid, J. C. (1973), *Poverty and Equality in Britain*, Penguin, London.

Laslett, P. (1965), *The World We Have Lost*, Methuen, London.

Le Grand, J. (1982), *The Strategy of Equality*, George Allen and Unwin, London.

Mathewman, J. and Lambert, N. (1982), *Tolley's Social Security and State Benefits*, Tolley Publishing Company, London.

McClements, L. (1978), *The Economics of Social Security*, Heinemann, London.

Meade Committee (1978), *The Structure and Reform of Direct Taxation*, George Allen and Unwin for the Institute for Fiscal Studies, London.

Parker, H. (1982), *The Moral Hazard of Social Benefits*, Institute of Economic Affairs, London.

Phelps-Brown, H. (1977), *The Inequality of Pay*, Oxford University Press, Oxford.

Pinker, R. (1979), *The Idea of Welfare*, Heinemann, London.

Pond, C. (1978), *Marcs 1: The Poverty Trap*, The Open University Press, Milton Keynes.

Rosa, J.-J. (1982), *The World Crisis in Social Security*, Bonnel, Paris.

Rowntree, B. S. (1901), *Poverty: A Study of Town Life*, Macmillan, London.

Rowntree, B. S. (1941), *Poverty and Progress*, Longmans, London.

Runciman, W. G. (1966), *Relative Deprivation and Social Justice*, Routledge and Kegan Paul, London.

Sinfield, A. (1981), *What Unemployment Means*, Martin Robertson, Oxford.

Titmuss, R. M. (1962), *Income Distribution and Social Change*, George Allen and Unwin, London.

Townsend, P. (1979), *Poverty in the United Kingdom*, Penguin, London.

Watts, H. W. and Rees, A. (1977), *The New Jersey Income Maintenance Experiment: Volume II Labour Supply Responses*, Academic Press, New York.

Williams, F. (1977), *Why the Poor Pay More*, Macmillan for the National Consumer Council, London.

Wilson, T. and Wilson, D. J. (1982), *The Political Economy of the Welfare State*, George Allen and Unwin, London.

Wynn, M. (1970), *Family Policy*, Michael Joseph, London.

ARTICLES

Atkinson, A. B. and Flemming, J. S. (1978), 'Unemployment, Social Security and Incentives', *Midland Bank Review*, Autumn.

Atkinson, A. B., Gomulka, J., Micklewright, J. and Rau, N. (1982), 'Unemployment Duration, Social Security and Incentives', *Journal of Public Economics*, (forthcoming).

Atkinson, A. B., Maynard, A. K. and Trinder, D. G. (1980), 'Evidence on Inter-Generational Income Mobility in Britain', Paper presented at the Sixth World Congress of the International Economic Association, Mexico City.

Atkinson, A. B. (1974), 'Poverty and Income Inequality in Britain', in D. Wedderburn (ed.), *Poverty, Inequality and Class Structure*, Cambridge University Press, London.

Atkinson, A. B. (1970), 'On the Measurement of Inequality', *Journal of Economic Theory*, 2.

Beckerman, W. (1979), 'The Impact of Income Maintenance Payments on Poverty: 1975', *Economic Journal*, 89.

Benjamin, D. K. and Kochin, L. A. (1979), 'Searching for an Explanation of Unemployment in Inter-war Britain', *Journal of Political Economy*, 87.

Bradshaw, J. (1980), 'Child Benefit – Is CPAG's Policy Right?' *Poverty*, 45.

Bradshaw, J. and Bradley, K. (1979), 'Can a Housing Allowance Work?', *Roof*, May.

Brown, C., Gilroy, C. and Kohen, A. (1982), 'The Effect of the Minimum Wage on Employment and Unemployment', *Journal of Economic Literature*, 20.

Brown, C. V., Levin, E. and Ulph, D. T. (1976), 'Estimates of Labour Hours Supplied by Married Male Workers in Great Britain', *Scottish Journal of Political Economy*, 23.

Browning, M. J. (1982), 'Pensions and Saving: Some UK Evidence', *Economic Journal*, 92.

Clark, S. and Hemming, R. (1981), 'Aspects of Household Poverty in Britain', *Social Policy and Administration*, 15.

Collard, D. (1980), 'Social Dividend and Negative Income Tax', in C. Sandford, C. Pond, and R. Walker, (eds.), *Taxation and Social Policy*, Heinemann, London.

Creedy, J. and Disney, R. (1981), 'Eligibility for Unemployment Benefits in Great Britain', *Oxford Economic Papers*, 33.

Davies, R., Hamill, L., Moylan, S. and Smee, C. H. (1982), 'Incomes In and Out of Work', *Employment Gazette*, Department of Employment, London.

Danziger, S., Haveman, R. and Plotnick, R. (1981), 'How Income Transfers Affect Work, Savings, and Income Distribution', *Journal of Economic Literature*, 19.

Dilnot, A. and Morris, C. N. (1981), 'What Do We Know About the Black Economy?', *Fiscal Studies*, 2.

Dilnot, A. W. and Morris, C. N. (1982), 'The Tax System and Distribution 1979–82', in J. A. Kay (ed.), *The 1982 Budget*, Basil Blackwell for the Institute for Fiscal Studies, Oxford.

Disney, R. (1981), 'Unemployment Insurance in Britain', in J. Creedy (ed.), *The Economics of Unemployment in Britain*, Butterworths, London.

Donnison, D. (1979), 'Is a Single Housing Benefit for Everyone on Low Incomes Feasible?', *Housing Centre Trust*, London.

Donnison, D. (1981), 'A Rationalisation of Housing Benefits', *Three Banks Review*.

Ermisch, J. (1981), 'Paying the Piper: Demographic Changes and Pension Contributions', *Policy Studies*, 1.

Ermisch, J. (1982), 'Measuring the Benefits from Subsidies to British Owner-occupiers and Tenants: Theory and Application', Policy Studies Institute.

Feldstein, M. S. (1974), 'Social Security, Induced Retirement and Aggregate Capital Accumulation', *Journal of Political Economy*, 82.

Fiegehen, G. C. and McGwire, L. (1982), 'The Income and Incentive

Effects of the Housing Benefits Reform', Paper for the SSRC Social Security Workshop.

Goss, S. and Lansley, P. S. (1981), 'What Price Housing? A Review of Housing Subsidies and Proposals for Reform, *SHAC Research Report*, 4.

Gough, I. and Stark, T. (1968), 'Low Incomes in the United Kingdom', *Manchester School*, 36.

Green, G. F. (1981), 'The Effect of Occupational Pension Schemes on Saving in the United Kingdom: A Test of the Life Cycle Hypothesis', *Economic Journal*, 91.

Harvey, R. and Hemming, R. (1983), 'Inflation, Pensioner Living Standards and Poverty', *Oxford Bulletin of Economics and Statistics*, 45.

Hemming, R. and Harvey, R. (1983), 'Occupational Pension Scheme Membership and Retirement Saving', *Economic Journal*, 93.

Hemming, R. and Hills, J. (1983), 'The Reform of Housing Benefits', *Fiscal Studies*, 4.

Hemming, R. and Kay, J. A. (1981), 'Contracting Out of the State Earnings Related Pension Scheme', *Fiscal Studies*, 2.

Hemming, R. and Kay, J. A. (1982), 'The Costs of the State Earnings Related Pension Scheme', *Economic Journal*, 92.

Holland, D. M. (1969), 'The Effects of Taxation on Effort', *Proceedings of the 62nd National Tax Association*, October.

Joshi, H. (1982), 'The Effect of Children on Women's Propensity to Earn Pension Rights', Centre for Population Studies, London School of Hygiene.

Judge, K. (1980a), 'Is There a Crisis in the Welfare State?' PSSRU Discussion Paper, 164, University of Kent.

Judge, K. (1980b), 'Beveridge: Past, Present and Future', in C. Sandford, C. Pond, and R. Walker (eds.), *Taxation and Social Policy*, Heinemann, London.

Kay, J. A., Morris, C. N. and Warren, N. A. (1980), 'Tax, Benefits and the Incentive to Seek Work', *Fiscal Studies*, 1.

Kay, J. A. and Sandler, C. (1982), 'The Taxation of Husband and Wife: A View of the Debate in the Green Paper', *Fiscal Studies*, 3.

King, M. A. (1980), 'An Econometric Model of Tenure Choice and the Demand for Housing as a Joint Decision', *Journal of Public Economics,* 14.

King, M. A. and Atkinson, A. B. (1980), 'Housing Policy, Taxation and Reform', *Midland Bank Review*, Spring.

Lansley, P. S. (1982), 'Alternatives to Housing Benefit', *Poverty*, 53.

Lister, R. (1975), 'Social Security: The Case for Reform', Poverty Pamphlet, 22, *Child Poverty Action Group*, London.

Maki, D. and Spindler, S. A. (1975), 'The Effect of Unemployment Compensation on the Rate of Unemployment in Great Britain', *Oxford Economic Papers*, 27.

McClements, L. (1977), 'Equivalence Scales for Children', *Journal of Public Economics*, 8.

McCormick, B. and Hughes, G. (1982), 'The Influence of Pensions on Job Turnover', *Journal of Public Economics* (forthcoming).

Metcalf, D., Nickell, S. and Floros, N. (1982), 'Still Searching for an Explanation of Unemployment in Inter-war Britain', *Journal of Political Economy* (forthcoming).

Morris, C. N. (1981), 'The Age Allowance', *Fiscal Studies*, 2.

Morris, C. N. and Warren, N. (1980), 'The Reduced Rate Band', *Fiscal Studies*, 1.

Morris, C. N. and Warren, N. (1981), 'Taxation of the Family', *Fiscal Studies*, 2.

Muellbauer, J. (1979), 'McClements on Equivalence Scales for Children', *Journal of Public Economics*, 12.

Nicholson, J. L. (1949), 'Variations in Working Class Family Expenditure', *Journal of Royal Statistical Society*, 112.

Nickell, S. (1979), 'The Effect of Unemployment and Related Benefits on the Duration of Unemployment', *Economic Journal*, 89.

O'Higgins, M. (1981), 'Income During Initial Sickness', *Policy and Politics*, 9.

Orshansky, M. (1965), 'Counting the Poor: Another Look at the Poverty Problem', *Social Security Bulletin*, 28.

Pauly, M. V. (1968), 'The Economics of Moral Hazard: Comment', *American Economic Review*, 58.

Piachaud, D. (1981), 'Children and Poverty', Poverty Research Series 9, *Child Poverty Action Group*, London.

Pond, C. and Playford, C. (1980), 'The Case for the Reduced Rate Band', Low Pay Unit, London.

Rimmer, L. (1980), 'The Intra-Family Distribution of Income', Study Commission on the Family, London.

Robinson, A. and Wainwright, S. (1981), 'Specialist Claims Control', *Poverty*, 49.

Sen, A. K. (1976), 'Poverty: An Ordinal Approach to Measurement', *Econometirca*, 44.

Sen, A. K. (1979), 'Issues in the Measurement of Poverty', *Scandinavian Journal of Economics*.

Takayama, N. (1979), 'Poverty, Income Inequality and their Measures: Professor Sen's Axiomatic Approach Reconsidered', *Econometrica*, 47.

Thurow, L. C. (1981), 'Equity, Efficiency, Social Justice and Redistribution' in *The Welfare State in Crisis*, Organization for Economic Co-operation and Development, Paris.

Wilson, J. (1981), 'A Comprehensive Disability Income Scheme', *Poverty*, 48.

Wilson, P. (1981), 'Free School Meals', Occasional Paper 23, *Office of Population Censuses and Surveys*, London.

Zabalza, A., Pissarides, C. A., Piachaud, D. and Barton, M. (1979), 'Social Security and the Choice Between Full-time Work, Part-time Work and Retirement', *Journal of Public Economics*, 13.

Zabalza, A., Pissarides, C. A. and Piachaud, D. (1980), 'Social Security, Life-cycle Saving and Retirement', in D. Collard, R. Lecomber, and M. Slater (eds.), *Income Distribution: the Limits to Redistribution*, Scientechnica, Bristol.

GOVERNMENT OFFICIAL PUBLICATIONS

Beveridge Report (1942), *Social Insurance and Allied Services*, HMSO, London.

DHSS (1969), *National Superannuation and Social Insurance: Proposals for Earnings Related Social Security*, HMSO, London.

DHSS (1971), *Strategy for Pensions: The Future Development of State and Occupational Provisions*, HMSO, London.

DHSS (1971), *Two-Parent Families*, HMSO, London.

DHSS (1974), *Better Pensions (fully protected against inflation): Proposals for a New Pension Scheme*, Cmnd. 5713, HMSO, London.

DHSS (1981), *Social Security Act 1975: Reform of the Industrial Injuries Scheme*, HMSO, London.

D.o.E. (1981), *Assistance with Housing Costs*, Department of the Environment, London.

DE and DHSS (1981), *Payments of Benefits to Unemployed People*, Department of Employment and Department of Health and Social Security, London.

Finer, M. (1974), *Report of the Committee on One-parent Families*, HMSO, London.

Government Actuary (1978), *Occupational Pension Schemes 1975, Fifth Survey by the Government Actuary*, HMSO, London.

House of Commons Social Services Committee (1982), *Age of Retirement*, HMSO, London.

House of Lords Select Committee (1982), *Report on Unemployment*, HMSO, London.

Inland Revenue (1972), *Proposals for a Tax Credit System*, HMSO, London.

Inland Revenue (1980), *The Taxation of Husband and Wife*, HMSO, London.

Kemsley, W. F. F., Redpath, R. V. and Holmes, M. (1980), *Family Expenditure Survey Handbook*, HMSO, London.

Layard, R., Piachaud, D., Stewart, M. and others (1978), *The Causes of Poverty*, Royal Commission on the Distribution of Income and Wealth, Background Paper No.5, HMSO, London.

Ministry of Pensions and National Insurance (1966), *Financial and Other Circumstances of Retirement Pensions*, HMSO, London.

Ministry of Social Security (1967), *Circumstances of Families*, HMSO, London.

OECD (1980), *The Tax/Benefit Position of Selected Income Groups in OECD Member Countries*, Organization for Economic Co-operation and Development, Paris.

OPCS (1980), *Population Projections 1978–2018*, Office of Population Censuses and Surveys, HMSO, London.

Pearson Commission (1978), *Royal Commission on Civil Liability and Compensation for Personal Injury*, HMSO, London.

RCDIW (1978), *Royal Commission on the Distribution of Income and Wealth Report No.6: Lower Incomes*, HMSO, London.

Select Committee on Tax Credit (1973), *Report and Proceedings of the Committee*, HMSO, London.

SSAC (1982), *First Report of the Social Security Advisory Committee 1981*, HMSO, London.

Treasury and Civil Service Committee (1982), *The Structure of Personal Income Taxation and Income Support*, Minutes of Evidence, HMSO, London.

INDEX